Dear Beccy,

We hope you enjoy this car

Thank you for yr support of our work.

With best wishes,

Go

DD DAY 2021.

Tape Leaders
A Compendium of Early British Electronic Music Composers

Ian Helliwell

CONTENTS

1. Electronic Music Composers A-Z
2. Experimental Amateurs
3. Electronic Music Groups
4. EMS – Electronic Music Studios
5. The BBC Radiophonic Workshop
6. Tape Leaders CD
7. Information, Credits and Index

First published in the UK by Sound On Sound in 2016
This edition published by Velocity Press in 2021
velocitypress.uk
tapeleaders.co.uk
ianhelliwell.co.uk

Copyright © Ian Helliwell 2016, 2021
Collages, design and editing by Ian Helliwell

Ian Helliwell has asserted his right under the Copyright, Designs and Patents Act 1988 to be identified as the author of this work
All rights reserved. No part of this publication may be reproduced, in any form or by any means, without permission from the publisher
ISBN: 9781913231125

Janet Beat in her home studio, 1970s-80s

READER'S GUIDE

This compendium is designed as an illuminating reference manual for British-based composers, who created experimental work with electronics and magnetic tape. It concentrates on the formative period up to 1970, before widespread exploration with tape recorders, tone generators and harder edged electronic sounds, began to be eclipsed by keyboard synthesizers, and the number of composers increased well beyond inclusion in a manageable sized volume. While there is a wide range of publications about electronic music, this is the first time a book has put into perspective, not only the few acknowledged figures working in the field, but attempted to include all other active tape music composers, discovered during more than six years of research.

The focus here is on individual music-makers in Great Britain who created experimental tape pieces, rather than jobbing composers who wrote mainstream music to order, and occasionally incorporated electronic textures into otherwise conventional compositions. 'Experimental' is a subjective and often ambiguous term, but in this context, elements such as dissonance, tape manipulation, sound collage, electronic tone generation and machine-made timbres, are those that underpin the basis for inclusion. To qualify for an entry, a composer will have worked on an experimental tape composition prior to 1971.

The anomalous position in the UK in the early post-war period, is marked by the fact that British-based composers had generated the fourth largest body of electronic music in the world by the late 1960s, yet very little of this was acclaimed or widely recognised. The bulk was functional, instructional or in conjunction with other media, and only a small amount of music was released separately on record for the public to listen to at home. This has contributed to the misguided impression that little electronic composition was going on, and what there was appeared to be concentrated around the BBC Radiophonic Workshop. In fact the majority of the composers featured had no connection with the celebrated BBC department, and many worked independently in self-built studios.

Striving to be comprehensive, while acknowledging that further research is needed, this book intends to show a more balanced and accurate picture through an A-Z format; attempting to document all the early experimental electronic music-makers in Britain becoming active during the 1950s and 60s. It will reveal the many interconnections between various composers, and show the similarities, crossovers and differences in their individual careers. Although it will never be possible to identify and trace all the hobbyists, some recognition of their output is essential, as amateur backroom tinkering with tape recorders in home studios, is an integral part of the British story.

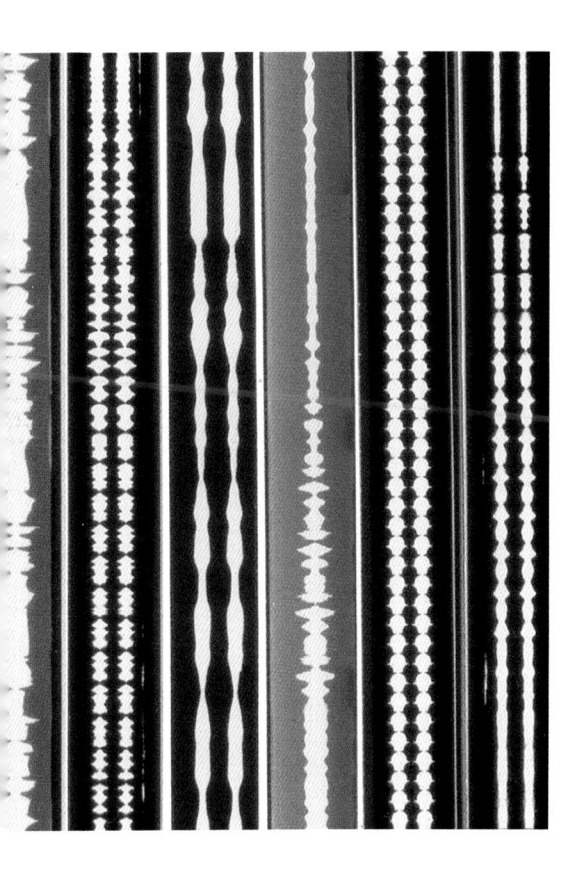

My long held interest in making and listening to electronic music, and frustration with the dearth of information on early British composers, created the idea for this compendium. The International Electronic Music Catalog, assembled by Hugh Davies and published in 1968, has been an essential resource and provided a starting point for getting things moving. Two of my projects – The Tone Generation audio series, and the film Practical Electronica, concerning FC Judd and early British tape music – helped turn what initially seemed a fanciful notion, into a feasible objective. Working without funding or support, I have still been able to make significant headway, and in pursuing my own independent research interests, investigations have unearthed many intriguing and forgotten figures, and facts that I have not previously read about or ever seen properly documented. It is fair to say that several entries in this compendium are somewhat scant, and question marks remain. Wherever possible I have tried to contact composers, relatives or those involved with electronic music in this early period, and include all the most interesting and accurate information. Over time this will be revised and updated as new facts and discoveries inevitably come to light, with research continuing as an ongoing project.

The wholly subjective ratings are out of ten. 'Obscurity', refers to how well known and celebrated a composer is, and acknowledges the difficulty in tracing reliable biographical details. 'Commitment', gauges involvement and passion for electronic music, including the number of tape pieces composed. Electronic music (EM) recording availability is rated Excellent, Good, Limited or Poor, and the earliest electronic works for each entry are marked 'unconfirmed', where they are based on slender evidence. CDs mentioned are those that contain interesting examples of electronic music, and do not represent any kind of discography. They are signposts for further listening and ones which I believe are worth investigating.

The grey boxes which appear at points throughout the book, contain extra background information relating to adjacent composer profiles, and give a broader contextual understanding. Composers are listed with the names they were born with or known by, during their early electronic music-making period; subsequent name changes are acknowledged within the text of their profile entry.

Ian Helliwell, March 2016 (updated July 2021).

TAPE LEADERS - INTRODUCTION

The wealth of early British electronic music has remained in the shadows for decades, and even at the time it was first made, outlets and audiences were often very limited. In an age of nostalgia and retro fixations for post war culture, much of this pioneering and forward looking work still remains hidden, with only a small selection of carefully compiled anthologies made available in recent years. It will become apparent when examining the profiles of different composers, that there were key figures such as **Tristram Cary**, **Daphne Oram** and **Peter Zinovieff**, who were extremely well connected, and often points of contact for those looking to engage with electronic music. A number of others such as **Roy Cooper**, **Brian Dennis** and **Malcolm Pointon** were little known, and concerned with disseminating electronic and tape sounds to students, hobbyists and ordinary people. Many more came from a classical music background, and were drawn only temporarily to electronic music, before returning to more accepted and conventional instrumental composing. At the same time, a large proportion of individuals operated alone in low-tech home studios, without professional equipment and often in isolation, unaware that people in other parts of Britain were working along very similar lines.

As well as an instructional and functional impulse in British electronic music – composing to fit a purpose rather than for the pure artistic satisfaction – there is a strong connection with engineering and construction, and a resourcefulness derived from World War II austerity for making much out of limited means. Before synthesizers were developed and became affordable, tone generators, filters, ring modulators and reverberation units were often home constructed. Composers looking for a certain kind of electronic sound would temporarily become engineers, while they soldered together a device to suit their special requirement. Tape recorders were also self-built, though with mass production from a large range of British manufacturers, they sold in their hundreds of thousands from the mid-1950s onwards, generating a great deal of interest in the potential for capturing and editing sounds. This led to many people of all ages and backgrounds building their own basic home studio set-ups or recording 'dens', long before most schools, colleges and universities caught on, and began to offer courses and facilities.

It is worth considering both the perception and reception of electronic music by the general public, concert goers, music critics and the composers themselves. There is a sense of ambivalence about whether electronics really were a legitimate foundation for composing, and whether or not the results were satisfying and credible, and could even be classified as music. Against this backdrop, a certain hostility or suspicion is quite natural for any new form of creative activity, but allied to a general scepticism in the British consciousness about affected artiness, and unwelcome modernist ideas coming in from the continent, a strong streak of conservatism was inherent from the outset. This inevitably had a confidence sapping effect on some British electronic composers; they could expect to face indifference, incomprehension or stinging criticism, and tape concerts staged on the same terms as conventional instrumental music, hardly helped allay listeners' doubts. Even a serious electro-acoustic piece such as Collages, by acclaimed composer **Roberto Gerhard**, which combined a full orchestra with electronic sound, still received some fierce condemnation at its premiere in 1961. One distinguished critic denounced the tape part as, "*heavy rhythmic breathing of some monster, and similar to a hostile jeering mob.*" Another said that the electronics were simply "*nothing more uplifting than deficient plumbing.*"

A lack of visual stimulation was, and still is, a problem for electronic music performance, and needs to be addressed in order to engage with anyone that may be interested in experimental sounds, but who expects something above and beyond listening to a hi-fi system at home. A straightforward concert hall setting with an absence of players or performative gestures, may not be the best circumstances in which to experience electronic music, whereas its effectiveness can be heightened when used in conjunction with other media, such as special lighting, kinetic sculpture, dance, film, TV, radio, theatre or art show. Nonetheless, it must be pointed out that four concerts of British electronic music during 1968-69 – three at the Southbank, and one at the London Planetarium – attracted very large crowds and were exceedingly popular. So while critics and the music establishment may have been underwhelmed, it is clear there was a great appetite amongst the switched-on concert going public, for the new sound worlds of electronic music.

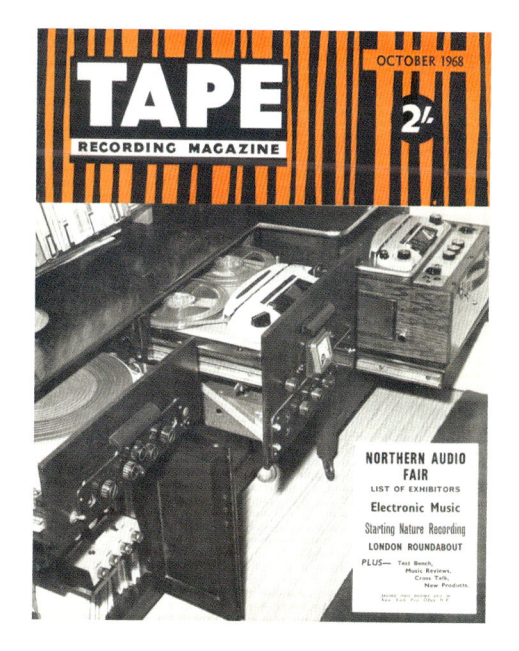

A further handicap that faced electronic experimenters in Britain, was the lack of institutional support, and an accessible national studio to facilitate the composing and dissemination of electronic music. The **BBC Radiophonic Workshop** was a closed shop geared towards servicing BBC productions, and did not exist to directly foster interest in tape experiments, or have the remit to commission new compositions from outside its small department. As a result there was a concerted drive by the British Society for Electronic Music at the end of the 1960s, to establish a purpose-built centre in London, and there was noticeable disappointment that this never came to fruition. It is, though, debateable how much impact it would have had, as a national studio would more likely have benefited those already in strong, influential positions, or involved with, or trained in academia. This would hardly have helped the self-taught lone experimenters and backroom boys, who carried out work in home studios in the provinces, and operated completely outside the British music establishment. However, as Tristram Cary eloquently argued in a magazine article in 1971, music graduates found it difficult to continue their experiments after university, and Britain was trailing behind other countries in being able to offer first class studio and concert facilities that serious composers required. He highlighted the support given by Philips to Dutch electronic music, and made a plea to companies here – EMI, Plessey and Pye – to offer similar backing.

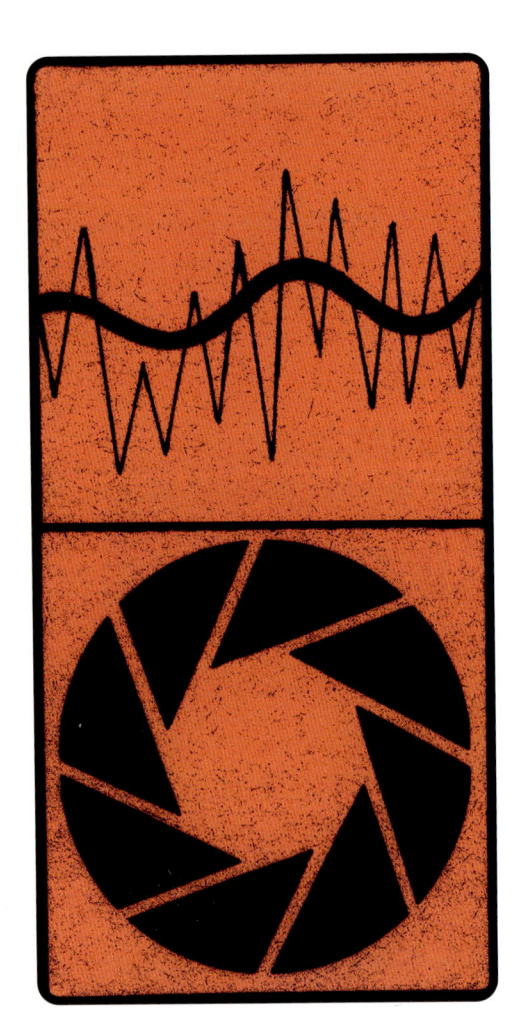

Experimentation across the arts was in the air during the 1950s-70s period. Electronic music was very new, futuristic and cutting edge, and an obvious attraction for all those British composers seeking unexplored territory, and for the first time, the chance to truly manipulate sound. Despite great initial enthusiasm, many of them gave up their early experimentation with tape and electronics, and concentrated on writing for conventional instruments for the remainder of their careers. Some may have felt hindered by their expectations not being met, and the difficulty in translating ideas into the electronic medium, while others may have considered the poor critical reception to their efforts as a signal to pursue other more popular outlets.

The equipment of that time was certainly quite primitive by modern standards. It was far more difficult to realise sophisticated multi-layered recordings, especially for those working at home with domestic and home-made apparatus. Nevertheless, it would be foolish to over-emphasise the degree of time and hardship involved in reaching worthwhile results. These were perfectly achievable, as much depended on the approaches and techniques adopted by each individual composer. Tape splicing with razor blade and sticky tape is undoubtedly labour intensive and time consuming, when it involves cutting up literally hundreds of small pieces of tape and splicing them together. On the other hand, making tape loops and recording them from one machine to a master tape on another, is easily workable, (and a process the author still carries out). Using tone generators or a radio to create sounds, recording them onto tape in the desired order and pausing the recorder while a new sound is found, also eliminates constant splicing. Whichever techniques are employed, the essence lies with ideas, imagination, skill and patience, as well as the sheer fascination with the sounds that can be conjured up; aspects that will always apply in making electronic music.

Over the years there has been a serious lack of early British electronic music album releases, and whole bodies of work have remained unheard for decades; unknown and in danger of being discarded and lost forever. Without any prospect of salvage, many tapes have inevitably been thrown away as they appeared to be of no consequence to their originators or next of kin, and of ostensibly little interest to the outside world. As tapes languish in cupboards and lofts with scant documentation to highlight their relevance or even their existence, the wider mission to unearth, explore and preserve this fascinating area of recent British musical history is more pressing than ever. A number of composers have sadly died while Tape Leaders has been in production, yet a lack of engagement persists with this early experimental phase of electronic music. Interest in a broad-based, and more representative picture, amongst broadcasters, historians, larger record labels and book publishers, has been distinctly lacking. This compendium seeks to address the problem, and starts from an unashamedly positive and enthusiastic position; nothing less than the overlooked, pathfinding British-based experimenters deserve.

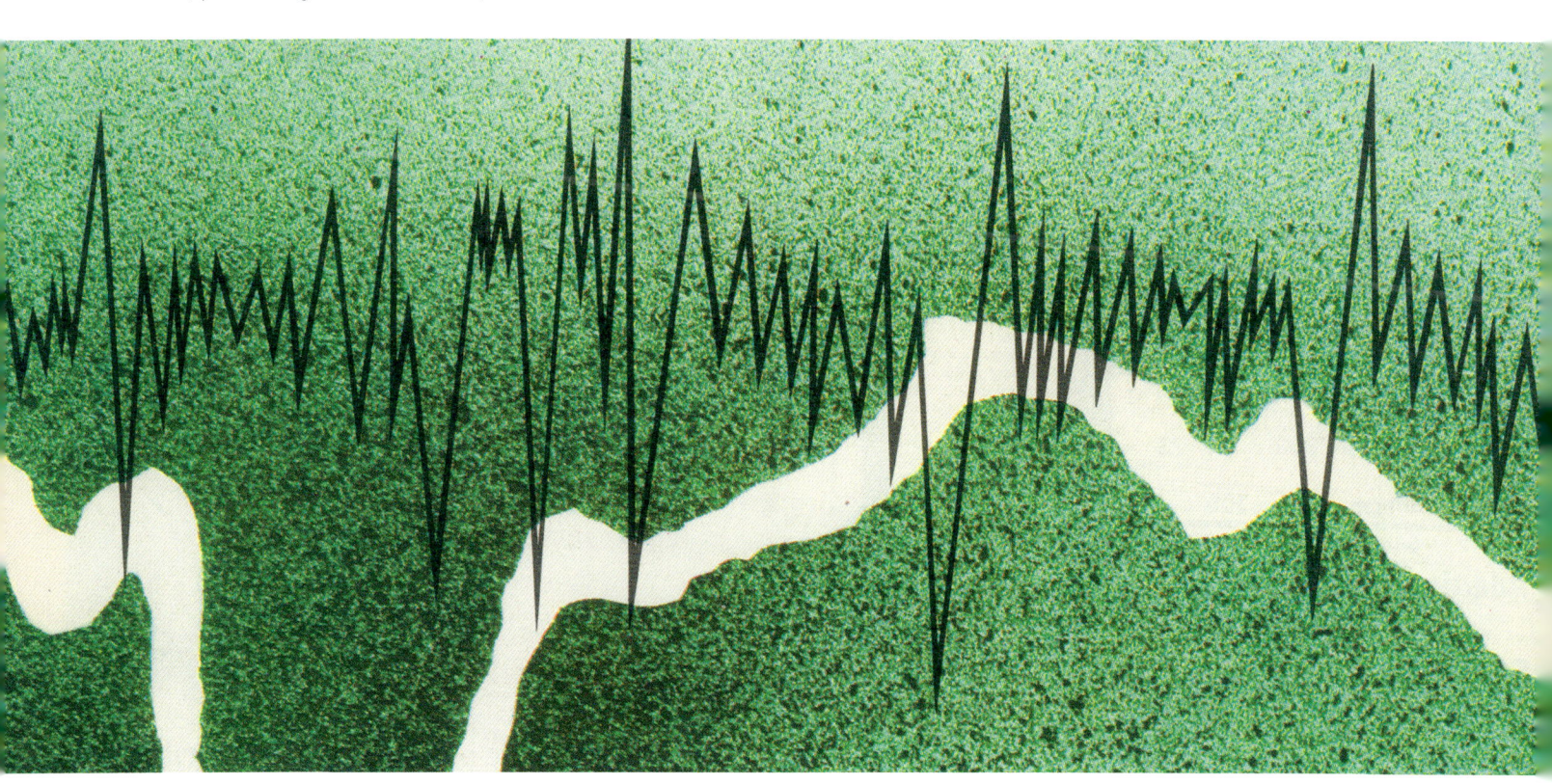

ELECTRONIC MUSIC COMPOSERS A-Z

Daevid Allen	(1938-2015)
Barry Anderson	(1935-1987)
John Baker	(1937-1997)
Laurie Scott Baker	(1943)
Don Banks	(1923-1980)
Janet Beat	(1937)
David Bedford	(1937-2011)
Ernest Berk	(1909-1993)
Harrison Birtwistle	(1934)
Michael Blake	(1930-?)
Desmond Briscoe	(1925-2006)
George Brown	(1947)
John Buller	(1927-2004)
William Burroughs	(1914-1997)
Tristram Cary	(1925-2008)
Lawrence Casserley	(1941)
Malcolm Clarke	(1943-2003)
Cyril Clouts	(1926-1989)
Bob Cobbing	(1920-2002)
Justin Connolly	(1933)
Roy Cooper	(1930-?)
Edward Cowie	(1943)
Howard Davidson	(1949)
Hugh Davies	(1943-2005)
Brian Dennis	(1941-1998)
Delia Derbyshire	(1937-2001)
Michael Dress	(1935–1975)
Grahame Dudley	(1942)
Terence Dwyer	(1922)
Jack Ellitt	(1902-2001)
Brian Eno	(1948)
Malcolm Fox	(1946-1997)

Ron Geesin	(1943)
Roberto Gerhard	(1896-1970)
Anthony Gilbert	(1934)
Ranulph Glanville	(1946-2014)
Stanley Glasser	(1926-2018)
Ken Gray	(1943-1994)
Peter Grogono	(1944-2021)
Graham Hearn	(1942)
Donald Henshilwood	(1930-2009)
Brian Hodgson	(1938)
James Ingram	(1948)
Wilfred Josephs	(1927-1997)
FC Judd	(1914-1992)
Peter Keene	(1953)
Basil Kirchin	(1927-2005)
Raymond Leppard	(1927-2019)
Desmond Leslie	(1921-2001)
John Lifton	(1944)
Ronald Lloyd	(1929-2008)
David Lloyd-Howells	(1942-2015)
Anna Lockwood	(1939)
David Lumsdaine	(1931)
John Herbert McDowell	(1926-1985)
Joe Meek	(1929-1967)
John Metcalf	(1946)
Jacob Meyerowitz	(1928-1998)
Thea Musgrave	(1928)
George Newson	(1932)

Daphne Oram	(1925-2003)
Richard Orton	(1940-2013)
Morris Pert	(1947-2010)
David Piper	(1943)
Malcolm Pointon	(1940-2007)
Andrew Powell	(1949)
Howard Rees	(1945-2011)
John Marlow Rhys	(1935-2011)
Alan Ridout	(1934-1996)
David Rowland	(1939-2007)
Leonard Salzedo	(1921-2000)
Peter Schmidt	(1931-1980)
Humphrey Searle	(1915-1982)
Robert Sherlaw Johnson	(1932-2000)
James Siddons	(1948)
Roger Smalley	(1943-2015)
Tim Souster	(1943-1994)
Alan Sutcliffe	(1930-2014)
Robert Swain	(1947)
John Tavener	(1944-2013)
Stephen Trowell	(1948)
Edgar Vetter	(1913-1988)
David Vorhaus	(1943)
Margaret Lucy Wilkins	(1939)
Marc Wilkinson	(1929)
Edward Williams	(1921-2013)
Keith Winter	(1940)
Trevor Wishart	(1946)
Geoffrey Wright	(1912-2010)
Peter Zinovieff	(1933-2021)

EXPERIMENTAL AMATEURS

Denis Affleck	(1906-1976)
Ralph Broome	(1928-1998)
Paul Carnell	(1944)
Steve Duckworth	(1948)
Kevin Edwards	(1952)
Leslie James Hills	(1911-1988)
Trevor Holmes	(1944)
Ian Loveday	(1954-2009)
George West	(1938)
Peter West	(1952)
Brian Whibley	(1931-2003)
Barry Witherden	(1949)
Stuart Wynn Jones	(1919-1991)

ELECTRONIC MUSIC GROUPS

The Beatles	(1960-1970)
Gentle Fire	(1968-1975)
Half Landing	(1965-1968)
Hawkwind	(1969->>)
Intermodulation	(1969-1976)
Light/Sound Workshop	(1962-1968)
Music Plus	(1970-197?)
Naked Software	(1970-1973)
Quiet Pavement Ensemble	(1968-197?)
Unit Delta Plus	(1965-1967)
White Noise	(1968->>)

FREE

GIVEN FREE WITH PRACTICAL ELECTRONICS

6 inch 33⅓ r.p.m. **RECORD** "ELECTRONIC SOUNDS AND EFFECTS"

Specially made as sound accompaniment to this month's big feature:—

ELECTRONIC MUSIC TECHNIQUES

Electronic music defined—how it is composed and produced—electronic tone sources and storage devices—professional techniques—circuits and hints for the amateur. With the FREE Record to guide you, this special article shows how *you* can find a fascinating new creative field in this exciting musical form.

PRACTICAL ELECTRONICS — OCTOBER ISSUE OUT NOW 2/6

MAKE SURE OF YOURS TODAY!

plus 7/6 P. & P. £11.11.0

ELECTRONIC MUSIC COMPOSERS A-Z

1

tape recorder

JUNE 1967 TWO SHILLINGS

SONY TC-350A AND WHM FLUTTERMETER REVIEWS • A SIMPLE TAPE
REPORT ON THE 1967 AUDIO FAIR • SERVICING THE THREE-SPEED

TAPE
RECORDING MAGAZINE

SEPTEMBER 1968
2/-

MIXERS and MIXING
Talking about Stars
Editing — More Expert Advice
ELECTRONIC MUSIC
ETC. ETC.

amateur
TAPE RECORDING

VOL. 3 No. 6   PRICE 2/-   JANUARY 1962

full details of the "Winston"
of Tape Recorders write to ➤ **WINSTON ELECTRONICS LTD**
GOVETT AVENUE SHEPPERTON MIDDLESEX
Telephone: Walton-on-Thames 26325

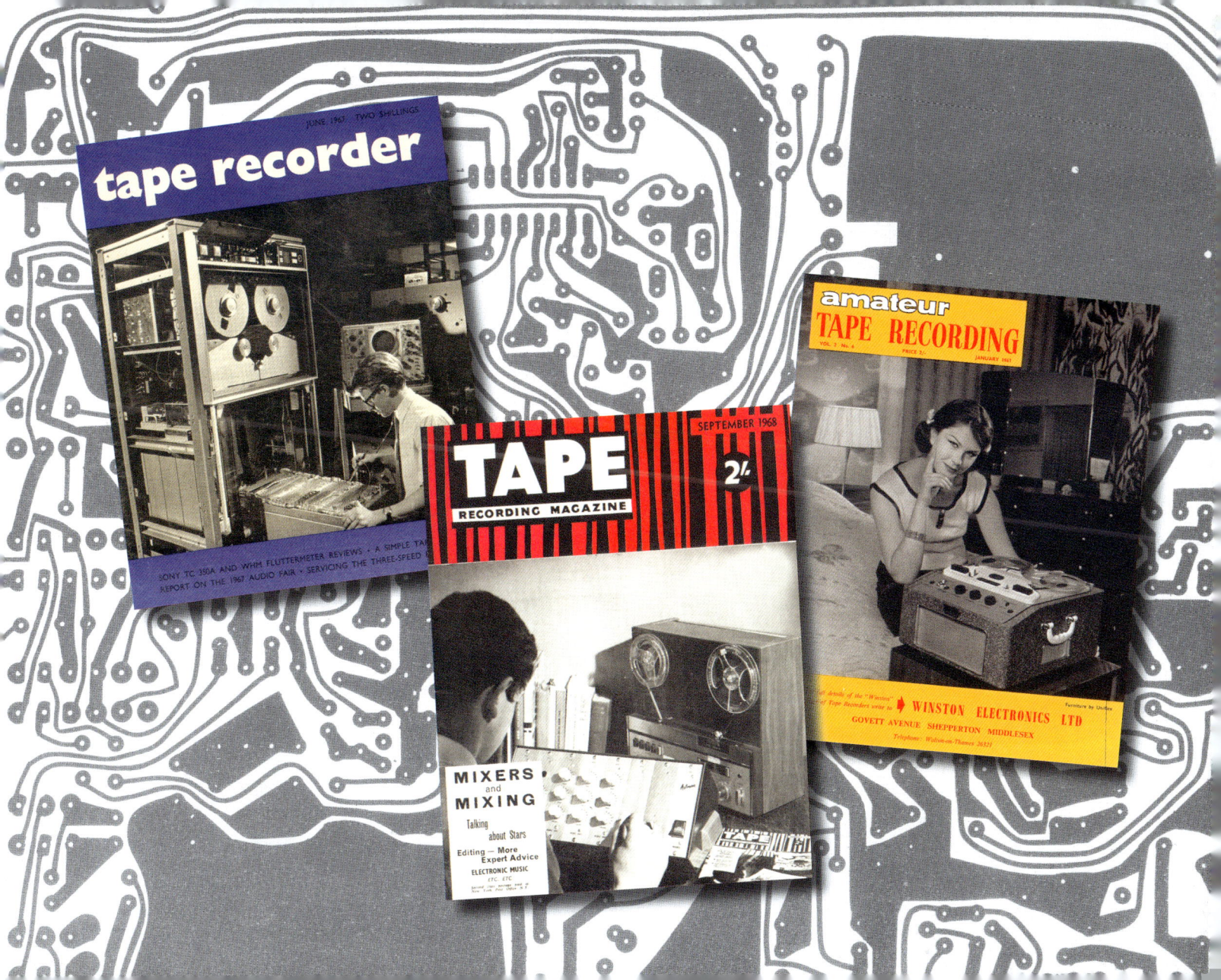

Daevid Allen (1938-2015)

Born: Melbourne, Australia
Earliest Electronic Work: Machine Poets tapes (1962)
Commitment Factor: 5
Obscurity Quotient: 4
EM recording availability: Poor

Growing up in Australia and working in a Melbourne bookshop, the young Christopher David Allen was inspired by the US Beat Generation writers, took up poetry and guitar, and formed the Dave Allen Trio. Leaving Australia in 1960 he travelled to Paris, where he had several inspirational encounters. After meeting US minimalist composer and tape loop exponent Terry Riley, he moved into a room at the Beat Hotel recently vacated by Allen Ginsberg. Fellow residents included Brion Gysin and **William Burroughs**, who were working on text and audio cut ups, and the flickering light Dream Machine. Allen experienced the psychedelic flicker effects first hand, and Burroughs later asked him to form a jazz trio to play during a dramatisation of his book, The Ticket That Exploded. After this, Allen hooked up with Burroughs again in the Machine Poets, a performance group in which he made his first tape loops. The outfit appeared at the ICA in London in 1962, and at the Paris Biennale at the Musee d'Arte Moderne.

Allen's next move was to Britain, and in 1965 he had a fortuitous breakthrough into BBC radio, with a commission for a one hour tape collage titled, The Switch Doctor. This was introduced by producer and poet George MacBeth, written and assembled by Allen, with contributions from future wife Gilli Smyth, and bassist and tape loop experimenter Hugh Hopper. The recording was realised with the facilities of the **Radiophonic Workshop**, and finally broadcast on the BBC Third Network in 1967.

During the mid-60s, Allen worked on a number of tape pieces, including What Do You Want (1964), The Pacific Rim (1964), The Twittering Machine (1965), and She Loves Me Not (1964), based on She Loves You, by **The Beatles**. At this time he was renting a room in Canterbury, and became friendly with his landlord's son, 16 year old Robert Wyatt. Together with Kevin Ayers and Mike Ratledge, they formed the group Soft Machine, and contacted Burroughs for permission to use his 1961 novel's title for their band name. Allen made introductory tapes for playing at the group's gigs, but following a tour of Europe, he was refused re-entry to the UK due to changes in visa restrictions he was unaware of, and he returned to Paris and split from Soft Machine before the recording of their first album. He went on to form the group Gong in 1969, and recorded his first solo LP Banana Moon, the following year. Gong have remained together in various configurations with shifting personnel, while Allen maintained his involvement and continued writing and performing up until his death from cancer.

```
OUTPUT TRANS. EL84 etc. 5/-; MIKE TRANS. 50:1 5/-.
SPEAKER COVERING MATERIALS. Samples Large S.A.E.

SOUND ACTIVATED
PSYCHEDELIC
LIGHT BOX

Fascinating light patterns
of Green, Blue, Red and
Amber. Works with any
mono or stereo amplifier
or radio output.
Input required 0.2 watts.
A.C. mains operated. Size 13
× 13 × 4in.
£12.10.0 Post Free

ALL EAGLE PRODUCTS
SUPPLIED AT LOWEST PRICES
ILLUSTRATED EAGLE CATALOGUE 5/-. Post Free.
```

Barry Anderson (1935-1987)

Born: Stratford, New Zealand
Earliest Electronic Work: Piano Pieces 1, 2 and 3 (1969-74)
Commitment Factor: 8
Obscurity Quotient: 7
EM recording availability: Limited

Anderson's mother was a proficient pianist and he began piano lessons at the age of six; by his teens he was playing concerts of classical repertoire. At 17 he won a scholarship and came to London from New Zealand to pursue piano, viola and composition at the Royal Academy of Music from 1952-56, and later studied piano in Zurich and Lucerne. He discovered the music of Bartok and Stravinsky, and at the end of his studies decided to stay in England and teach, rather than pursue a career as a concert pianist. After a spell living in Gloucestershire he moved back to London in 1962, to focus on his rapidly developing interest in composition. During the 1960s he heard Karlheinz Stockhausen's, Kontakte (1959-60), which left a big impression with its mix of tape sounds and live instruments. It appears his earliest work with electronics occurred with piano in combination with filtering and ring modulation; his Piano Pieces 1, 2 and 3, are sections of a larger composite work, and feature virtuosic piano passages with electronic processing.

Securing a post at the South Bank Institute in London (now part of Morley College), gave him access to facilities to properly pursue his experimental interests, and he established the West Square Electronic Music Studio in 1971, in a college building in Elephant and Castle, South London. (This was a former school where Charlie Chaplin had once been a pupil.) The basic equipment included tape recorders and an **EMS** Synthi, and as the director of the studio, Anderson encouraged and performed new works, with his own Syntaxis Mix, for 8-channel tape, and Topograph, for three percussion groups, fillers and ring-modulators, both composed in 1973. The West Square Electronic Music Ensemble was established that year, and gave its first professional performance at St. John's, Smith Square in Westminster in 1975.

Anderson was co-founder in 1979 of the Electro-Acoustic Music Association of Great Britain (EMAS), and for several years from 1981 onwards, he worked intensively at IRCAM in Paris on The Mask of Orpheus, for **Harrison Birtwistle**; he was instrumental in creating the computer synthesized electronic sequences for the opera. With the completion of the epic project, he then threw himself into his own music, again at IRCAM, and by the end of recording he was very likely suffering from exhaustion. He died aged 52 shortly after a Radio France broadcast of his final work Arc, written for string quartet, bass clarinet and tape.

CD: Arc and Other Electronic Works (Continuum, 1989).

John Baker (1937-1997)

Born: Leigh-on-Sea, Essex
Earliest Electronic Work: Electro Twist (1965)
Commitment Factor: 6
Obscurity Quotient: 4
EM recording availability: Excellent

With a natural flair for music and an early keyboard talent, Baker studied composition and piano at the Royal Academy of Music, joined the BBC in 1960, and transferred three years later to the **Radiophonic Workshop**. He had a passion for jazz and performed live, and was interested in the combination of instruments and tape. His many signature tunes during the 1960s have a distinctive jaunty pop style, characterised by simple techniques such as blowing across bottles and plucking rubber bands, allied to intricate tape manipulation and splicing. He was one of the most recognisable Radiophonic composers of the 60s, but also undertook freelance work outside of the BBC at home in Leigh-on-Sea. Under the pseudonym John Matthews, he carried out various independent commissions, and was employed by advertisers and the Southern Library of Recorded Music. Along with Radiophonic colleague **Brian Hodgson**, he worked on the short, Boy and Bicycle (1965), the first film by director Ridley Scott.

In 1968 a selection of his tracks appeared on the BBC Radiophonic Music album, and the following year he appeared being interviewed for the TV documentary, The Same Trade As Mozart. Vendetta, a Mafia crime spy thriller series, first aired on the BBC in 1966, featuring a number of episodes with Baker's electro-acoustic music.

By the early 70s his taxing workload led to alcohol dependence, and he became increasingly withdrawn. He had bouts of illness and absence from work, and finally his career at the BBC was terminated in 1974. Although he continued to play the piano, quite often in a lounge jazz idiom, he never returned to electronic music before his death aged 59.

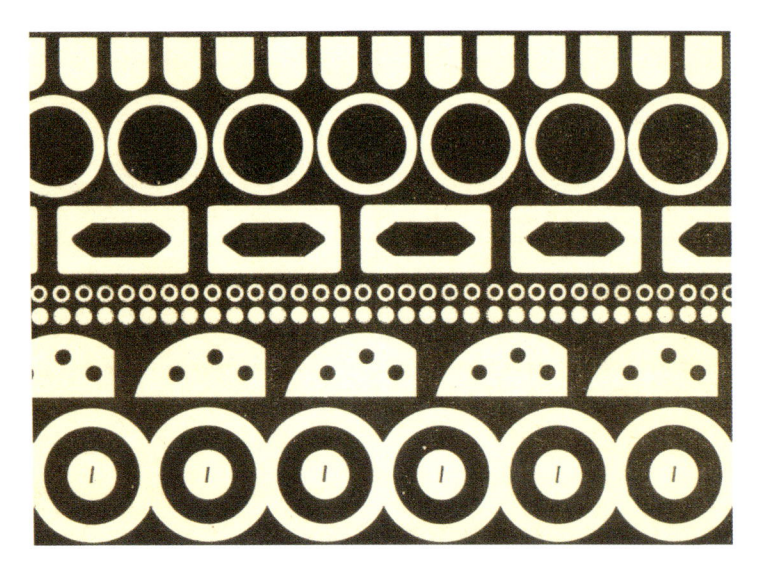

CDs:
The John Baker Tapes 1 & 2 (Trunk, 2008)
BBC Radiophonic Music (BBC, 2008) – includes 18 tracks by John Baker.
John Baker: The Vendetta Tapes (Buried Treasure, 2015)

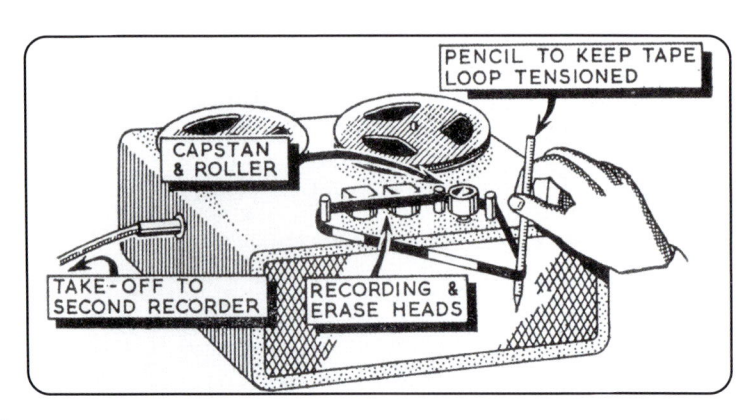

Laurie Scott Baker (1943)

Born: Sydney, Australia
Earliest Electronic Work: Tape Loop Studies (1968-69)
Commitment Factor: 6
Obscurity Quotient: 6
EM recording availability: Good

After leaving school at 15, Laurie Scott Baker worked on the Sydney Morning Herald newspaper, which gave him experience in graphics that would prove useful later in life when developing new musical notation. He studied harmony and double bass from 1959-60, and kept up a regular club gig at a jazz venue in Sydney. It was during this period that he first used contact mics and tape to extend the possibilities of the double bass, and look ahead to the new horizons opened up by electronics.

He was interested in the work of modern jazz players as well as contemporary classical composers, and left Australia in 1964 to pursue his musical interests. Arriving in London in spring the following year, he sought out left field musicians, attended the Little Theatre Club sessions of John Stevens, and hooked up with composer Cornelius Cardew. Becoming immersed in London's modern music scene, he wrote his own compositions which would often involve graphic notation, and at the same time found regular session work, including a lengthy stint in the West End production of Hair. Starting in 1968, the residency at the Shaftesbury Theatre lasted several years, and in that period he introduced **EMS** synthesizer generated electronic sounds, into the freeform opening section of the musical. Taking part in many high profile concerts, he joined the Scratch Orchestra in 1969, and People's Liberation Music in 1972. Active with the Recreation Ground Theatre Company, he was also a member of the Progressive Cultural Association, as well as the Musician's Union.

Baker assembled his own electronic studio and created tape loop pieces, and at the end of the 60s received a demonstration from **Tristram Cary** of the prototype VCS3 synthesizer, and purchased one of the first production models. He was also friendly with EMS designer David Cockerell, and at one point the pair carried out a bioacoustic experiment by wiring up house plants. In touch with **Brian Dennis** and **Hugh Davies**, he was well connected and worked with a variety of groups and performers, including Maggie Bell, Alex Harvey, Harry Beckett and Robert Wyatt. He provided Synthi contributions for Bob Downes Open Music, and Manfred Mann's Earth Band on the title track of their 1973 album Messin'.

By 1970 he had broken through into film and TV scoring, and that year wrote two songs for the feature film, Secrets. In 1977 he scored the first of two animations by Geoff Dunbar, and by the 1980s had found full-time employment at the BBC as a dubbing mixer, which involved a very brief attachment to the **Radiophonic Workshop**. He has subsequently worked on commissions for BBC radio drama, and set up the record label Musicnow, releasing his own music and an album by Brian Dennis. In 2013 his exhibition, Graphic Music Scores 1965-1970, ran for several months at the SNO Contemporary Art Projects gallery in Sydney, Australia.

CD: Laurie Scott Baker: Gracility (Musicnow, 2009).

Laurie Scott Baker at the VCS3, early 1970s

Don Banks (1923-1980)

Born: South Melbourne, Australia
Earliest Electronic Work: Equation (1968)
Commitment Factor: 8
Obscurity Quotient: 6
EM recording availability: Limited

Although an Australian born composer with a lifelong passion for jazz, Banks played an important role in early British electronic music, having moved to London in 1950 to pursue his composition studies. After working briefly with Milton Babbitt in Salzburg, Austria, he won a scholarship to study with Luigi Dallapiccola in Florence, Italy in 1953. After this he settled back in London, though there was one further significant period of tuition three years later, when he attended a summer school at Gravesano, Switzerland. This was at the villa of the noted conductor Hermann Scherchen, who had established a private electronic music studio in 1954.

Returning to London, Banks began to work in film and TV music, while producing serious compositions that would establish him as a prominent figure in the British music scene. Similar to his friend **Tristram Cary**, his musical output covered a variety of forms, including jazz, chamber, orchestral and electronic music. To support himself and family, he worked extensively in commercial fields, and along with **Desmond Leslie** and **Roberto Gerhard**, he had a piece included in the Doctor Who story The Space Museum (1965). He built up a composing relationship with Hammer Films, scoring The Evil of Frankenstein (1964); Nightmare (1964); The Reptile (1966); Rasputin, the Mad Monk (1966); and The Mummy's Shroud (1967); amongst others. In all, he wrote soundtracks for 19 feature films, 22 documentaries and more than 60 episodes of various television serials. Developing a connection with Halas & Batchelor Cartoon Films, he scored a variety of short films and adverts.

During the early 1960s, as well as pursuing the 12 tone method of composing, Banks became interested in electronics and electro-acoustic music. His output includes a number of pieces that fuse synthesized sounds with instruments, such as Intersections (1969), and Benedictus (1976), for voices, jazz quartet, synthesizer, electric piano and tape. As Banks was friendly with John Dankworth and Cleo Laine, it was the Dankworth Ensemble with the London Sinfonietta, who first recorded his electro-acoustic composition Meeting Place (1970). The piece Commentary (1971), for piano and two channel tape, includes recorded speaking parts with the voices of Banks and Harvey Matusow.

Through his connection to Tristram and **EMS**, and allegedly with the sum of £50, he instigated the development of the Don Banks Music Box, the progenitor of the VCS3 synthesizer. This original which Banks took with him when he relocated back to Australia, resides in the Powerhouse Museum in Sydney, though it has not been kept in a playable condition. In November 1970 he gave a presentation on electronic instruments for BBC Radio 3, and in 1968 his piece Equation, a 'third stream' work for small jazz group, was taped and then analysed by computer at EMS; the first time this type of waveform synthesis was used in Britain.

He was chairman of the Society for the Promotion of New Music at the end of the 1960s, and a founding member of the British Society for Electronic Music, serving on the committee which included Tristram Cary, **Peter Zinovieff** and **Hugh Davies**. They were all involved in a concert of British electronic music at the Queen Elizabeth Hall in February 1969, which included Equation, and work by **Donald Henshilwood**, **Justin Connolly**, **Lawrence Casserley**, **Harrison Birtwistle** and **Ernest Berk**.

Following a visit to Australia in 1970, Banks returned permanently two years later, and in October 1973 he was appointed Head of Composition and Electronic Music Studies, at the Canberra School of Music. He became a consultant in the development of electronic music studios in high schools and colleges, and in 1977 he took up a position at the New South Wales State Conservatorium of Music, three years before his untimely death of cancer.

CD: Don Banks: Nexus (ABC, 2007) Includes Meeting Place.

Janet Beat (1937)

Born: Streetly, Staffordshire
Earliest Electronic Work: Untitled tape (1957)
Commitment Factor: 8
Obscurity Quotient: 7
EM recording availability: Poor

A childhood fascination with sounds of the countryside signalled the beginning of Janet Beat's lifelong interest in music, science and the arts. Machine-made noises were also a formative influence, and the family engineering business and industry of the West Midlands, opened up factory visits and first-hand exposure to the sounds of industrial processes. Contrary to parental expectations, she attended Birmingham School of Music to pursue the horn, and then studied music at Birmingham University. It was there in the late 1950s, that she first became aware of electronic music by Henk Badings and Karlheinz Stockhausen. Unable to find any courses or tuition for tape experimentation, or much encouragement from tutors, she sought advice from university technicians, and set about teaching herself with the purchase of a Brenell open reel recorder, and books about tape editing techniques.

Janet Beat in her home studio

Her first two untitled musique concrète pieces date from 1957, and incorporated household sounds such as sewing machine, typewriter and vacuum cleaner. Two works of Aural Sculpture from 1958-59, were based around car sounds, lawn mower, electric mixer, water and creaking floorboards. One of her later compositions from this formative period, Piece for JR (1968), explored purely electronic sources using a signal generator with ring modulation, but the recording no longer exists – unfortunately all her early tapes were damaged in a flood and did not survive.

While teaching at Worcester College of Education, she established a course for electronic music making, and during the 1960s she worked as a freelance horn player. In 1972 she joined the staff of the Royal Scottish Academy of Music and Drama (RSAMD) in Glasgow, and also made contact with **Daphne Oram**, who provided help and advice on circuit designs, and backed the setting up of an electronic music studio at the Academy. Beat visited **EMS** in Putney and received a perfunctory synthesizer demonstration from **Peter Zinovieff**; she nevertheless purchased a suitcase Synthi A, and used it for her electro-acoustic experimentation throughout the 1970s. When the RSAMD moved to a new building in 1987, she initiated the installation of a fully equipped recording studio. She is a founder member of the Scottish Society of Composers, and the Scottish Electro-Acoustic Music Society. In 1988 she formed the group Soundstrata, to perform contemporary music, and in 1991 retired from full-time teaching to concentrate on composing.

Brenell BRENELL ENGINEERING CO., LTD
1a DOUGHTY STREET, LONDON W.C.1.
Telephone: HOLborn 7356/8

David Bedford (1937-2011)

Born: London
Earliest Electronic Work: Piece I (1962) Recorded in Italy
Commitment Factor: 2
Obscurity Quotient: 4
EM recording availability: Limited

Born into a musical family, Bedford began composing at an early age, attended Trinity College in London, and studied with Lennox Berkeley at the Royal Academy of Music from 1958-61. With a grant from the Italian government, he was able to study with Luigi Nono in Venice, and at the RAI Electronic Music Studio in Milan during 1961, where he began work on Piece I. Back at home in London he qualified as a music teacher, and maintained a keen interest in astronomy and science fiction. In 1968 he devised a musical arrangement for a show, From Marie Antoinette to the Beatles, at London's Roundhouse, which was stage managed by an associate of the Soft Machine. This led to an introduction with Kevin Ayers, former guitarist of the group, who was looking for an arranger for his Joy Of A Toy album. Bedford arranged, played keyboards, and became a member of the Whole World backing group, which also included Mike Oldfield and Lol Coxhill.

From 1963, Bedford had two or three commissions to do every year, and this continued through the Whole World period. His piece The Garden of Love, for pop band and instruments, was performed at the Queen Elizabeth Hall by the London Sinfonietta, alongside Kevin Ayers and the Whole World. Piece for Mo (1963), was conducted by Bedford from a specially constructed console, which gave signals to performers via the flashing of coloured lights. Other works designed for educational use include Music for Albion Moonlight (1965), and Whitefield Music (1966). In 1978 came one of his most celebrated compositions, The Rime of the Ancient Mariner, a music theatre piece which can be performed by players of varying musical ability.

After three albums with Ayers, Bedford went on to orchestrate several Mike Oldfield compositions, and collaborated with a variety of musicians in the 1970s, including Roy Harper, the Edgar Broughton Band and Steve Hillage. In later years he worked as arranger and/or conductor for a diverse selection of artists, such as Billy Bragg, Elvis Costello, Frankie Goes to Hollywood, A-ha, the Jesus and Mary Chain, and Madness. His film work includes orchestrations for The Killing Fields, Supergrass, Absolute Beginners and Orlando. He was Composer-In-Residence at Queen's College, London from 1969-1981, and heavily involved with youth music education throughout his life. Maintaining contact with **Brian Dennis** amongst others, he was concerned with introducing new initiatives and progressive teaching methods into the classroom.

Ernest Berk (1909-1993)

Born: Cologne, Germany
Earliest Electronic Work: End of the World Op. 1 (1957)
Commitment Factor: 10
Obscurity Quotient: 6
EM recording availability: Good

One of the most prolific and colourful of all the British pioneers of electronic music – a dancer, choreographer, teacher, composer and nudist – Berk met his first wife Lotte Heimansohn while they both trained under Mary Wigman at a dance school in Cologne, and they married in 1933. Though born in Germany, his passport was British, allowing the couple and their daughter an escape to England upon the rise of the Nazis. They settled in London and were later to divorce, and both opened their own studios. Lotte Berk invented her world renowned exercise method, while Ernest established his studio for electronic music in 1955, at 249 Camden Road, London, N7. He was looking for sound that would match the experimental type of dance he wanted to pursue, and in the mid-50s he was drawn to electronic music, as a form that could better express his ideas than conventional musical styles. In his Camden studio with tape recorders, percussion and tone generators, he created dozens of electronic pieces; far more productive than almost any of his contemporaries.

His musical works during this period enjoyed a high profile amongst his fellow British experimenters, and in 1968 two of them were played at the Queen Elizabeth Hall and the London Planetarium, alongside pieces by **Tristram Cary**, **Stuart Wynn Jones**, **Peter Zinovieff** and **Brian Dennis**. For a February 1969 concert of British electronic music at the QEH, the Financial Times reviewer Dominic Gill described Berk's Sychrome as revealing, "*students from three drama schools writhing expressively to an electronic accompaniment like beautiful maggots.*"

With his second wife Ailsa, he established a new studio at 52 Dorset Street, London, in 1970, and gave tuition in modern dance and electronic composition, as well as performances with the Ernest Berk Dance Theatre Commune. He also taught at the Guildhall School of Music and Drama, from where a number of the Commune members were drawn. Striving for a total theatre experience, he was interested in dance, electronic music, poetry, film and lights, combining into an exciting synthesis. The Dance Theatre Commune appeared at many live events, and performed at The Roundhouse in London, on day 5 of the ICES-72 festival.

In the early 70s Berk released a privately pressed album with two side long electronic tracks, Initiation and Gemini; both ballet scores. He composed music for several movies, including an abstract short by artist John Latham, and three films by British director and editor David Gladwell; among them the brilliant and beguiling An Untitled Film. Intriguingly Berk is credited with music for the feature length Last of the Long-haired Boys (1968), a World War II drama which failed to get a UK cinema release. He made a number of pieces for library music labels, including Conroy, Rediffusion, Morgan and the CBS EZ Cue library.

Working with a variety of dancers, choreographers, poets and composers, Berk collaborated musically with John Tilbury and **Basil Kirchin**. In 1962 he recorded Kali Yuga at the studio of **Desmond Leslie**, and dedicated to him the piece Anecdote 1. He made around 200 recordings, and his tapes and some equipment and papers were bequeathed to the Historical Archives of the City of Cologne. However, due to a catastrophic structural collapse of the museum building in 2009, it appears that some, if not all of his materials were tragically damaged.

Unlike the overwhelming majority of his peers, Berk carried on making uncompromising electronic music even as a pensioner well into the 1980s, using more or less the same analogue equipment that he had started with in the 50s; tape recorders, tone generators, microphones, filters, voices and percussion. He is unique in Britain for his pioneering work fusing experimental electronics and dance, and unlike his American counterparts such as Alwin Nikolais, his major contribution to this form is yet to be properly acknowledged.

Photos courtesy of Mick Dunn

Harrison Birtwistle (1934)

Born: Accrington, Lancashire
Earliest Electronic Work: Four Interludes for a Tragedy (1968)
Commitment Factor: 4
Obscurity Quotient: 3
EM recording availability: Good

Encouraged by his mother who bought him a clarinet when he was seven, Birtwistle's musical interests were fostered with lessons from the local military bandmaster, and after joining the band, he played in accompaniments to Gilbert and Sullivan productions. In 1952 he entered the Royal Manchester College of Music on a clarinet scholarship, and hooked up with fellow composers Peter Maxwell Davies and Alexander Goehr. Together they formed the New Music Manchester group, dedicated to the performance of modern compositions. Birtwistle left the college in 1955 and carried out two years National Service, followed by a spell teaching at schools in Wiltshire. A Harkness Fellowship gave him two years of study in the USA, where he became Visiting Fellow at Princeton University.

Back in Britain in 1969 he collaborated for the first time with **Peter Zinovieff**, who worked on the tape parts for three pieces: Four Interludes for a Tragedy, Linoi and Medusa. The first version of Medusa, for instruments and tapes; one of synthesized sounds and the other featuring distorted saxophone, also included a part for a **Hugh Davies** Shozyg. It was first performed at the University of Sheffield in 1969 by Zinovieff and the Pierrot Players; the group Birtwistle had co-founded with Maxwell Davies.

Known primarily for his instrumental works, Birtwistle nonetheless included electronic tape in several other pieces, and in 1971 he composed Chronometer, made purely from the sounds of various clock mechanisms, with Big Ben providing the central ostinato. These sounds were recorded and assembled by Zinovieff and analysed by computer at **EMS**, with assistance from **Peter Grogono**. The collaborations with Zinovieff also included the soundtrack for Sidney Lumet's terrific, gritty police drama The Offence, starring Sean Connery. It proved to be Birtwistle's first and last film score, and aside from Chronometer, all his other early electronic works were left unpublished or withdrawn. The libretto for his gargantuan opera The Mask of Orpheus (1973-86), was written by Zinovieff, though the long and protracted process in bringing the opera to fruition – due to the complex staging requirements, and the commission passing between several different organisations – meant a lengthy hiatus after the first two acts were completed by 1975. During this time EMS folded, and Zinovieff had begun pursuing other interests aside from electronic music, so Birtwistle approached the IRCAM studio in Paris in 1981 to pick up the threads. Exploring computer synthesized voices, the project gained a further collaborator, with **Barry Anderson** working with Birtwistle at IRCAM, to create around around an hour's worth of tape music by 1983. Three years later The Mask of Orpheus was finally premiered at the London Coliseum by English National Opera.

Birtwistle became musical director of the National Theatre in London in 1975, and he was knighted in 1988. From 1994 to 2001 he was Henry Purcell Professor of Composition at King's College, London. He gained minor notoriety in 1995, when his piece Panic, premiered at the Last Night of the Proms at the Royal Albert Hall, caused outrage amongst the narrow-minded in the audience.

Michael Blake (1930-?)

Born: Untraced
Earliest Electronic Work: Decomposition Mark 1 (1959)
Commitment Factor: 5
Obscurity Quotient: 10
EM recording availability: Poor

Decomposition Mark 1, was recorded for a theatre work at an ad hoc studio in London belonging to Steven Grant. Decomposition Marks 2-4, were created during 1963-64 in Paris at the Theatre des Champs Elysees, and Mark 5, in 1965 in Geneva. There is also a listing for a piece entitled Decomposition of **William Burroughs**, from 1966, recorded back in Paris at the Theatre La Boheme. The search for information continues.

Desmond Briscoe (1925-2006)

Born: Birkenhead, Merseyside
Earliest Electronic Work: All that Fall (1956)
Commitment Factor: 7
Obscurity Quotient: 5
EM recording availability: Limited

Starting his musical career as a drummer, Briscoe first performed on radio in Children's Hour, and got his break into the BBC in Manchester at 16, as a programme engineer. After World War II military service, he returned to the BBC this time in London, as a programme assistant for radio drama, controlling sound effects and balancing. He was enthusiastic about musique concrète from Paris, and was thus recruited by influential radio producer Donald McWhinnie, for the sound design of All That Fall, by Samuel Beckett, broadcast in 1957. Briscoe worked on other well received radio productions, which helped cement the need for a permanent BBC facility for the production of experimental sound. Alongside **Daphne Oram**, he was a senior studio manager at the **Radiophonic Workshop** at its inception in 1958, and took over as studio head on Oram's departure, remaining there for the rest of his career. A further renowned electronic contribution came on TV in 1958, with the sci-fi serial Quatermass and the Pit, and he established his own studio in Staines, Surrey the following year. Working there he created electronic sounds for a number of noteworthy British feature films, including The Haunting, Children of the Damned, and The Ipcress File. In 1966 a selection of his electronic pieces appeared on the LP, Electronic Sound Pictures, in the Listen, Move and Dance series. A track from this, Group Shapes, cropped up in the Doctor Who story The Moonbase (1966).

Briscoe was on the panel of judges – alongside Oram and **Tristram Cary** – for the Tape Recorder magazine's amateur music contest in 1959. At the 4th National Tape Recording Course held at the Rose Bruford Training College in Sidcup, Kent in April 1961, he was among several tutors including **FC Judd**, who gave instruction on tape recording and electronic music. For the 1969 BBC TV documentary The Same Trade As Mozart, he described the basic physics of sound, and the fundamental waveforms used in synthesis. During a trip to the USA in 1970, he visited Robert Moog and discussed the current state of synthesizer development, looking to equip the Workshop with more up to date sound generators. Ironically during a visit to the University of Wisconsin, he worked with students on three radio projects, using a recently acquired British VCS3 synthesizer. Back in London he advised on the purchase of **EMS** equipment, overseeing the procurement of the VCS3 in 1970, and the Synthi 100 the following year. In May 1971 he presented an impressive concert at the Royal Festival Hall, for the Institute of Electrical Engineers, which featured six VCS3s, film, lasers, smoke and oscilloscope projections, as well as a **Delia Derbyshire** piece created on the Synthi 100.

Although mainly desk bound and embroiled in administrative tasks, Briscoe still managed to make electronic music during the 1960s and 70s; he contributed to ghostly TV drama The Stone Tape (1972), and the Nicholas Roeg feature The Man Who Fell To Earth (1976). A year before his retirement in 1984, he co-wrote the book The BBC Radiophonic Workshop – The First 25 Years, giving his personal perspective on the studio's history, and in 2003 he appeared in the documentary Alchemists of Sound.

George Brown (1947)

Born: Cardiff
Earliest Electronic Work: Musique Concrète experiments (1965-66)
Commitment Factor: 5
Obscurity Quotient: 8
EM recording availability: Poor

Studying composition with Richard Hall at Dartington College of Arts from 1965-66, Brown carried out initial experiments with tape manipulation, and met his harpsichord playing future wife Helena; marrying her in 1969. He studied at the Royal College of Music from 1966-70, with **Humphrey Searle** and Alexander Goehr his tutors for composition, and Edwin Roxburgh for conducting and contemporary music. Signing up for **Tristram Cary**'s new RCM electronic music course in 1967 – alongside **Lawrence Casserley** and **Howard Davidson** – he later joined a new evening class in electronic music at Goldsmiths College run by **Hugh Davies**, and helped him build and install some of the studio equipment.

Also in 67 he received a commission for a ballet score, The Little Dog Laughed, from Ballet Rambert, and with choreography by Jonathan Taylor, it was first performed in March 1968 at the Jeanetta Cochrane Theatre. The score was for string quintet, percussion, piano and tape, and as the RCM studio was yet to be fully operational, the tape part was made at the **BBC Radiophonic Workshop**, with the assistance of **Delia Derbyshire** and **David Vorhaus**.

In 1969 Brown provided the electronic background music and effects for a stage production of Richard III, and continued making short tape pieces (now withdrawn). His composition, Splurge: the whole world is in a state of chassis, for small ensemble with live electronic transformation, gained a RCM prize that same year, and a number of performances. Another tape piece, Prisms, commissioned for the 1970 Cheltenham Music Festival, received its premiere along with electronic work by Tristram Cary, Howard Davidson, Milton Babbitt and Karlheinz Stockhausen. Brown generated the basic sound material for Prisms, at Cary's studio in Fressingfield, Suffolk, with the treatment and final assembly carried out at the RCM. Later that year, in order to play composer-violinist George Whitman's microtonal compositions, Brown and his wife formed a performance trio with Whitman, and accompanied him on a specially adapted **EMS** VCS3 synthesizer. Especially early on in his career, Brown was particularly active in avant-garde music, working with Stockhausen, Morton Feldman and **Harrison Birtwistle**. He put together a version of Birtwistle's Medusa, for ensemble, Shozyg and tape, and conducted one of its rare performances.

Brown took over running the electronic music studio at Goldsmiths College in the 1970s, and during the time **John Buller** was involved, he was on the committee of the Macnaghten Concerts until its demise in the mid-90s. Since the 1980s, as George Mowat-Brown, he has spent most of his musical life lecturing on contemporary music, and teaching composition; firstly at the University of Surrey, and then predominantly for the Open University.

He has continued to write a small number of musical works, but without institutional access to electronic studio facilities, he has focussed on acoustic instruments. Besides music, he is something of an authority on classic British cars, in particular Rovers and the Hillman Imp. The epidemiology of multiple sclerosis in Scotland, is another of his areas of special interest.

John Buller (1927-2004)

Born: London
Earliest Electronic Work: The Cave (1970)
Commitment Factor: 3
Obscurity Quotient: 8
EM recording availability: Poor

Enjoying a musical childhood, Buller was a chorister at St. Matthews, Westminster, and in 1946 he had an early composition accepted by the BBC. Deciding against a career in music, he became an architectural surveyor, and it was not until he was in his thirties that he resumed serious music studies. In 1965 he attended a summer school led by **Harrison Birtwistle**, and he joined the Macnaghten Concerts Committee, serving as chairman from 1971-76. In the early 1970s he gave up surveying work completely, and his piece The Cave, for flute, clarinet, trombone, cello and tape, was premiered in London by the Nash Ensemble in 1972. From 1975-76 he was Composer-in-Residence at the University of Edinburgh, holding a similar post at Queens University, Belfast from 1985-86.

Over the years his work has received broadcasts and high profile performances; in 1978 The Mime of Mick, Nick and the Maggies, was staged at the Roundhouse, and The Theatre of Memory, was commissioned by the BBC for the 1981 Proms. Buller tended to work slowly and methodically, though wrote further electro-acoustic pieces including Le Terrazze (1974), for 14 instruments and tape, and Towards Aquarius (1983). After a spell living in France, he returned to live in Dorset, but signs of Alzheimer's were becoming apparent and starting to inhibit his composition. His final significant work Illusions, a 12 minute orchestral piece, was premiered at the Cheltenham Music Festival in 1997.

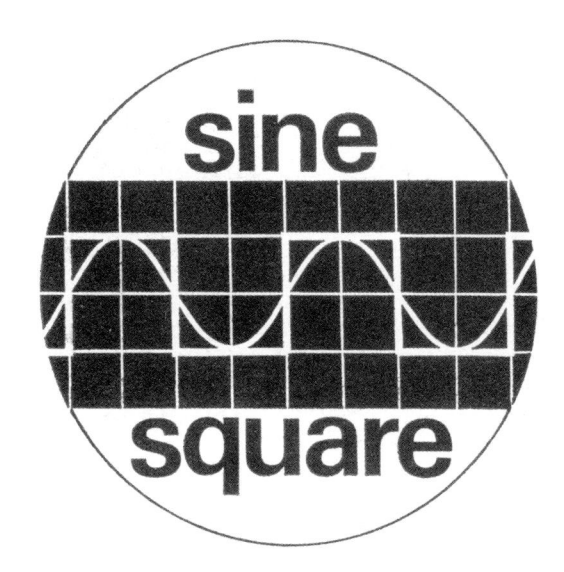

The Macnaghten Concerts were established in 1931 by Iris Lemare, Elizabeth Lutyens and Anne Macnaghten, to foster contemporary classical music, and ran until 1937. The initiative was a voluntary organisation registered as a charity, and revived in 1952 as the New Macnaghten Concerts. It promoted performances of avant-garde compositions, and from 1960, included presentations of electronic music. In November 1968 a series of concerts in London aired electro-acoustic works by Karlheinz Stockhausen, which involved **Hugh Davies**, **Richard Orton**, and the Arts Laboratory Ensemble with **Howard Rees** on clarinet. For the printed programme to accompany the series, **Brian Dennis** created a special text montage entitled Hello Stockhausen! In 1971 the Macnaghten Concerts executive committee featured **John Buller** as Treasurer, **Justin Connolly** as Chairman, with members including Hugh Davies and Michael Nyman. The charity was formally wound up in 2001.

William S. Burroughs (1914-1997)

Born: St. Louis, Missouri, USA
Earliest Electronic Work: Tape experiments (early 1960s) Recorded in Paris
Commitment Factor: 2
Obscurity Quotient: 2
EM recording availability: Good

Grandson of inventor and founder of the Burroughs Adding Machine Company, and nephew of a publicist for the Rockefeller family, William Seward Burroughs was evidently from a wealthy background. In 1932 he attended Harvard University studying English, and later travelled to Vienna for a spell at a medical school, all the while receiving a generous allowance from his parents. On his return to America he eventually enlisted in the US Navy in 1942, though was allowed a swift discharge on medical grounds, and made his way to New York.

By 1944 he was living with Joan Vollmer, and sharing with fellow writer Jack Kerouac. He became a heroin addict and was subsequently busted on a drugs charge and fled to Mexico, where Vollmer and their son joined him. In 1951 Burroughs accidentally shot and killed her during a drunken game, and was arrested for homicide. Skipping bail he returned to the USA, and by that time had written his first two novels and collaborated on a book with Kerouac. In 1954 he left for Tangier, and spent the next four years working on his breakthrough novel Naked Lunch. He moved to Paris, found a room at the Beat Hotel, and encountered Brion Gysin (1916-1986) and the cut-up technique; used most significantly in his books that make up The Nova Trilogy (1961-64).

British filmmaker and distributor Anthony Balch (1937-1980), got to know Burroughs, Gysin and Ian Sommerville (1940-1976) at the Beat Hotel, and Balch made three short films with them: Towers Open Fire (1963), The Cut-Ups (1967) and Bill and Tony (1972). Sommerville was a Cambridge mathematics graduate and boyfriend of Burroughs, and his technical expertise facilitated experiments with audio tape as well as flickering light. By the mid-60s the pair had left Paris for London, and through his connection to the Indica Gallery, Sommerville met **Beatles** member Paul McCartney, and became in-house recording engineer for McCartney's basement studio at 34 Montagu Square in London. Aside from McCartney himself, Burroughs was the other main user of the studio, and in collaboration with Sommerville, he conducted various tape experiments with backwards sounds, overdubbing and manually pulling the tape across the record heads. He would read extracts from his written texts or newspaper reports, or use radio broadcasts as random sound sources. Eventually the Montagu Square flat was let to Jimi Hendrix, and later John Lennon and Yoko Ono, and Burroughs left London in 1974 to continue his celebrated literary career based in the USA.

Tristram Cary (1925-2008)

Born: Oxford
Earliest Electronic Work: Experimental studies (1947-1955)
Commitment Factor: 10
Obscurity Quotient: 3
EM recording availability: Excellent

The son of novelist Joyce Cary, Tristram attended Westminster School from 1938-42 where he met Michael Flanders and Donald Swann; Swann introduced him to Stravinsky's music, which Tristram cited as a significant inspiration. He was studying at Christ Church, Oxford when he was called up for military service in 1943, serving in the Royal Navy until 1946. Trained to work with radar, this specialist knowledge of electronics combined with his passion for music, was to have the most profound effect on his future career.

Once he was demobbed from the Navy, he soon began experimenting with war surplus electronic equipment, which he could salvage very cheaply from second hand shops in London. By 1947 he was independently constructing his own very basic electronic music studio in the basement of his parent's house in Oxford, at a time when the celebrated work in Paris and Cologne was in its infancy. He was clearly in the vanguard of the new music, and before tape recorders were readily available, he invested in a disc cutting lathe, working with 78 rpm discs alongside his collection of oscillators.

Graduating from London's Trinity College of Music in 1950, the following year he got married and moved to a house in Earl's Court. Earning an income giving evening classes, and a job at a gramophone shop in the West End, it was not until 1955 that he received his BBC breakthrough. The Japanese Fishermen, was one of the earliest British radio plays to feature electronics, realised three years before the founding of the **Radiophonic Workshop**. From this point in the mid-1950s Tristram was able to concentrate on commissions, and support himself and his family, composing for film, TV, radio, kinetic sculpture, exhibitions and the concert hall. Also in 1955 came his score for The Ladykillers; the first of many films which include Time Without Pity, The Flesh Is Weak, Tread Softly Stranger; and for Hammer: Quatermass and the Pit (1967), and Blood From the Mummy's Tomb (1971). In addition he provided special electronic sound for Sebastian, and Here We Go Round the Mulberry Bush.

Like **Daphne Oram** and **George Newson**, Tristram visited the Brussels World's Fair in 1958, where the Richard Williams animation The Little Island, was screened, featuring his soundtrack. During the late 1950s and 60s he was much in demand, and in April 1966 as a member of the Composers' Guild of Great Britain, he invited fellow Guild members to his Fressingfield studio in Suffolk, to experience tape experimentation first hand. Those attending included **Thea Musgrave**, **Anna Lockwood**, Alan Rawsthorne, and Ernest Tomlinson. His electronic music was heard in animations for Halas & Batchelor; at the British Pavilion for Expo 67 in Montreal; and on the radio in the award winning play The Ballad of Peckham Rye. He established the Royal College of Music electronic studio in 1967, with **Lawrence Casserley**, and **Howard Davidson**, among the first students to sign up for his new course.

He joined **Peter Zinovieff** and David Cockerell in forming **EMS** and developing the VCS3, the first British production synthesizer, for which Tristram designed and built the prototype cabinet. (This original instrument is now in the possession of his eldest son John.) As a champion of British avant-garde tape music, he helped to promote and organise concerts, including an electronic music programme at the Queen Elizabeth Hall in January 1968, where his pieces 3 4 5, and Birth Is Life Is Power Is Death Is God Is... were played. The concert also featured work by **Delia Derbyshire**, Peter Zinovieff, Daphne Oram, George Newson, **Jacob Meyerowitz** and **Ernest Berk**. His Suite – Leviathan '99, a concert version of radio soundtrack music he created for a Ray Bradbury play, was premiered at the same venue in 1972, along with a performance from Ernest Berk's Dance Theatre Commune. With an invitation to lecture in Australia, and friendships with composers **Don Banks** and **Grahame Dudley**, during the early 1970s Tristram

Tristram Cary and a section of the score for Trios

was tempted to relocate down under. He was visiting senior lecturer at the University of Melbourne in 1973; visiting composer at the University of Adelaide in 1974; becoming Senior Lecturer and finally Dean of music in 1982. His electronic studio which had moved to Earls Court and then to Fressingfield, made its way to Australia; most of it being incorporated into the expanding teaching studio at Adelaide University. In 1986 he left the University to resume self-employment, operating as Tristram Cary Creative Music Services. During 1988-90 he concentrated on writing a major book on music, published in London in 1992 as The Illustrated Compendium of Musical Technology. The University of Adelaide awarded him the position of Honorary Visiting Research Fellow, in which capacity he continued his computer music research, and in 2001 he gained the degree Doctor of Music. He retained dual citizenship, and in 1991 was awarded the Medal of the Order of Australia for services to Australian music.

Making significant contributions to the Doctor Who series during its classic years of the 1960s and 70s, his uncompromising electronic score for the second ever Who adventure in 1963, provided a menacing backdrop for the enduring appeal of the Daleks. He composed for several other stories during the 60s, and his final contribution was in 1972 for the Jon Pertwee tale The Mutants, made at his Fressingfield studio with tape and EMS synthesizers. Although he wished for more recognition for his instrumental music in the concert hall, he still looked upon his Doctor Who work with pride. Tristram was a pivotal figure in early British electronic music, and is justly celebrated for his pioneering explorations in the field, while being personally remembered for his helpfulness and generosity.

CDs:
Tristram Cary: Soundings (Tall Poppies, 2000).
Tristram Cary: Devils' Planets (BBC Music, 2003).
Tristram Cary: It's Time For Tristram Cary (Trunk, 2010).

Lawrence Casserley (1941)

Born: Little Easton, Essex
Earliest Electronic Work: The Final Desolation of Solitude (1968)
Commitment Factor: 10
Obscurity Quotient: 6
EM recording availability: Good

As a youngster, Casserley sang in church choirs, later discovering jazz and classical music. In 1952 he and his family moved to the USA, and from 1962 he was attending the Chicago Musical College, studying percussion, flute and piano, alongside conducting and composition. At the college he first encountered a performance of Karlheinz Stockhausen's Kontakte, which opened his mind to the potential of electro-acoustic music. He returned to Britain in 1966 and started as a post-graduate student at the Royal College of Music in London, studying composition with Herbert Howells. While continuing courses in conducting and percussion, Howells recommended him for a new class in electronic music established by **Tristram Cary** in 1967. At that stage the RCM tape studio was nowhere near finished, and for the first two terms, Casserley and fellow students **George Brown** and **Howard Davidson** made visits to Tristram's Fressingfield studio in Suffolk, as well as the **BBC Radiophonic Workshop**, and **Peter Zinovieff**'s computer studio in Putney.

By the autumn of 1968 the RCM studio was ready, and Casserley was able to set about creating his first tape work, but with the complete montage realised at Fressingfield. The Final Desolation of Solitude, was premiered at a concert of tape music at London's Queen Elizabeth Hall in early 1969, in a tremendous line up that included Cary, Zinovieff, **Alan Sutcliffe**, **Don Banks**, **Donald Henshilwood**, **Hugh Davies**, **Harrison Birtwistle** and **Ernest Berk**. Later that year he experimented at the **EMS** studio, and acquired an EMS sound synthesizer. This was one of several prototypes the company built; the first going to Don Banks, and the second initially to **Delia Derbyshire** to test out. It had however, been promised to Casserley, and he had to travel up to the Kaleidophon studio in Camden where Derbyshire was based, to wrest control of this rare precursor to the VCS3. He also made some of his own gear from the popular home construction projects range, Heathkit, and purchased a second hand Revox tape recorder. This basic equipment allowed him to pursue his interests in live electronic processing and performance, and as well

Lawrence Casserley standing next to Per Hartmann in the mid-1970s

as presenting his own compositions, he performed in concerts of work by Stockhausen. In 1970 he was invited by **Grahame Dudley** to organise an electronic studio, and teach classes at the newly opened Cockpit Arts Centre. Out of this came the performance group Sound, Light and Space, involving Eddie Franklin-White and others interested in audio-visual arts and music theatre. The outfit performed at the Cockpit Theatre, and the Roundhouse in London during the ICES-72 festival. Casserley left the Cockpit in 1972, and the following year, he collaborated with **Bob Cobbing**; working with him on live performances and the recording of the piece 15 Shakespeare Kaku. In the mid 1970s he formed the company Synthesiser Music Services, alongside Per Hartmann and Stephen Deutsch, and developed a version of the Minisonic synthesizer project, originally designed by GD Shaw.

At the RCM, Casserley had become Tristram Cary's teaching assistant, then Professor-in-Charge of Studios and Adviser for Electro-acoustic Music, before finally taking early retirement in 1995. Pursuing his performing career, he has focussed on the development of real time electro-acoustic sound, and has been particularly associated with improvised music through his work with the groups Hydra, Tube Sculpture and Electroacoustic Cabaret. Hydra was formed together with Eddie Franklin-White, and gave performances in the 1970s fusing projections, smoke and lasers, together with electronic and instrumental sound.

Along with composer/performer Simon Desorgher, he formed Eye Music Trust in 1984, to promote contemporary music to a wider audience, and present the Colourscape environments. These are reminiscent of the futuristic designs seen at World's Fairs; fabulous walk-in inflatable structures of colour and light developed in 1971, which regularly tour the UK and overseas, and often include electronic performances in their presentations. Casserley's own music is now almost entirely made by live real time improvised transformations of sounds generated by fellow musicians. For this he uses his self-designed Signal Processing Instrument, though on occasions he can still be persuaded to dust off his VCS3.

Malcolm Clarke (1943-2003)

Born: Leicester
Earliest Electronic Work: The Insect Play (1961)
Commitment Factor: 8
Obscurity Quotient: 5
EM recording availability: Good

Clarke studied for A-Levels in Music, Art and Physics, and became a member of the Leicester Tape Recording and Hi-fi Club during the 1960s. In 1961 while still a teenager, he scored a local school production of the Capek satirical work The Insect Play, by recording Pyrex dishes on the strings of a grand piano, and then changing tape speeds and editing the results. He delivered a talk to his tape club about musique concrète and the techniques he used for the play's soundtrack, and that same year gave a lecture titled Sound – its properties and effects. Joining the **BBC Radiophonic Workshop** in 1969, he was initially struck by the paucity of modern electronic sound equipment, though the Workshop was soon to receive delivery of **EMS** synthesizers. One of his early and most notable assignments came in 1972, for season nine of Doctor Who.

The series included remarkable scores created on EMS equipment for two stories; The Sea Devils and The Mutants. These effective excursions into experimental soundscapes were composed by Clarke and **Tristram Cary** respectively, allowing both composers to introduce dissonant electronic sounds into a hugely popular children's TV series, greatly enhancing the atmosphere of the episodes. Clarke had an experimental edge and carried out a good deal of work with the Radiophonic Workshop's giant EMS Synthi 100; he is shown in the BBC documentary, The New Sound of Music, demonstrating the synthesizer's capabilities. He didn't get another chance to score Doctor Who until 1982, by which time both the series and the Workshop were well past their prime. Working there long after its cutting edge and relevant period, he finally left in 1994. He appears being interviewed in the BBC documentary Alchemists of Sound, broadcast in 2003, and died suddenly of a heart attack later that year.

CD: Doctor Who at the BBC Radiophonic Workshop: Volume 2
   (BBC Music, 2000) Includes the complete Sea Devils soundtrack.

Cyril Clouts (1926-1989)

Born: Cape Town, South Africa
Earliest Electronic Work: Orders of Motion: Walking and Dancing (1963)
Commitment Factor: 6
Obscurity Quotient: 7
EM recording availability: Poor

The father of Cyril Clouts and his twin brother Sydney, was born in Inverness, Scotland, and his Jewish family emigrated to South Africa and settled in Cape Town. Although Sydney Clouts is an acknowledged and respected poet, very little has been written about the career and compositions of Cyril. Studying Political Philosophy, Social Anthropology, Economic History and Logic and Metaphysics, he left the University of Cape Town two and a half years into his degree, to join the Israeli army during the Arab-Israeli war of 1948. On his return he attended the University part-time to study music, while working as a clerk for the Cape Town City Council.

He left South Africa for London in 1954, and in September that year enrolled at the Guildhall School of Music to continue his studies. By 1956 he was devoting himself to composition full-time, writing pieces for orchestra, wind instruments, percussion and prepared piano. He went on to explore electronics and tape, and equipped his small home studio with a Heathkit sine-square wave generator, and a Magnetophon tape recorder. Before his marriage in 1957, he shared a flat in north London with his friend **Jacob Meyerowitz**, a fellow Cape Town émigré, who similarly established a home tape studio at the start of the 60s.

In 1964 Cyril was asked to write music for a stage production at the Lamda Theatre, and attended a course in conducting at Morley College. Although operating mainly outside the music establishment, he met overseas composers Milton Babbitt, Pauline Oliveros and John Cage, and visited the **BBC Radiophonic Workshop**. Interested in movement and composing for dance, he struggled to get commissions and performances of his work throughout his career, and was turned down by US choreographers Martha Graham and Merce Cunningham. However, he did have one of his pieces choreographed back in South Africa at the Space Theatre in Cape Town, around 1974. In March 1969 the first of a substantial series of his articles looking at electronic music, ran in the magazine Tape Recording, under the title Project Alpha. Here he examined in great detail but in a rather sober style, the nature of sound and how it can be shaped with electronic music techniques. Curiously, he warned on the "*dangerous*" use of tape loops, as he felt they produced a "*facile effect of repetition.*" He referred to non-western music and African drumming when looking at rhythm, and referenced the film The Seven Samurai (1954), to illustrate forms of movement in sound and vision. He was very interested in movie music, and in 1973 wrote to British director Lindsay Anderson for advice on a short film soundtrack.

Apart from his composition Orders of Motion (1963), he created several other electronic pieces; Time Stream 2 (1964), Intervals of Motion (1965), and Ribbon 1: Now (1966-67), which was played at London's Arts Lab. The slim volume Sydney Clouts: Collected Poems, was co-edited by Cyril and Sydney's wife, and published in 1984. Five years later, on a visit to Cape Town with his wife Rose, he was unfortunately knocked down by a car and died from his injuries.

Rose and Cyril Clouts, 1957

Cyril and Rose Clouts, Brighton Beach circa 1960

Images from Project Alpha by Cyril Clouts

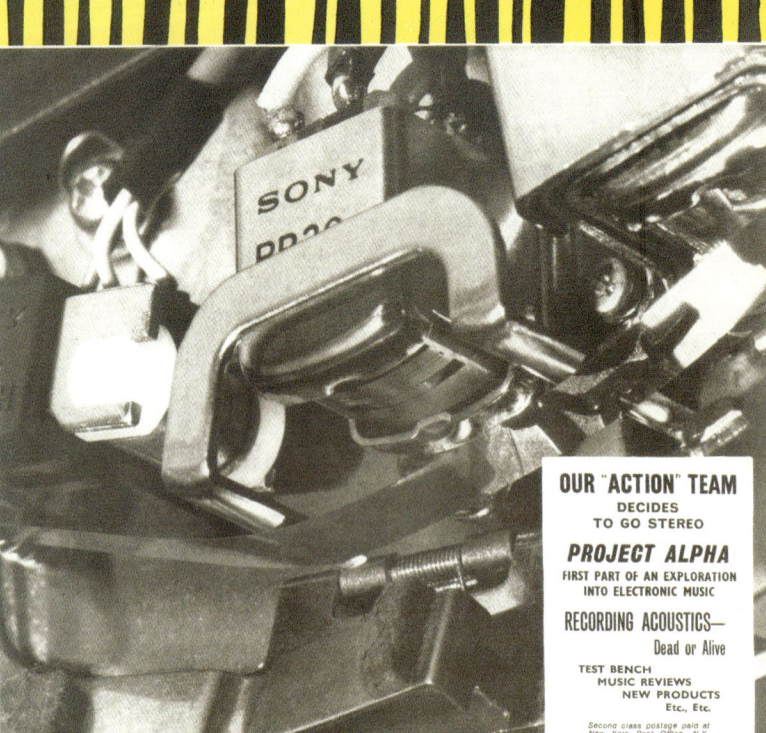

CYRIL CLOUTS CONCLUDES HIS
EXPLORATION INTO EXPERIMENTAL MUSIC
PROJECT ALPHA

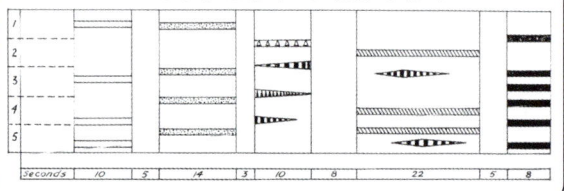

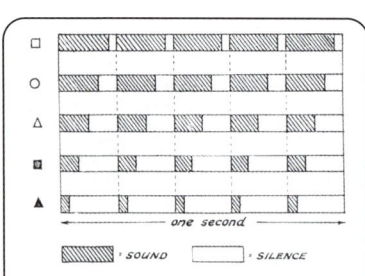

Fig. 1. A change of ratio between sound and silence applied to five sets of pulses at a rate of five pulses per second.

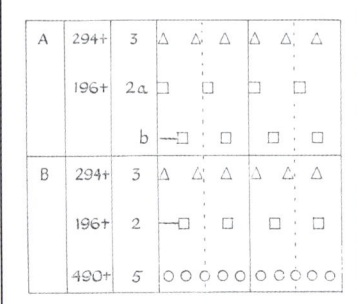

Fig. 2. An initial experiment in the articulation of motion.

36

Bob Cobbing (1920-2002)

Born: Enfield, London
Earliest Electronic Work: Are Your Children Safe In the Sea
 (with Anna Lockwood, 1966)
Commitment Factor: 3
Obscurity Quotient: 5
EM recording availability: Good

Brought up in a strict religious household, Cobbing attended Enfield Grammar School and received training in accountancy as well as teaching. Starting in the mid-1940s, he became a full-time secondary school teacher in north London; art, literature and music were his chosen subjects. His involvement with the Hendon Experimental Art Club began in 1951, inspiring him to write poetry, and establish the Writers Forum. This published hundreds of titles from 1963 until his death in 2002, ranging from his own poetry work, to undiscovered and upcoming writers and internationally recognised poets. They were printed on a mimeograph mechanical duplicating machine using ink forced through stencils, which in itself became a creative tool for the graphic manipulation of text. His early poems were performed mainly in libraries and small venues, and in 1964 he discovered the possibilities of the tape recorder to further develop concrete poetry – focussing on the sound of the words and their extension via tape manipulation techniques.

After organising film events at Hendon, he gave up teaching in 1965 and found a job at the Better Books shop at 94 Charing Cross Road in London. He took over as manager and established the Cinema 65 film club, showing foreign, alternative and experimental movies. At that stage an underground music, film, and counter cultural arts scene was developing, and Cobbing was on a committee to engineer the formation of what became the London Filmmakers Co-op (LFMC), initially based at Better Books.

The Destruction In Art Symposium, which ran during September 1966, included events at the bookshop organised by Cobbing and Gustav Metzger, and the following month the LFMC was formally constituted, with **Anna Lockwood**'s husband Harvey Matusow as chairman, and Cobbing as one of the secretaries. He collaborated that year with Lockwood on a short vocal and tape piece, Are Your Children Safe In the Sea, and in 1967 they both contributed to the soundtrack of experimental short Marvo Movie, by Brighton filmmaker Jeff Keen.

With the ousting of Matusow from the LFMC, and the closure of the Better Books literature department in 1967, activity shifted to the newly opened Arts Lab in Drury Lane, and the eventual split of those involved in the LFMC organisation into two factions. Cobbing endeavoured to set up a new book shop and cinema under the name Boooooks, but in 1968 a police raid effectively scuppered the project, and in November that year he resigned from the LFMC.

Despite the curtailment of his film programming activities, his forays into concrete poetry continued unabated, and as the prime British exponent, he forged links with European counterparts such as Henri Chopin, Ake Hodell and Francois Dufrene. His 1965 piece, ABC In Sound, was recognised by the BBC, and a version was recorded with the **Radiophonic Workshop** to extend and manipulate his voice. It was broadcast on the BBC Third Programme in August 1968. That same month he was involved with the Festival of Sound, in the Pavilion in the Park initiative in London, which presented international sound poetry and experimental electronic music from members of **Gentle Fire**. The flyer for the event gives details of a working group, convened by Cobbing and Lockwood, meeting each week to explore the intersection between poetry, music and electronics.

Cobbing also collaborated with **Lawrence Casserley**, and as well as recording the piece 15 Shakespeare Kaku, the pair did a number of live shows together in the early 1970s. In later years he continued wholeheartedly with live performance and a range of collaborators, including the group BirdYak, which involved Hugh Metcalfe, Lol Coxhill and Cobbing's wife Jennifer Pike.

CD: Bob Cobbing: The Spoken Word (British Library, 2009).

```
              FESTIVAL  OF  SOUND
              pavilion in the park
                august 22 to 28
                 10am to 10pm
SOUND ENVIRONMENT  VOICE BOX FOR AUDIENCE PARTICIPATION
& EACH DAY SPECIAL PERFORMANCES   LIVE & ON TAPE    AT
            11.30   3  &  7.30     of
SOUND POETRY  RELATED CONCRETE AND ELECTRONIC MUSIC  &
ANTICOMPOSITIONS  SOUND ISOLATIONS  BELL PIECES  SOUNDS
          OF HENRI CHOPIN  BOB COBBING
          ANNA LOCKWOOD   HUGH DAVIES

                   and many others
SOUND POEMS ON TAPE by ERNST JANDL of Austria PAUL DE VREE
of Belgium OKE HODELL of Sweden ALLEN GINSBERG BRION GYSIN
& MICHAEL McCLURE of U S A HENRI CHOPIN FRANCOIS DUFRENE
BERNARD HEIDSIECK GIL WOLMAN ROBERTO ALTMANN JEAN-LOUIS
BRAU of France ANNA LOCKWOOD BOB COBBING ANDREW RAWLINSON
ADRIAN NUTBEEM of England     and numerous additions  plus
works by
CHRISTIAN WOLFE ROBERT ASHLEY JOHN CAGE HUGH DAVIES    and
performances by STUART JONES RICHARD BERNAS PATRICK HARREX
```

Festival of Sound programme, 1968

Justin Connolly (1933)

Born: London
Earliest Electronic Work: Obbligati II (1967)
Commitment Factor: 2
Obscurity Quotient: 7
EM recording availability: Limited

Educated at Westminster School, London, Connolly briefly studied law at the Middle Temple before deciding on a career in music. At the Royal College of Music his tutor was Peter Racine Fricker, and following graduation, he travelled to Yale University in the USA on a Harkness Fellowship, where he took classes with jazz pianist and tape composer Mel Powell. In the late 1960s he briefly taught at Yale before returning to Britain for a teaching post at the RCM, later moving to the Royal Academy of Music, and taking up chairmanship of the Macnaghten Concerts committee. A period of ill health led to a lengthy composing hiatus during the 1980s, and he retired from teaching in 1995.

During the late 1960s and early 70s he composed a number of pieces for instruments and tape, in conjunction with **Peter Zinovieff** and the **EMS** studio, including Obbligati II, Variations, Triad IV, Tesserae D, and Triad VI. He appears in the 1969 BBC documentary The Same Trade As Mozart, discussing his then current collaboration with Zinovieff. Their three part work M-Piriform, based on text by Samuel Beckett, was premiered at the Queen Elizabeth Hall in a major concert of British music. Also in 1969, Obbligati II for flute, clarinet, violin, cello, piano and tape, was featured in the Project: Electronic Music concert, at the Royal Festival Hall in London, to launch the British Society for Electronic Music. Connolly's further tape pieces, Poems of Wallace Stevens (1970), Tesserae 4 (1971), and Tetramorph (1972), were all realised at EMS with assistance from **Peter Grogono**.

Connolly continues to compose and currently lives in Greenwich, but upon being contacted, he now disavows any mention of his former work with electronics and tape.

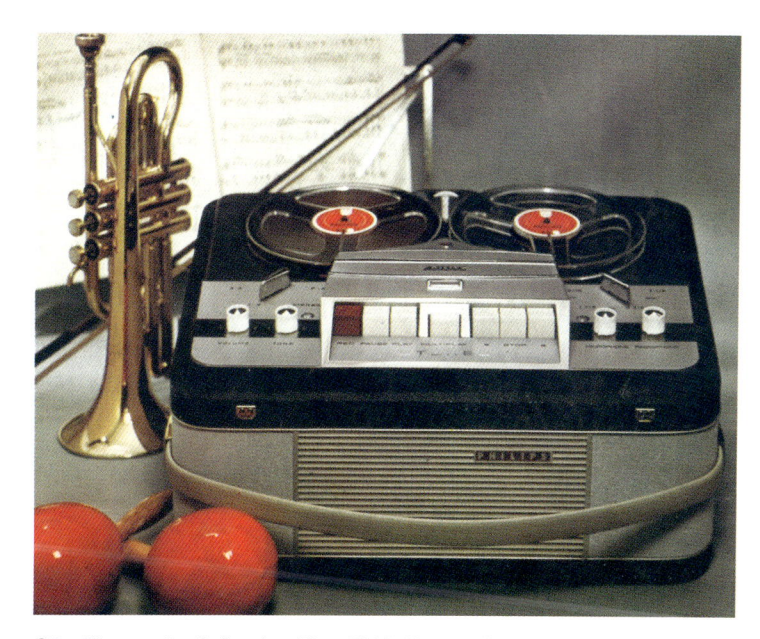

CD: Electronic Calendar The EMS Tapes (Space Age Recordings, 2015) Includes Connolly and Zinovieff's M-Piriform.

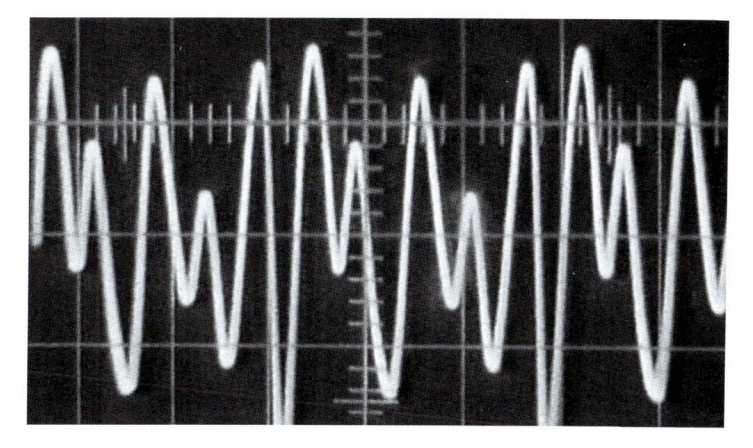

Roy Cooper (1930-?)

Born: Untraced
Earliest Electronic Work: Untitled (1964)
Commitment Factor: 6
Obscurity Quotient: 8
EM recording availability: Poor

A north country teacher establishing his own tape studio in Wakefield, West Yorkshire in 1963, Cooper taught at Adwick comprehensive school near Doncaster during the 60s. He was in the vanguard of a progressive initiative in music education, adopting a child centred approach which incorporated and encouraged new sounds from tape recorders and electronics; a policy which attracted attention from the press and the BBC. The Music In School series for television included an edition focussing on new sounds, and featured Cooper being interviewed. It showed him demonstrating equipment, with his pupils in the classroom, and a filmed sequence involving their experimental soundtrack.

Adwick High School grew out of a merger and opened in a new building in 1965, with a progressive headmaster, and Cooper appointed head of music. His department was well equipped with traditional musical instruments, though initially it only had a single Ferrograph tape recorder. In close contact with **Daphne Oram**, he arranged for her to visit and lecture at the school, and her company, Essconics Ltd. to supply multivibrator circuits, filters, reverberation units and microphone mixer. However, a further school merger in 1968 ushered in a new headmaster at Adwick, and a change in the educational ethos. Cooper's experimental ideas and a planned school electronic studio, were now unwelcome, and he left at the end of the academic year.

In September 1969 he took up a new post at Bingley College of Education in Yorkshire, and continued with music education. In a letter from May 1970, he invited Oram to Bingley, and discussed an educational book they had been planning to co-author, but which never came to fruition. He mentioned that he was "*still thinking around the subject of light modulated set ups using possibly Sinclair modules, photoelectric cells, which would then voltage control the synthesizer.*" He also told her about his modern jazz group which he described as moving quite "*far out,*" while "*experimenting with electronics here and there.*" He was involved with introducing jazz music to inmates at Wakefield Prison, and had run a jazz club while he was at Adwick School.

After leaving Bingley he joined a team at York University in 1973, to work on a Schools Council research project led by John Paynter. There is a credit for a tape work, A Night at the Opera, from 1967, a son et lumiere for 4 soundtracks, lighting and geometric objects, but a number of blanks remain in Cooper's profile.

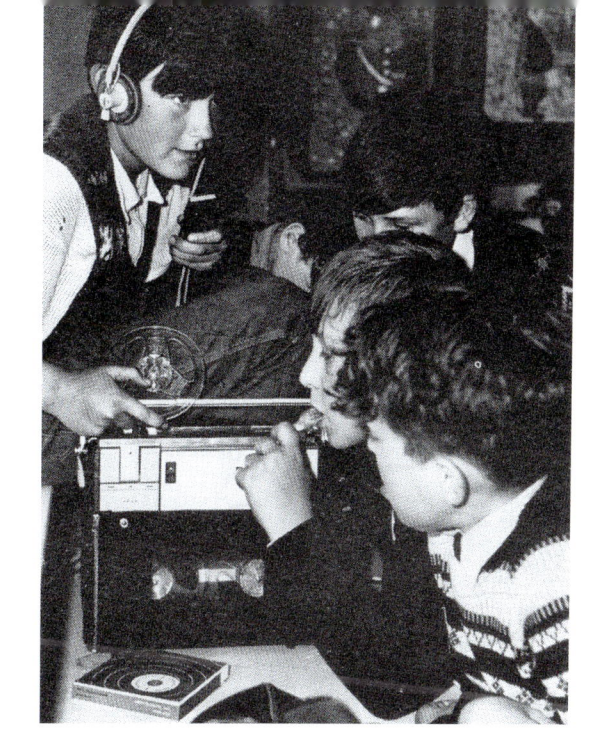

For the January 1963 issue of Tape Recording magazine, teacher Glyn Harris penned an article titled, A Tape Recorder in the Junior School. He discussed how tape can be used effectively and creatively in the classroom, and explained about a project he had initiated at a London school. This involved a large abstract coloured mural at the school entrance as the starting point for movement, which then developed with the addition of sound. The children wanted more abstract accompaniment, and came up with an array of percussive sounds recorded on tape. Harris concluded his article describing the freedom that had been found. *"Finally it showed how the tape recorder really is a creative force in the school, if one can get away from the idea that it is only there to record scripted plays under studio conditions."*

Edward Cowie (1943)

Born: Birmingham
Earliest Electronic Work: Concerto for Bass Clarinet and Tape (1969)
Commitment Factor: 1
Obscurity Quotient: 7
EM recording availability: Poor

Spending his early life in the rural countryside of Suffolk as well as the Cotswolds, Cowie studied the violin and piano whilst still at school, and was already writing music by the age of 13. In London undertaking a physics degree, he continued studies in composition, and in 1964 became a pupil of Alexander Goehr. By the late 1960s, he was working both as a visual artist and a composer, and some of his early pieces were finding their way into concert programmes. In 1971 he was awarded a Chopin Fellowship to study under Witold Lutoslawski in Poland, and he also came under the influence of Sir Michael Tippett, who remained a close friend.

Cowie's Concerto for Bass Clarinet and Tape, was premiered at the Edinburgh Festival in 1970, and his career as a composer became firmly established with the first performance of his 1975 Proms commission, Leviathan, played by the BBC Symphony Orchestra. In 1984 he was awarded the first Granada Composer Fellowship with the Royal Liverpool Philharmonic Orchestra. Since that time, he has worked as a conductor with several major orchestras and ensembles in England and Australia, and he now lives and works in both Devon and France, with his visual-artist wife, Heather. He has doctorates in music and philosophy (the latter embodying theoretical physics), and through his time living and working in Australia, he holds dual British and Australian nationality.

His soundtrack work for television includes Edward Lear (1979), Ned Kelly (1983) and Leonardo (1984), and more recently a BBC commission marked his 70th birthday, with his Earth Music I – The Great Barrier Reef, premiered at the 2013 Proms. On his website which lists his compositions in a wide range of forms, there is no mention of his Concerto for Bass Clarinet and Tape.

Howard Davidson (1949)

Born: Sunderland
Earliest Electronic Work: Icarus for tape (1968)
Commitment Factor: 5
Obscurity Quotient: 6
EM recording availability: Poor

Beginning his musical career with the Leicestershire Schools Symphony Orchestra, Davidson went on to study clarinet with Colin Bradbury, and composition with **Tristram Cary**, at the Royal College of Music from 1967-70. He gravitated towards contemporary performance, including experiments with live electronics and tape, and alongside **Lawrence Casserley** and **George Brown**, he joined Tristram's RCM electronic music class. The discovery of the 1967 book New Sounds for Woodwinds, provided inspirational insights into extended techniques for his clarinet, which stood him in good stead for performing Casserley's Solos, Commentaries and Integrations. This stimulated the composition of several of his own pieces with electronic sounds and instruments, including Nautonium, for ensemble and tape (1969), April 39.187, for voice, ensemble and tape (1969), and Messier 13, for orchestra and tape (1970). For the Cheltenham Music Festival in 1970 he composed Omega Centauri, which was included in a concert alongside electronic pieces by Brown, Cary, Milton Babbitt and Karlheinz Stockhausen.

After graduating from the RCM he joined the Cockpit Arts Centre, which was heavily involved with music and arts education in London. He gave evening classes in electronic music and musique concrète, and as well as school visits, he organised and played in concerts with the Cockpit Ensemble and **Music Plus**, alongside **Howard Rees** and **Malcolm Fox**. His piece Tucance, for clarinet, cello and electronics, was played at the Cockpit by him and Music Plus in December 1971.

In 1974 Davidson moved to Brisbane, Australia, part of a 'brain drain' of composers from Britain – Tristram Cary, **Grahame Dudley**, Malcolm Fox and **Roger Smalley** – all migrating down under in the mid-70s. Establishing an electronic music studio at the Queensland Conservatorium of Music, Davidson equipped it with the first Buchla synthesizer seen in Australia, and remained for six years as a senior lecturer in electro-acoustic composition and music technology. Back in Britain he has forged a hugely successful career as a composer for TV, dance, theatre and radio, and with over 300 scores to his credit, some of his large scale works have been performed by leading British orchestras. While continuing to write music, he remains Professor of Composition at the RCM.

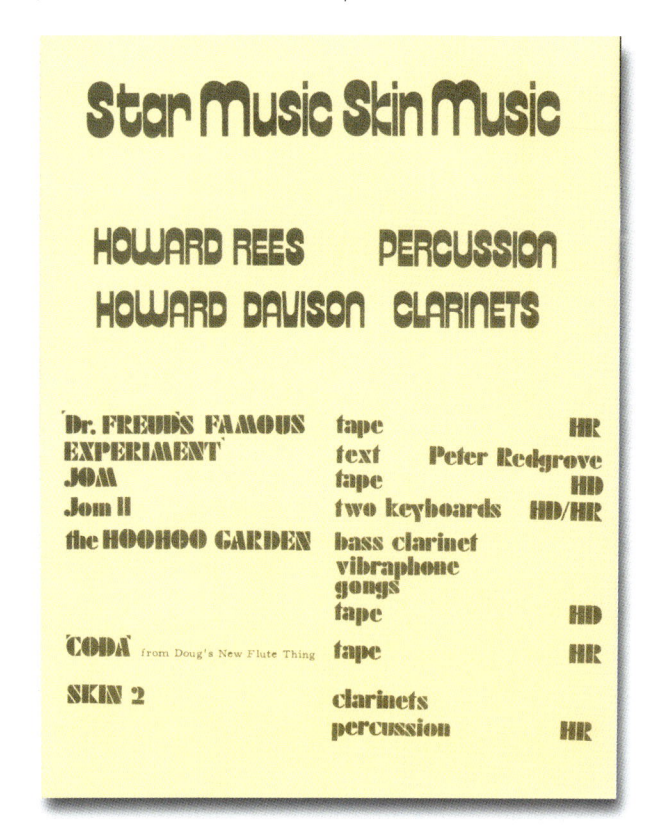

Hugh Davies (1943-2005)

Born: Exmouth, Devon
Earliest Electronic Work: Essay (1962)
Commitment Factor: 8
Obscurity Quotient: 4
EM recording availability: Limited

In January 1961 Davies attended a presentation of electronic music given by **Daphne Oram**, at the Mermaid Theatre in London, and his first tape work as a composer came a year later, when Oram invited him and Martin Gellhorn for a weekend stay at her Tower Folly studio. He inherited from her a commission to compile a discography of electronic music for a journal related to the National Sound Archive, marking the beginning of the research strand of his career. Following music study at Oxford University from 1961-64, the 21 year old Davies was taken on by Karlheinz Stockhausen as composing assistant, and a member of his live performance group. He stayed in Cologne during 1964-66, and was featured on the recording of Stockhausen's Microphonie 1, released on LP by CBS.

On returning to Britain he began teaching evening classes in electronic music towards the end of 1967, and the Goldsmiths College Electronic Music Studio (originally named the Electronic Music Workshop), was established by the beginning of 68. He remained the director until 1986, and was a research consultant until 1991, also holding a position as a visiting lecturer and part-time Researcher in Sonic Art, at the Centre for Electronic Arts, Middlesex University. In 1967 he had begun to establish his own small tape studio, augmenting his limited range of sound generators with everyday items, such as springs, combs and broken light bulbs.

The following year he started to make his own instruments for performance, amplifying their sounds with contact microphones. Shozyg became a generic name for his instruments built inside unconventional containers, and the first of these was housed within the final volume of an encyclopaedia, which covered everything from 'shoal' to 'zygote' with SHO-ZYG on the spine. The sounds were produced with finger contact, or by activation with various devices such as screwdrivers or electric motors. From 1969 he collaborated on occasions with British artist John Furnival, to explore the sculptural aspects of instrument building and presentation. At a major concert of electronic music at the Queen Elizabeth Hall in February that year, which included work by **Donald Henshilwood**, **Tristram Cary**, **Lawrence Casserley**, **Harrison Birtwistle**, **Peter Zinovieff** and **Ernest Berk**, Shozyg 1 (1968), was performed by John Tilbury and Gavin Bryars, on Shozyg and oscillators respectively.

During the 1970s, notated compositions and tape pieces became less a part of Davies's activities, and he focussed more on live performance, belonging to the groups **Gentle Fire**, **Naked Software** and Music Improvisation Company, with Jamie Muir, Derek Bailey and Evan Parker. He played with a variety of musicians including **David Rowland**, Han Bennink and Max Eastley, and was extremely well connected with other tape composers in Britain and abroad. His International Electronic Music Catalog published in 1968, is an essential resource for the understanding of the early development of electronic sound across the world – attempting to list every piece of tape music that had been composed up to 1967.

Richard Orton's book Electronic Music for Schools (1981), features a number of absorbing and useful chapters, including Making and Performing Simple Electroacoustic Instruments, penned by Davies. Further work included over 300 entries for The New Grove Dictionary of Musical Instruments (1984), and a book of his own creative writings, Sounds Heard (2002). He was the custodian of Daphne Oram's archive, and preparing a release of Gentle Fire recordings, at the time of his sudden death in 2005.

Brian Dennis (1941-1998)

Born: Marple, Cheshire
Earliest Electronic Work: Study for Tape with Piano (1962)
Commitment Factor: 5
Obscurity Quotient: 6
EM recording availability: Poor

With a musically trained mother, the young Brian Dennis was sent away to be educated at St. Edmund's School, Canterbury. After a year's study for a science degree at Cambridge, he became dissatisfied with the course, and won a scholarship to the Royal College of Music in 1961, spending four years studying with Peter Racine Fricker and John White. In his first year at the RCM he wrote Doria, for voice and piano, and became close friends with **Roger Smalley**, a fellow student and colleague in the Composers Ensemble. During this period he met Cornelius Cardew, whose music had been introduced to the Ensemble by pianist John Tilbury.

After college in 1965, Dennis attended the Cologne Course for New Music, taking classes with Karlheinz Stockhausen, Luciano Berio, Earle Brown and Cathy Berberian. A concert of electronic music held at the London Planetarium in 1968, featured his Dream Music, as well as pieces by **Ernest Berk**, **Stuart Wynn Jones**, **Peter Zinovieff**, and **Hugh Davies**. In the early 1970s he collaborated with composer **Grahame Dudley**, and British painter and op-artist Oliver Bevan, on a production at the Cockpit Theatre in London of Z'Noc. This was a 30 minute experimental piece by Dennis, in which musicians took cues from Bevan's kinetic display of abstract colours and shapes, created by projecting light onto three mobiles.

For secure employment he trained as a school teacher, and like **Roy Cooper**, Peter Warham and a number of other teachers, he was concerned with introducing contemporary ideas and electronic equipment into the classroom; his composition Music for Percussion and Tape (1965), was designed for a group of 12 school children to perform. After several years teaching at Shoreditch School, he was appointed Lecturer in Contemporary Music Education at St. Mark and St. John's College, Chelsea, where George Self was already on the staff. Together with **David Bedford** they attempted to standardise a form of simplified musical notation relying on clear cut graphic symbols for students to readily understand. Self had written the book New Sounds in Class, in 1967, and Experimental Music in Schools, penned by Dennis was published by OUP in 1970. The previous year he featured in the TV documentary The Same Trade As Mozart, being interviewed and shown in the classroom with his students. In 1971 he was appointed lecturer in Composition and Contemporary Music at Royal Holloway College, University of London, and his second book for teachers, Projects in Sound, was published in 1975. This contained useful musical ideas for the classroom, and some graphic scores designed by Oliver Bevan. Throughout his life Dennis maintained a keen interest in music, art, science and astronomy, and a fascination with Chinese poetry.

Music In School was a series made by the BBC, broadcast in 1969. Part 4 – A New Sound, was introduced by Peter Fletcher and featured **Brian Dennis** and **Roy Cooper** in the studio, giving explanations of their work with school children. Dennis was head of music at Shoreditch School at that time, and led a performance of a composition created by his students. It was based on the theme of heat, and built around a sustained organ cluster with a variety of percussion sounds. Cooper demonstrated a tape loop, multivibrator circuit and a sheet of steel with contact mics, and was filmed at Adwick School in a music lesson with pupils. The BBC cameras also visited Ivydale Primary School where the infants were shown with their teacher, incorporating tape recorders into their music making.

Delia Derbyshire at the Radiophonic Workshop in 1966

Delia Derbyshire (1937-2001)

Born: Coventry
Earliest Electronic Work: Time On Our Hands (1962)
Commitment Factor: 8
Obscurity Quotient: 2
EM recording availability: Excellent

Attending Barr's Hill School for Girls in Coventry, Derbyshire was a very promising young pianist, and was accepted to study at both Oxford and Cambridge. She opted for a mathematics scholarship at Girton College, Cambridge, but switched after a year to include music, graduating in 1959. She had gained a diploma in piano, and this secured her a position with the UN in Geneva, teaching piano to the children of diplomats, and working for the International Telecommunications Union. Back in Britain she applied to the BBC and was taken on as a trainee studio manager in 1960, working on the programme Record Review. Hankering after a post at the **Radiophonic Workshop**, where three month attachments were generally the rule at the time, Derbyshire commented that, "*the Workshop was purely a service department for drama. The BBC made it quite clear that they didn't employ composers, and we weren't supposed to be doing music.*" Nevertheless, her attachment in 1962 became permanent, and she emerged as one of the key Workshop personnel during the 60s.

Her earliest radiophonic tape work completed towards the end of 1962, was for a BBC TV programme Time On Our Hands, a docu-fiction pondering the state of Britain 25 years into the future, broadcast in March 1963. That year, with the assistance of Dick Mills, she arranged and recorded the Ron Grainer penned Doctor Who theme tune. Despite receiving no royalty or on screen credit, it was her crowning achievement, recognised throughout the world as a classic of electronic music. She created many other pieces for the BBC, ranging from jingles and call signals for Radio 2 and Radio Leicester, through to serious works for programmes in The World About Us, and Out of the Unknown series. Her career is also marked by outside work and collaboration, in particular with fellow radiophonic composer **Brian Hodgson**. They operated together in **Unit Delta Plus**, **White Noise** and briefly in Electrophon, as well as for music publishers KPM and the Standard Music Library. Together with Hodgson and **David Vorhaus**, at the Kaleidophon studio in Camden High Street, London, she created various soundtracks for adverts and plays, including productions of Hamlet, King Lear and Macbeth.

Derbyshire attended the Dartington summer school in 1962, and alongside **FC Judd**, she was one of the assistants to Italian composer Luciano Berio. She also helped with radiophonic effects for **Roberto Gerhard** and his 1964 BBC radio production Anger of Achilles, and two years later assisted **George Newson** with The Man Who Collected Sounds. In 1967 she collaborated with the Hornsey **Light/Sound Workshop**, to provide electronic music environments for displays of light and kinetic sculpture on the West Pier in Brighton. Amongst a wide range of projects, she worked with playwright and poet Barry Bermange on his Inventions for Radio (1964-65), and with singer-songwriter Anthony Newley on the 1966 electronic pop curio Moogies Bloogies.

With the arrival of new staff and equipment at the Radiophonic Workshop in the early 70s, her more abstract style and favoured working methods were being superseded, and she left the BBC in 1973. It was intended that she would join Brian Hodgson in his Electrophon studio, but aside from a limited contribution to the Legend of Hell House film score, the plan did not work out due to her variable health. For the rest of the 70s and 80s she worked in jobs outside music, and it was in the late 1990s that she was encouraged back to experimenting with electronic sounds, by a younger generation of musicians. A number of films and plays for radio and theatre are based on her well-trodden life story, and her tape collection is housed at the University of Manchester.

CD: BBC Radiophonic Music (BBC/Grey Area of Mute, 2008).
   Includes 10 tracks by Delia Derbyshire.

Michael Dress (1935-1975)

Born: Berlin, Germany
Earliest Electronic Work: Exit the King (1963)
Commitment Factor: 4
Obscurity Quotient: 9
EM recording availability: Poor

Growing up in Germany before moving to London, Michael Dress showed an early musical talent, and at the age of 16 he trained to be an organist at the Church Music Academy in Spandau. Like **Ernest Berk** he studied dance under Mary Wigman, and his interest in settings of satirical poetry led him away from the religious based Academy. In London during the late 1950s he met fellow German, Agnes Bernelle, who was married to **Desmond Leslie**, and who performed as the first non-stationary nude on the British stage in a production of Oscar Wilde's Salome. Dress took on the role of Bernelle's musical director, and together they developed a set of songs for performance, which were later released as part of an album.

Dress composed an opera for the BBC and music for theatre productions and films, including several notable features: Rotten to the Core (1965), A Touch of Love (1969), The Mind of Mr. Soames (1970), Quackser Fortune Has a Cousin in the Bronx (1970), and The House That Dripped Blood (1971). He also scored several BBC plays in the late 60s, and a radio adaptation of Bertolt Brecht's In the Jungle of Cities. Information about his electronic music is scant, though he is credited with several tape pieces for the theatre, and music for a sculpture by artist and designer Yolanda Sonnabend. In the late 60s he visited **Ron Geesin** at home in his Notting Hill studio, in connection with tape music. Before his premature death he devoted much energy to visual art, creating a series of 13 oil paintings based on the life of Jesus.

Write now for details of the complete range
TAPE RECORDERS (Electronics) LTD.
784-788 High Road, London, N.17. Telephone : TOTtenham 0811-3
Cables : Taperec London

Below and opposite, 35mm polarized slides by Ian Helliwell

Grahame Dudley (1942)

Born: Sydney, Australia
Earliest Electronic Work: Mibu Kyogin (1969)
Commitment Factor: 6
Obscurity Quotient: 7
EM recording availability: Poor

Studying first at the New South Wales Conservatorium of Music, Dudley won a scholarship to the Elder Conservatorium in Adelaide, where he was taught by visiting British composer Peter Maxwell Davies. He left Australia and arrived in London in 1968, and studied with **Tristram Cary** at the Royal College of Music, and also with Pierre Boulez, who was partly based in London at that time. He visited the Dartington summer school in 1969, and that same year he composed Mibu Kyogin, which involved gong, bell, horn, temple block, trombone and tape delay system, plus visual accompaniment and kinetic light by artist Oliver Bevan.

Dudley was invited to join the newly established Cockpit Arts Centre in Marylebone, London, which officially opened in 1970. He was appointed Director of Music at the venue, and with advice and backing from Cary, he initiated the first open access electronic music studio in the country. Bringing in young experimental composers **Lawrence Casserley** and **Malcolm Fox**, he engineered the formation of groups **Music Plus** and the Cockpit Ensemble, and an offshoot, Sound, Light and Space. These outfits saw Dudley and the Cockpit at the leading edge of electronic music performance and mixed media presentation, with an integral part of their concerts being the combination of live electro-acoustic sounds, projections, props, sculpture, light effects and movement.

In 1973 Malcolm Fox took over as Director of Music from Dudley, who had decided the time was right for a return to Australia, where he took up a post teaching Music Education and Composition at Adelaide University. He was soon able to provide encouragement for both Fox and Tristram Cary to emigrate to join him on the staff there, and during the 70s he was involved in performing Tristram's dice and Synthi piece Trios (1971). In 1985 he was commissioned to write The Snow Queen, a youth opera performed in Adelaide, Brisbane, Melbourne and Newcastle. Five years later he returned to new music ensemble playing by forming the group Lights, which gave many performances of compositions by Australian composers. Since his retirement from teaching, Dudley continues his involvement with modern music via the regular radio show Ear to the Ground, broadcast by Radio Adelaide.

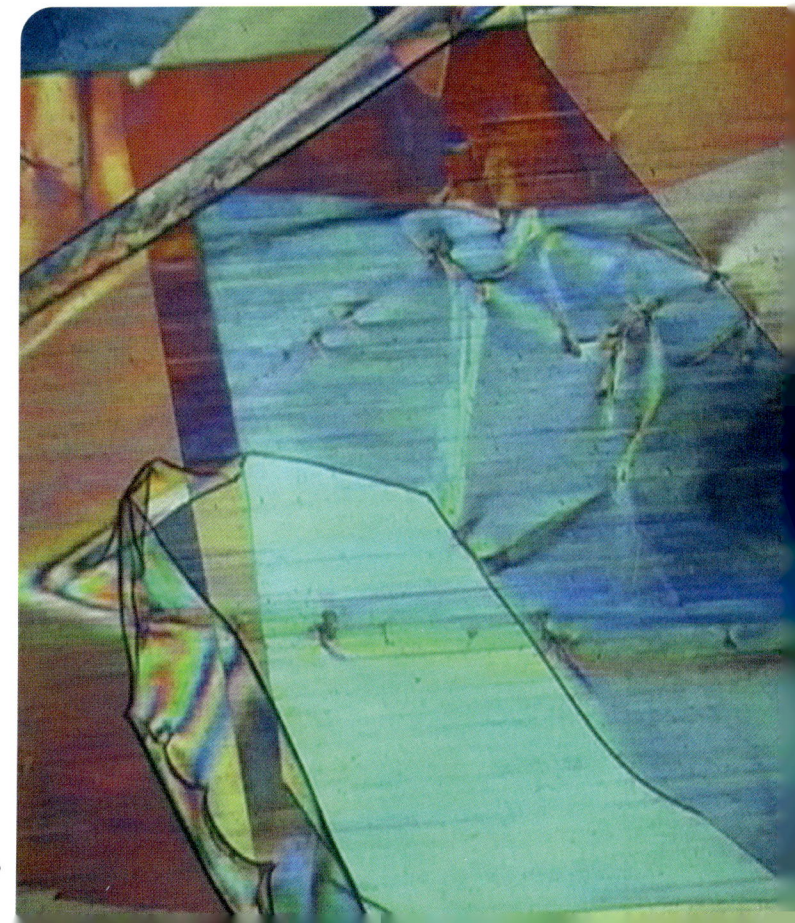

Terence Dwyer (1922)

Born: Leicester
Earliest Electronic Work: The Congo (1969)
Commitment Factor: 5
Obscurity Quotient: 7
EM recording availability: Poor

In the 1940s and 50s Dwyer taught at schools in the Leicester area, and as something of a late starter with electronic and tape sounds, he was already into middle age before realizing there was a sizeable gap in his largely self-taught, classically orientated musical knowledge. In 1963 he was appointed Head of Music at Loughborough College of Art, to teach music as a complimentary study, and with his department's generous budget he purchased Ferrograph and B&O tape recorders plus microphones. In tandem with his teaching he was able to set about tinkering with tape, and some of his early experiments were incorporated into a cantata; his first electro-acoustic composition The Congo (1969).

He started devising projects for his Loughborough art students, and sought guidance from similarly bearded and bespectacled **Tristram Cary**. Tristram advised that an instructional book was in the pipeline, though this never materialised, and Dwyer seized the initiative with Composing with Tape Recorders, published by Oxford University Press in 1971. This beginner's guide to musique concrète was highly influential, and followed hot on the heels of instructional books by George Self, John Paynter, and tape composer and teacher **Brian Dennis**.

Around 1969, Dwyer visited the **BBC Radiophonic Workshop**, and was given a guided tour by former Leicestershire denizen **Malcolm Clarke**. The Workshop took delivery of the massive Synthi 100 in 1971, and Cardiff University, under the direction of **Keith Winter**, installed this same **EMS** synthesizer model. The following year Dwyer took a sabbatical from teaching at Loughborough to do a Master's degree at Cardiff, in Electronic Music and Contemporary Music Analysis. At the start of the 1970s he established a small home studio, composing pieces for tape alone, and in conjunction with voice or instruments, including percussion, oboe, cor anglais, flute and string orchestra. The EMS Synthi A was at the heart of his studio, supplying electronic sounds, as well as more importantly for Dwyer, the transforming of external sources using envelope shaping and ring modulation.

After the publication of Composing with Tape Recorders, he received numerous invitations for lectures, seminars and weekend courses on working with tape, and his follow up book on the subject, Making Electronic Music, came out in 1975. Not long after, and with a catalogue of 15 tape pieces to his name, his enthusiastic experimentation with electronics inexplicably ground to a halt. In his twilight years, Terry Dwyer Esq. has resided in the synthetic sounding Leicestershire village of Quorn, where his hobbies have included golf, bridge, bowls and music.

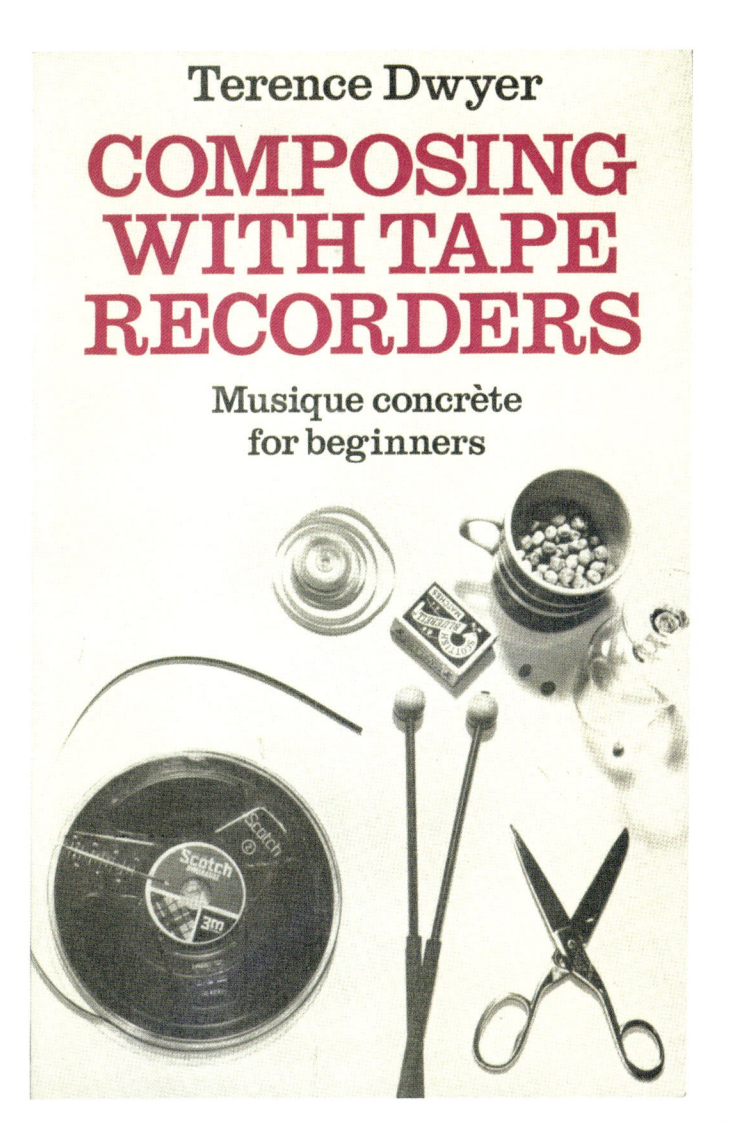

Jack Ellitt (1902-2001)
Born: Manchester
Earliest Electronic Work: Journey # 1 (c. 1930s)
Commitment Factor: 6
Obscurity Quotient: 7
EM recording availability: Limited

With his very early years spent in England, Ellitt and his parents emigrated to Sydney, Australia, and by the age of 16 he had won a scholarship to the New South Wales Conservatorium of Music, where he continued studying the piano and played bassoon. During the 1910s he met New Zealand filmmaker and artist Len Lye in Sydney, and after Lye boarded a ship heading towards Britain, Ellitt followed and joined him in London in 1927. Lye is justly acclaimed for his pioneering animated work drawing abstract images directly onto film, though Ellitt's sound experiments have languished in the shadows.

He worked closely in a technical capacity for animation and sound synchronisation on Lye's shorts, made for the GPO film unit during the 1930s, and wrote music for his colleague's first film Tusalava (1929). He was concerned with escaping from traditional musical values with new and imaginative forms; looking ahead to the potential of collage with everyday noises, using 'sound construction' as exemplified in his much later tape piece Etude for Voice, Bird Sounds and Tap Water.

Experiments with photographing and exposing images and waveform patterns onto film, were being undertaken in the Soviet Union and Germany in the 1930s, and by 1933 Ellitt had already begun exploring variable area soundtracks. He applied inks and assorted marks by hand, to generate different tones once the film was run through a projector, and built himself an animation camera rostrum. This synthetic sound technique was widely recognised and came to prominence, through the Canadian state sponsored films of Norman McLaren, who before he emigrated, was working in London at the GPO film unit at the same time as Ellitt. Although not precisely dated, Ellitt's remarkable sound collage, Journey #1, is reckoned to be from the early 1930s, and edited together from strips of 35mm sound film, as this predates the invention of magnetic tape, and comes more than a decade before the musique concrète from Paris. The piece is said to be for a sci-fi themed film project with Len Lye titled Quicksilver, and while the music was completed, the film remained unfinished.

By the early 1940s the two men had gone their separate ways, and Ellitt pursued employment as an editor and director in the movie industry, working for the BBC, ICI and the National Coal Board amongst others. He lived with his wife near Wadhurst, East Sussex, and equipped his small home studio with tape recorders, a film editing machine and various home-made devices. After retirement around the start of the 1970s, he furthered his sound experiments, while closely guarding his privacy; he allegedly shunned contact with electronic music makers during the 60s, including **Hugh Davies**, who was very likely in the process of compiling his International Electronic Music Catalog. He does though appear on camera in the Channel 4 documentary Doodlin': Impressions of Len Lye, made in 1987. Ellitt moved back to Australia in his twilight years, and had already started to destroy some of his earlier work he was unhappy with. Following a very long life and dedication to the art of sound, it is heartbreaking that the bulk of his surviving papers and recordings were thrown away after his death.

CD: Artefacts of Australian Experimental Music 1930-1973 (Shame File Music, 2007). Includes Ellitt's Journey #1.

> Born in Stirling, Scotland in 1914, celebrated animator Norman McLaren, conducted synthetic sound experiments while at the GPO film unit in London from 1936-37, during the making of the documentary Book Bargain. He left Britain for the USA shortly after the outbreak of World War II, and went on to join the National Film Board of Canada.

Brian Eno (1948)

Born: Woodbridge, Suffolk
Earliest Electronic Work: Tape manipulations (c.1966)
Commitment Factor: 5
Obscurity Quotient: 1
EM recording availability: Good

Equipped with four O-Levels from the Catholic grammar school, St. Joseph's College, Eno enrolled at Ipswich School of Art in 1964, and an important early influence was his tutor Tom Phillips; a London based painter and musician who had compositions performed by **Gentle Fire**, and was a founding member of the Scratch Orchestra. He helped to open up the worlds of literature and avant-garde music for Eno, who decided to attend the celebrated Royal Albert Hall International Poetry Incarnation, in 1965. Phillips also introduced him to creative the possibilities of tape recorders in music, and starting at Winchester School of Art in 1966, Eno collaborated in musical performance art group Merchant Taylor's Simultaneous Cabinet, and gave solo performances of his manipulated tape experiments. His early pieces include Delay and Decay (1967), Water Music (1968), Father Johnson (1968), and the soundtrack for the captivating short experimental found footage film, Berlin Horse (1970), by British filmmaker Malcolm Le Grice. Eno also formed the short lived group Maxwell Demon, with a guitarist, and himself on vocals and signal generator, and first appeared on record with the LP release of Cornelius Cardew's, The Great Learning.

He became a member of the incompetent ensemble The Portsmouth Sinfonia, and through an opportune meeting on a London tube train with saxophone player Andy Mackay, his career took an unexpected turn into high profile rock and pop, when he joined the line-up of Roxy Music. He used tapes and an **EMS** VCS3 synthesizer to process the group's sound and provide electronic tonalities, as well as a strong stage presence with his flamboyant glam rock attire. He left after the second Roxy Music album For Your Pleasure, in 1973, and that year collaborated with King Crimson guitarist Robert Fripp on No Pussyfooting; the first

HOW TO CATCH A SOUND WAVE

Our "Series Four" microphones will catch anything without damage or distortion. No need to use transformers, each microphone is multi-impedance and will work into 25 Ohms, 200 Ohms, 600 Ohms and 50K Ohms. Imagine how useful that is when you change recorders.
These four microphones have been produced to extract the last drop of performance from your recorder or P.A. System. Combining Lustraphone dependability with superb performance and exciting styling. These instruments will give you pride of ownership for years to come.
4.20 Dynamic Omnidirectional 4.30 Dynamic Cardioid
4.40 Studio Ribbon 4.50 Professional Miniature Ribbon
See the "Series Four" Microphones at leading Hi-Fi dealers – or write direct to LUSTRAPHONE LTD for free illustrated literature giving full description and specification.
A comprehensive "Selection and Instruction" pamphlet is also available free on request.

lustraphone
THE FOREMOST NAME IN MICROPHONES
Lustraphone Limited,
Regents Park Road, London N.W.1   01-722 8844

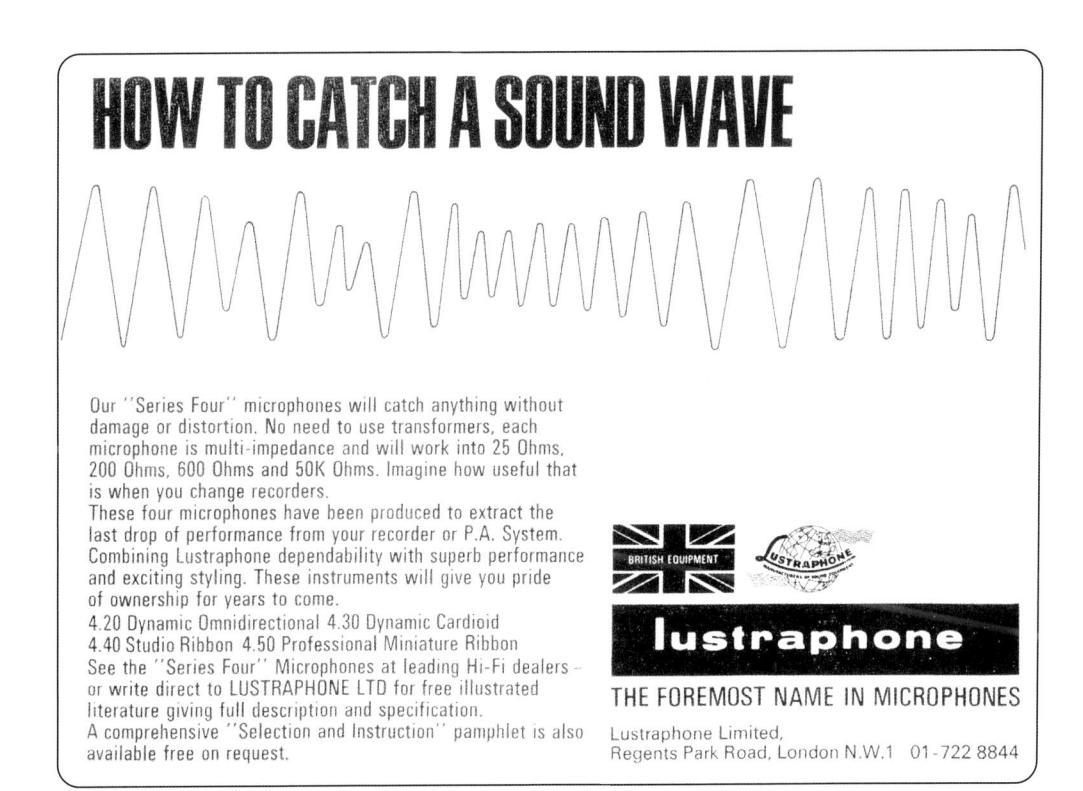

of four LPs released by the pair. Evening Star continued the formula of treated guitar, tapes and synthesizer; it was issued in 1975, the same year that Eno founded Obscure Records. The label released 10 albums up until 1978, featuring several leading lights in contemporary music, including Gavin Bryars, Max Eastley, John Cage, Michael Nyman and Harold Budd. Contributions to Obscure recordings came from **Howard Davidson**, **Howard Rees** and the Cockpit Ensemble. Music For Airports (1978), by Eno signalled the start of Ambient and the demise of Obscure. Through the mid-70s he released four pop based albums, and following on from Robert Fripp, he collaborated with or produced many other groups and artists working in the rock and pop field, most notably Quiet Sun, John Cale, David Bowie, Devo and Talking Heads. Less judiciously but more profitably he has worked with U2, James, Coldplay, and Paul Simon. Together with **Peter Schmidt** he developed Oblique Strategies, a deck of cards with directions or insights for problem solving, and he has branched out into the wider art world with generative visual works and installations. In 2010 he was the uninspiring guest director of the annual Brighton Festival, and he continues to be much in demand for a broad range of artistic opportunities. His quiet room containing ambient sound and visuals, was funded in 2013 by the private sector £34 million, Montefiore Hospital in Brighton & Hove.

Malcolm Fox (1946-1997)

Born: Windsor, Berkshire
Earliest Electronic Work: Variants (1969)
Commitment Factor: 7
Obscurity Quotient: 8
EM recording availability: Poor

Attending in combination the University of London and the Royal College of Music (RCM), Malcolm Fox studied with a range of established composers including **Tristram Cary**, Gordon Jacob, **Humphrey Searle** and Alexander Goehr. He investigated the music of Wagner, and subsequently became an authority on the subject, and joined Tristram's class at the RCM electronic music studio in 1967. During the second half of the 1960s he composed several pieces while a student; he wrote the score for the 1968 Ballet Rambert production Remembered Motion, and the following year his work Variants, was scored for cello, tape and electronics.

After graduation, he followed fellow RCM alumni **Grahame Dudley**, **Howard Davidson** and **Lawrence Casserley**, to the Cockpit Arts Centre in London, and from 1972-74 he was the Director of Music at the Cockpit Theatre. As leader of the electro-acoustic Cockpit Ensemble, he staged concerts of avant-garde music in conjunction with Dudley, and performances with the group **Music Plus**. For the ICES-72 festival in London, he played with Music Plus in a programme which included his composition Yeti.

In 1974 he secured a position at the Elder Conservatorium of the University of Adelaide, where Dudley and Cary were also based, and moved permanently to Australia to become Senior Lecturer in Music. Despite his individual approach, he worked his way up to become Dean of the Music Faculty. His opera for children, Sid the Serpent Who Wants to Sing (1976), became a highly popular success, while he continued using tape in Hajek Variations (1977), Refractions (1978), and an electronic ballet score The Journey, written in 1983.

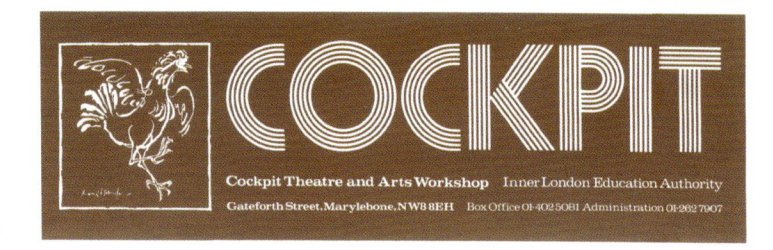

COCKPIT

Cockpit Theatre and Arts Workshop   Inner London Education Authority
Gateforth Street, Marylebone, NW8 8EH   Box Office 01-402 5081   Administration 01-262 7907

THE COCKPIT ENSEMBLE   director MALCOLM FOX

THE COCKPIT ENSEMBLE aims to introduce senior pupils to the sounds of modern music

Projects have been designed with 5th and 6th form pupils and College of Education students in mind. They may be easily adapted to suit 4th formers

Projects suggest possible fusions with the other arts and cover the whole spectrum of musical ability, from the unmusical pupil to the advanced instrumentalist

THE COCKPIT ENSEMBLE can visit your school any TUESDAY or FRIDAY starting January 23rd

photo: MARTIN HENLEY

Ron Geesin (1943)

Born: Stevenston, Ayrshire
Earliest Electronic Work: Doctored (1965)
Commitment Factor: 6
Obscurity Quotient: 3
EM recording availability: Good

Learning mouth organ and banjo as a lad, Geesin also took up piano and in 1961 he joined the dixieland jazz band The Original Downtown Syncopators, after seeing them at a gig in Glasgow. He was pianist with the group for the next four years, leaving to move down south, first to Crawley, then to Notting Hill in North London. Buying an open reel recorder, he started experimenting with tape music and began to make a name for himself as a composer. A number of commissions came his way during the mid-60s, including commercials for Trebor Mints, Phensic and Nescafe.

Releasing his first solo album A Raise of Eyebrows, in 1967, he also began working on short film soundtracks with upcoming British director Stephen Weeks, and neighbour Stephen Dwoskin. He scored Chinese Checkers, and Alone, for Dwoskin in 1964, and subsequently created several pieces for broadcast on John Peel's Top Gear radio show. In 1968 he moved to Ladbroke Grove, a bohemian area of London where he encountered various artists, musicians and filmmakers. Pink Floyd asked him to work on their 1970 album Atom Heart Mother, and he wrote and arranged the orchestral parts and co-wrote the title track. He also collaborated with the Floyd's Roger Waters on the soundtrack to The Body, a brilliant documentary film about human bodies and behaviour, for which Geesin recorded a wide variety of bio-musical sounds.

The John Schlesinger movie Sunday Bloody Sunday (1971), provided a decent pay packet and a breakthrough into feature film scoring, and he worked again with Stephen Weeks in 1974 for the sinister film Ghost Story. In 1972 he created electronic and tape manipulated tracks for the LP Electrosound, released on the library music label KPM, and set up his own imprint, Ron Geesin Records, to release his solo album As He Stands. The BBC

Ron Geesin at the Synthi A

SUNDAY BLOODY SUNDAY

educational series The Do It Yourself Film Animation Show, with Bob Godfrey, featured Geesin as a guest in 1974, and during the 70s he was approached by Desmond Briscoe, with a view to a post at the **Radiophonic Workshop**. Quite possibly due to Geesin's iconoclastic and irrepressible nature, this did not happen, and by that stage he was settled with his family well outside of London in a house in the country near Heathfield, East Sussex.

Besides studio recording, Geesin creates site specific sound works; these have included music for the British Pavilion at Expo 70; his Tune Tube, an interactive walk-through tunnel; and the quadraphonic Singing Bridge, for the Science Museum. From 1996-2003 he was a Senior Research Fellow in Sound at the University of Portsmouth, and in 1998 he created two public interactive events in the city: Sound-A-Maze for Shock Waves Festival, and Sea Sound, the University of Portsmouth's exhibit for the International Festival of the Sea. For the 2007 Doctor Who New Beginnings DVD box set, he assisted with the 16-track master tape transfer, and it turned out his wife Frances had been a costume creator on The Keeper of Traken, one of the stories in the set. Geesin still performs and composes, and as well as a liking for various types of wood, he has an unabashed passion for adjustable spanners – kitting out his own 'Spannarium', whilst writing a niche book about his singular spanner specialism.

Geesin splicing

Roberto Gerhard (1896-1970)

Born: Valls, Spain
Earliest Electronic Work: The Prisoner (1954)
Commitment Factor: 7
Obscurity Quotient: 5
EM recording availability: Good

In his early years Gerhard studied piano and composition, and following the death of his teacher Felipe Pedrell in 1922, he became a pupil of Arnold Schoenberg in Vienna. Returning to Barcelona in 1928, he devoted his energies to new music through concerts and journalism, while also collecting folksongs and old Spanish music. Supporting the Republican cause throughout the Spanish Civil War, as musical adviser to the elected government, he was forced into exile after the victory of Franco's facists in 1939, and came to England and settled in Cambridge later that year.

During the 1950s, he developed a radical approach to composition, and his work with electronics showed him at the forefront of the avant-garde, and one of the earliest established composers in Britain to begin working with tape. He was active by 1954, and that year he made tape effects for Bridget Boland's play The Prisoner. He received commissions from the BBC, and was thus granted access to the **Radiophonic Workshop**, and the use of technicians and equipment. After moving house in 1958, he established a permanent home studio at 14 Madingley Road, Cambridge, with four high quality tape recorders, and a large library of taped sounds he had recorded from a variety of sources. An edited selection of his electronic tracks was issued as a Southern library music 7" record in 1964, and extracts appeared in early episodes of Doctor Who, including the stories The Space Museum, The Time Meddler and The Tomb of the Cybermen.

Gerhard wrote the score for Lindsay Anderson's classic 1963 feature film This Sporting Life, though fell out with the director over the music for the title sequence. The soundtrack was highly effective, and that same year Gerhard worked on a rather different film – DNA in Reflection – an experimental short made by two students at the Cambridge Laboratory of Molecular Biology. This involved a type of kaleidoscope, for an abstract study based on a plastic model of the double helix molecular chains. Complete with his soundtrack of tape manipulated sounds, it was screened in 1969 at a Macnaghten Concerts presentation of live electronic music from **Gentle Fire**, plus films featuring electronic scores. Gerhard's sound was better known as a concert tape piece under the name Audiomobile No. 2 DNA, and was included in the event Project: Electronic Music, held at the Royal Festival Hall in London.

His 1960 work Symphony No. 3 (Collages) was commissioned by the Koussevitsky Foundation, scored for tape and orchestra, with the electronic section completed at the Radiophonic Workshop. The piece received its premiere in 1961 played by the BBC Symphony Orchestra, with the tape recorder operated by Workshop member Dick Mills. Made for BBC radio, The Anger of Achilles, scored for orchestra, soloists, choir and magnetic tape, won Gerhard the Prix Italia in 1965, with **Delia Derbyshire** finalising the radiophonic parts.

From the early 1950s, he suffered from a heart condition which eventually ended his life in 1970. A research project started in 2012 based at the University of Huddersfield, has organised, catalogued and digitised his electronic music tapes, held at the Cambridge University Library.

CD: Roberto Gerhard: Electronic Explorations from his Studio + the BBC Radiophonic Workshop 1958-1967 (Sub Rosa, 2014).

Films
AND ELECTRONIC MUSIC

TOWN HALL
EUSTON ROAD NW1
Thursday 13 November 1969 at 7.30

presented by
THE MACNAGHTEN CONCERTS

FILMS WITH ELECTRONIC SCORES AND LIVE ELECTRONIC WORKS

performed by

THE GENTLE FIRE

(Richard Bernas, Hugh Davies, Patrick Harrex, Graham Hearn, Stuart Jones, Richard Orton)

Trois Portraits de l'Oiseau-qui-n'existe-pas — *Francois Bayle*

Animated colour portraits of three 'non-existent' birds: *carnivorous bird*, *humming bird* and *song bird*, directed by Robert Lapoujade (1963). Production of the Service de la Recherche of the French Radio.

Kiss Combine — *Richard Orton*
(first performance)

Live electronic work composed in May 1969 and dedicated to the performers. Four tape channels provide a fluctuating sound-environment against which four musicians produce voice sounds at a large amplified glass plate.

DNA in Reflection — *Roberto Gerhard*

Scientific documentary in colour, produced in 1963. The music is probably the best-known English electronic composition, under its concert title *Audiomobile No.2*.

Antithese — *Mauricio Kagel*

Film directed by the composer for North German TV. 1965 film version of the 1962 theatre piece for solo actor with a wide range of electronic equipment of various kinds and vintages.

Five Short Films — *Robert Ashley & Gordon Mumma*

1. December 1962: A Film for Hooded Projector (music Manupelli)
2. I Love You Do Not Be Afraid (music Ashley)
3. Say Nothing About This to Anyone (music Mumma)
4. I Must See You Regarding a Matter of the Utmost Urgency (music Ashley)
5. If You Leave Me I Will Kill Myself (music Mumma)

Directed by George Manupelli, USA, 1963-4.

Appearance — *Toshi Ichiyanagi*
(first London performance)

Live electronic music composed in 1967 for one string instrument (electric guitar), one brass instrument (trumpet), one organ or bandoneon (piano accordion), two oscillators and two ring modulators.

Plus Vite — *Bernard Parmegiani*

Colour cartoon film on the increasing speed of 20th-century life. Directed by Peter Foldes, 1965, and produced by the Service de la Recherche of the French Radio.

Tickets: 6s 10s 15s 20s
On sale from 13 October at the Box Office, Town Hall, Euston Road, NW1
Box Office Tel 278/4444 ext. 281 and from all Camden Libraries and usual ticket agents. Cheques and postal orders payable to the London Borough of Camden

The Macnaghten Concerts (founded 1931) are in association with the Arts Council of Great Britain.

Anthony Gilbert, 1971

Anthony Gilbert (1934)

Born: London
Earliest Electronic Work: The Scene-Machine (1970)
Commitment Factor: 5
Obscurity Quotient: 7
EM recording availability: Poor

After working as a translator and interpreter, Gilbert studied piano and later received tuition from Matyas Seiber, (who was a regular composer for Halas & Batchelor Cartoon Films). He then attended Morley College in London, and studied with Alexander Goehr, and received some instruction from Gunther Schuller at Tanglewood in the USA. Gilbert's music was starting to be recognised and performed during the 1960s, and he was commissioned by brewer Watneys to compose Brighton Piece, for the first Brighton Festival in 1967.
Employment with music publishers Schotts, provided employment and a publishing deal for his compositions lasting until 1994, and he worked his way up to the company's head of production. From 1969-70 he ran a course at Goldsmiths Electronic Music Workshop, based around tape recorders and a VCS3, and completed his piece Treatment of Silence, scored for violin and tape. He participated in a summer course held at **EMS** in 1970, and was composition tutor in the Adult Studies Department at Goldsmiths from 1971-73. His one-act opera, The Scene-Machine (1970), with libretto by George MacBeth, involves solo singers, chorus, orchestra, pop group, and a passage with electronic tape.

Gilbert consolidated his teaching, taking a position at the Royal Northern College of Music (RNCM), where he remained until 1999. During his time at the college he established an electronic music studio, wrote works for a variety of commissions, and spent periods in Australia at the New South Wales Conservatorium. Being heavily involved with contemporary music, he served on committees of the SPNM, and the New Music Panel of NW Arts, and while at the RNCM he founded the ensemble AKANTHOS. Maintaining his keen interest in music, Tony Gilbert continues to compose at his home in Styal in Cheshire.

Ranulph Glanville (1946-2014)

Born: London
Earliest Electronic Work: Music for Exhibition (1966)
Commitment Factor: 6
Obscurity Quotient: 8
EM recording availability: Limited

With an early interest in serial music and the work of Olivier Messiaen, the young Glanville initially got started experimenting at home with reel to reel tape recorders. A music summer school programmed by **Harrison Birtwistle** was a further ear opener, and subsequently led to contact with **Hugh Davies**, Cornelius Cardew, **Peter Zinovieff** and Peter Maxwell Davies, (for whom he made some electronic sound).

Starting in 1964, Glanville studied Architecture and Music at the Architectural Association School in London, and organised concerts of contemporary music, including performances of pieces by Iannis Xenakis and John Cage, as well as gigs by the Yardbirds and Pink Floyd. (Noting the limitations of the Floyd's electronic equipment, he gave them a ring modulator he had constructed.) For an event at the AA School in 1966, he created a multi-speaker sound installation using unmatched loudspeakers, which gave different frequency responses from the same electronic source material. That year he was involved in a concert during a four day Experimental Music Festival at the Commonwealth Institute in London, which also featured **David Bedford**, John Surman and members of AMM.

His piece Nona Meyeah Teay – the title based on an anagram – reveals his interest in overlapping tape loops, blocks of sound, distortion and white noise, and dates from 1967. Being very interested in the integration of electronics, concrete sounds, live performance and theatricality, he formed **Half Landing**, one of Britain's first live electronic music groups, active from 1965-68. At the end of his architectural studies, Glanville's interests in design and cybernetics led him towards a fascinating career, which has included prescient designs for a form of internet shopping and a 1960s style laptop. With writing and regular international lecturing taking up much of his time, his electronic music took a back seat for many years, though his interest remained. In later life he returned to composition, fitted in amongst his many academic commitments.

CD: Not necessarily English Music (Electronic Music Foundation, 2001). Includes Glanville's Nona Meyeah Teay.

Stanley Glasser, early 1970s

Stanley Glasser (1926-2018)

Born: Johannesburg, South Africa
Earliest Electronic Work: Electronic sounds for Emperor Jones (c.1960)
    Recorded in South Africa
Commitment Factor: 4
Obscurity Quotient: 7
EM recording availability: Poor

After gaining a degree in economics in South Africa, Glasser came to England in 1950 and studied with Matyas Seiber at Cambridge University. His composition work was informed by his in-depth study of African folk songs, and back in his home country around 1960, he supplied electronic sounds for a stage version of Eugene O'Neill's Emperor Jones. In 1963 he returned to England to teach at Goldsmiths College, becoming Head of the Music Department in 1969, a position which lasted until his retirement in 1991. Amongst a number of posts held during his career, he became associate editor of the Composer magazine in 1967, and chairman of the Composers' Guild of Great Britain in 1975.

During 1967 **Hugh Davies** had proposed the establishment of an electronic studio at Goldsmiths, of which Glasser was a strong supporter. He quickly arranged for Davies to be engaged to give an evening class in electronic music, and once the sessions were up and running, Glasser was able to press for space to be allocated and a studio created. By January 1968 evening classes were being held at the Goldsmiths Electronic Music Workshop, which developed into a fully equipped studio, now a state of the art facility named in Glasser's honour. For the Musical Times in 1972 he wrote, "*the electronic music studio now possesses two VCS3s; if funds were to hand, this studio, for its present needs alone, would buy another four.*"

Besides the piece Coromantee (1970-71), he wrote Serenade (1974), for piano, 10 instruments and synthesizer, and music for the film The Last of the Few in 1959. He even has a credit for the Benny Hill Show, and composed in a wide range of contexts throughout his musical career. In his final years debilitating illness brought his activities to a close, and he died aged 92.

Ken Gray (1943-1994)

Born: Ilford, Greater London
Earliest Electronic Work: Audio sculpture studies (1970)
Commitment Factor: 6
Obscurity Quotient: 8
EM recording availability: Limited

Ken Gray and his Electrosculpture

An audiovisual artist, kinetic sculptor and teacher, Gray preferred the term 'communications engineer' rather than artist, to convey the essence of his creative exploits. He obtained a National Diploma in Civil Engineering from Southend on Sea Municipal College in 1964, and for a time worked as a marine surveyor. His artistic interests prompted him to take a foundation course at Brighton School of Art (which evolved into Brighton University) starting in 1968, and this led to him studying for a degree the following year in the painting department. He was inclined towards interactive art, kinetic sculpture and electronic sound, and by 1970 he was working with experimental tapes. For an art show Illusions, at Sussex University in March 1971, he provided equipment and electronic sounds, and a year later he had his first solo exhibition of electronic sculptures at the Zarach gallery in London, with this work going on to be shown in Germany.

For the Brighton Festival in 1976 he created Phantasmagoria Today, a walk-in futuristic interactive environment, with sculpture, lights and electronic sounds activated by touch. His aim was to heighten spectator experience, and physically involve normally passive viewers in the artwork. Another of his electrosculpture installations involved visitors being given metal rods with which to probe the exhibits, in order to generate electronic sounds and light.

He graduated from Brighton Polytechnic in 1973, and that year started renting The Pepperpot, a Victorian tower folly, from Brighton Council for £220 per year. Inside he housed his studio, and a photograph taken at that time shows him entering decked out as an urban spaceman; perhaps depicting a communications engineer travelling to and from other worlds. After gaining an MA at the Royal College of Art in 1976, he left Britain four years later and moved with his family to the USA, teaching art in Tennessee, and gaining a further master's degree at Memphis State University. In 1981 he moved to Anchorage, Alaska, and became associate professor of art at the state university. His premature death from cancer followed his last big art show; a group sculpture exhibition at the Anchorage Museum.

ILLUSIONS

Directed by John Epstein artist in residence
Musical director Francis Shaw
Design, construction, projection and music, Robert Burne, Sacha Kagan
students of Sussex University and Brighton Polytechnic

Gardner Centre Theatre
March 19 and 20 1971   10p

Ken Gray exhibiting his Electrosculpture

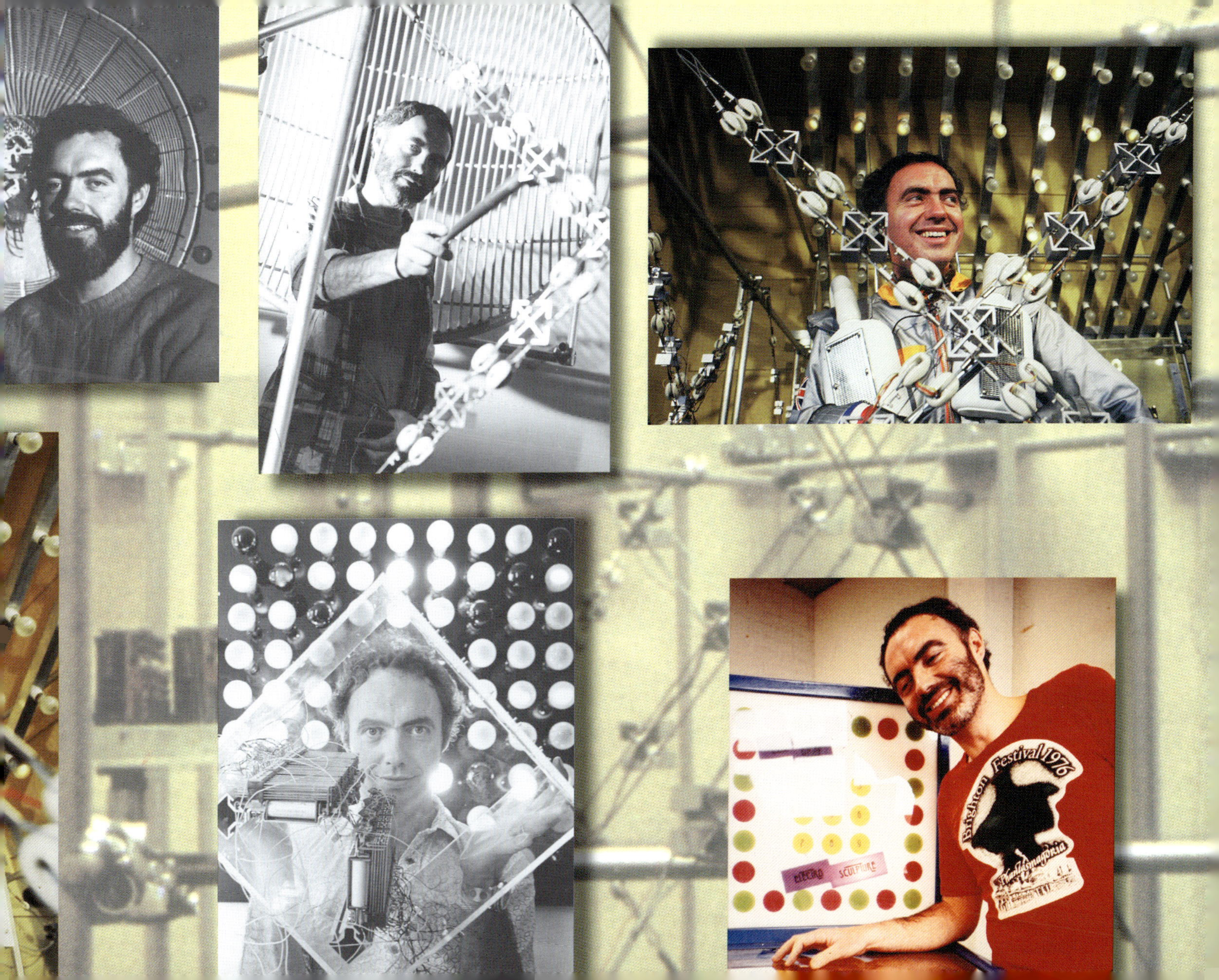
Brighton Festival 1976
ELECTRO SCULPTURE

Peter Grogono (1944-2021)

Born: London
Earliest Electronic Work: Tape studies (late 1950s)
Commitment Factor: 6
Obscurity Quotient: 6
EM recording availability: Limited

As a young teenager in the 1950s, Grogono was inspired to teach himself the piano, and amidst parental indifference, he managed to persuade his father to buy a tape recorder. His experiments with tape and piano sounds, began in earnest after he had listened avidly to the BBC Network 3 radio series Sound, first broadcast at the beginning of 1959, featuring contributions on electronic music by **Tristram Cary**. At Queens' College Cambridge studying mathematics from 1962-65, he joined both the film society and the film production unit, which gave him access to several different tape recorders, allowing for more serious experimentation, and the creation of a piece with multiple tape loops. After graduating, his experiments continued with a multi-speed Tandberg reel to reel recorder and a great deal of tape splicing. In the mid-60s he lived in Ealing and executed tape sounds for several local theatre productions, including a staging of Look Back In Anger.

His interests in computing had started at a young age, and involved constructing his own mechanical computer in the late 1950s. During the 60s he worked with the EDSAC 2 computer at Cambridge, and a 7094 at IBM in London. His second job was at EMI in 1966, where he wrote a computer program which could read and encode musical scores, and 'compose' music using statistical probability.

In February 1969 he was invited to attend a concert of electronic music at the Queen Elizabeth Hall in London; an event which presaged a major turning point in his life. The **EMS** company provided equipment for the concert, and was coincidentally based in Deodar Road in Putney, where Grogono happened to be moving to that weekend, to be nearer his new job with computing firm ICL. After the concert he made enquiries about working with EMS, and for a period continued at ICL while doing EMS work in the evenings; an arrangement that lasted until **Peter Zinovieff** offered him a full-time position. Working with PDP-8 computers, he wrote the music synthesis program MUSYS, and assisted a number of composers with the electronic realisation of their work. These included Francis Monkman of rock group Curved Air, **Justin Connolly**, **Anna Lockwood** and **Harrison Birtwistle**; Grogono adapted MUSYS to perform fast percussive chords for Birtwistle's Chronometer.

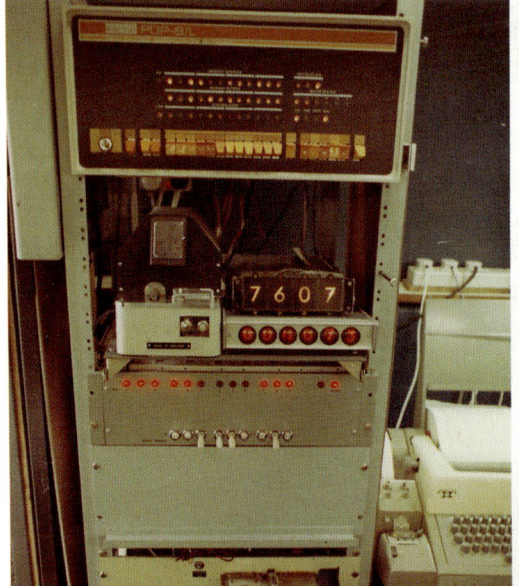

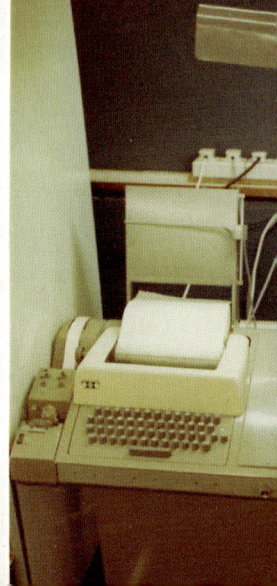

Experiments with his own music had to be carried out in his spare time, and Grogono vividly recalls the excitement of playing a PDP-8 digital computer tape on an Ampex analogue tape recorder; the piece Datafield, was created out of this experiment. He received his one and only commission at EMS while Zinovieff was away, and this came from US experimental filmmaker Stan Vanderbeek, who needed a soundtrack for a new short film concerning 'the creation'. Grogono recorded a baritone voice intoning the words "*In the beginning was the word*," and then used the processing capability of the EMS filter bank to create 14 minutes of music from the one phrase. (Unfortunately further information on the film has so far proved elusive.)

Grogono remembers a time in the early 70s with **Beatles** drummer Ringo Starr; "*I was impressively ignorant of the culture around me and did not understand the [EMS] secretary's startled look when I handed the phone to her with a nonchalant "it's for you – some guy called Richard Starkey." A few days later, I was at EMI's Abbey Road studios trying to get noises out of a VCS3 to please Ringo.*"

In 1973 he emigrated to Canada, and initially assembled his own studio with a tape recorder and home made electronic gear, plus a large sheet of resonant steel. During his career he developed programming languages and wrote software manuals, and his various interests included artificial life, computer animation and snooker. He was a professor at the Department of Computer Science and Software Engineering, at Concordia University, Montreal until his death in 2021.

MUSYS - the computer section

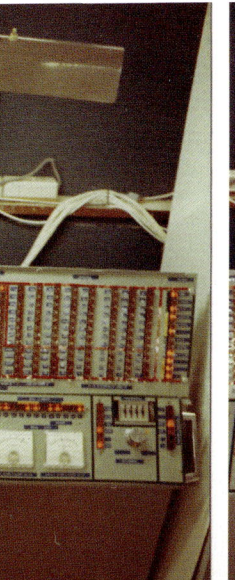

ELECTRONIC MUSIC STUDIOS
49 DEODAR ROAD LONDON S.W.15. 01-874-2363

Peter Grogno, Esq.,   10th September, 1969.
53 Deodar Road,
London, S.W.15.

Dear Peter,

This is to confirm our conversation of last night that I am giving you a sum of £1000 to work on programme for me for six months.

I will pay you in three equal instalments and expect you to remind me when they are due. There are no conditions attached to this except that your role basically will be to make Musys a fantastically sophisticated software package.

Ever yours,

Peter

Graham Hearn (1942)

Born: Battersea, London
Earliest Electronic Work: Contrapunctus (1968)
Commitment Factor: 6
Obscurity Quotient: 7
EM recording availability: Poor

Following study at Trinity College of Music from 1961-64, Hearn gained teaching experience at a Leeds comprehensive school until 1967, when he began studying for a doctorate in composition at the University of York. Around this time he became increasingly interested in electronic sound, and experimented in the newly established University electronic music studio, overseen by **Richard Orton**. His preference was for electro-acoustic composition, especially using found sounds and long playing records, and he composed Contrapunctus (1968), and Centrepiece (1970), with this type of material.

Contrapunctus involves LP records of a Bach fugue played by turntable operators according to instructions. Centrepiece is derived from the run-off locked groove sounds at the end of a vinyl record, a selection of which were made into tape loops. In performance the loops are played back on any number of tape recorders for as long as required. This aleatoric aspect is also discernible in his piece Listen-in (1970), for any sized group of performers each with a radio. All the receivers are switched on together, and the players attempt to reach a unified frequency by tuning in to the same wavelength.

Hearn became an experienced exponent of the VCS3, and played the synthesizer as part of live performance group **Gentle Fire**, formed with fellow York University students, plus Orton and **Hugh Davies**. While still studying at York, he taught part time at Harrogate School of Art, and from 1970 lectured full time at Harrogate College of Further Education in experimental music. He set up a small electronic studio there with a VCS3 and Revox tape recorders, and in 1979 he switched to Leeds College of Music, and established a slightly more sophisticated studio based around

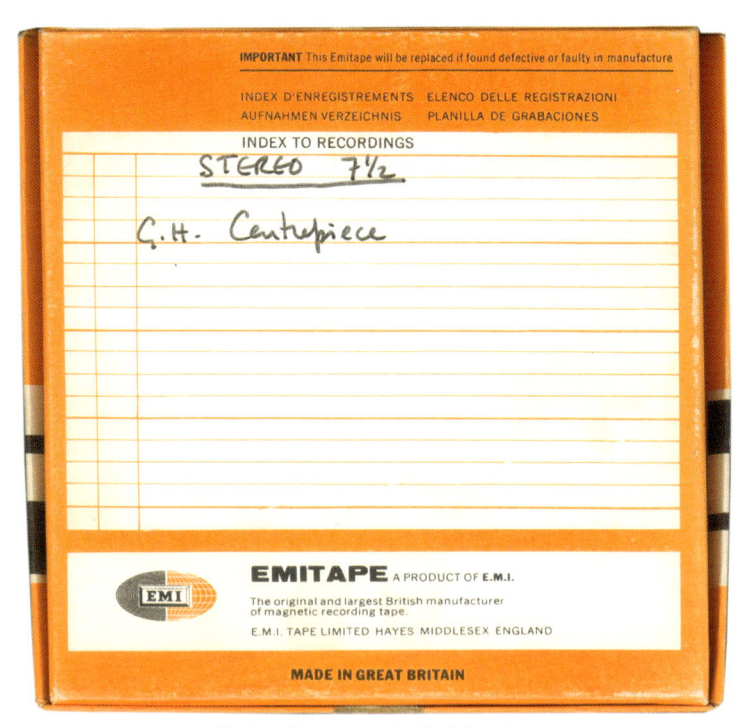

Graham Hearn - quarter inch tape box

EMS equipment. Teaching electro-acoustic music, mainly to jazz students, he invited in guest lecturers including **Trevor Wishart**, and after the demise of Gentle Fire he focused primarily on his college work. During the mid-1980s, the studio he had set up with classic analogue gear, was dismantled behind his back and replaced with all new digital equipment. He continued lecturing at Leeds College, covering jazz and 20th century music, until retiring in 2012. Since that time he has kept active with jazz as composer, arranger and pianist with a couple of local groups, and confesses that he has not ruled out a return to experimental music in the future.

Donald Henshilwood (1930-2009)

Born: North Bierley, Bradford, Yorkshire
Earliest Electronic Work: Improvisation (1961)
Commitment Factor: 7
Obscurity Quotient: 7
EM recording availability: Limited

Educated at Bingley Grammar School in Yorkshire, Henshilwood was a largely self-taught composer, though in the 1960s he undertook some studies with Witold Lutoslawski and Luciano Berio. Attending the Dartington Summer Schools from 1957-63, at the same time as **FC Judd**, **Delia Derbyshire** and **George Newson**, by 1961 he had established his home studio at 130 Frankby Road, West Kirby in Cheshire. He was equipped to record electronic music in popular and experimental idioms, and during the early 1960s he worked on pop songs with electronic sounds. During 1967 he upgraded his studio with the addition of extra amplifiers and a fourth tape deck, and was beginning to focus his attention away from popular music, except where electronics and tape were required.

In April 1968 his piece Sonata, featured in what appears to be the first ever major concert of electronic music held in the north west of the country, at Mountford Hall in Liverpool. It was included in a strong programme alongside works by **Tristram Cary**, Delia Derbyshire and **Brian Dennis**. A concert at the QEH in London in February 1969 saw another first-rate line up of British electronic music, and featured his piece Sonata 6. The previous month he was engaged in a further event at Liverpool University's Mountford Hall, titled The Eye and Ear Concert. This involved his tape work Delta (1968), and tracks by Berio, Pierre Henry and Rudolf Komorous, with accompanying dance, lights and visual effects, plus live sound transformation by the **Quiet Pavement Ensemble**.

He composed five symphonies, music for brass and wind ensembles, and created at least seven numbered electronic pieces during the 60s under the title Sonata; other tape works include Triplex (1968), and Galaxy (1969). A US radio programme featuring 'new electronic compositions from England', broadcast on station KPFA in 1972, featured tracks by **Richard Orton**, plus Henshilwood's Modulations (1972). In 1963 he provided a tape score for the theatre production Oedipus Rex, and in 1978 he worked with the Cheshire based Hillbark Players on their version of A Midsummer Night's Dream.

He continued composing throughout the 1980s and 90s, still living at the same Frankby Road address, but in his final years he suffered a stroke which curtailed much of his composing activity. Sadly it seems likely that all his original equipment and electronic music tapes were discarded or dispersed after his death.

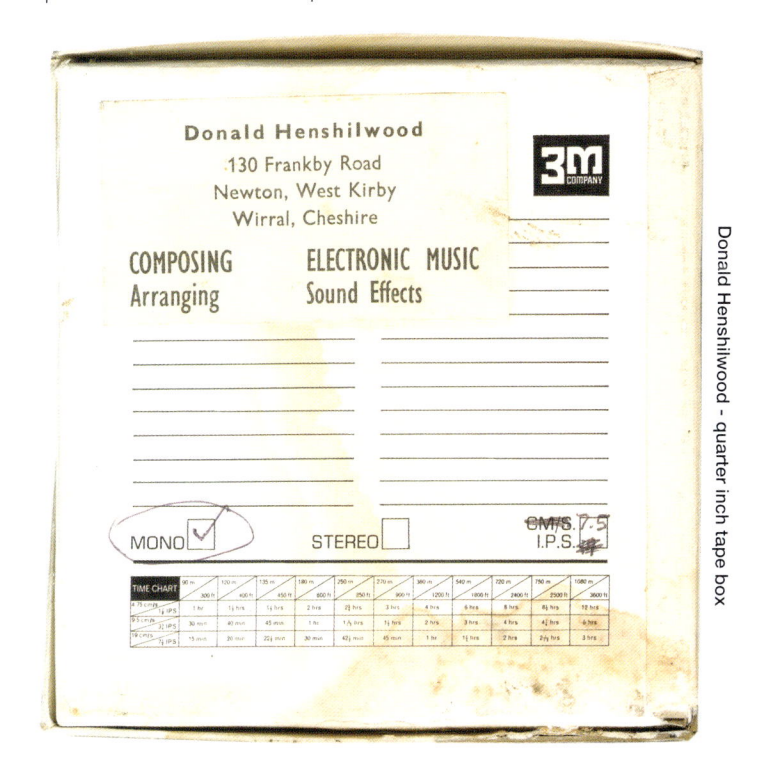

Donald Henshilwood - quarter inch tape box

> **DONALD HENSHILWOOD**
>
> ARRANGING   COMPOSING   RECORDING
> ELECTRONIC MUSIC and SOUND EFFECTS
> 130 Frankby Rd., Newton, West Kirby, Wirral, Cheshire. L48 9UX
> Phone 051-625 6742
>
> Dec. 6th 1968
>
> Dear George,
>
> As suggested at the S.P.N.M. weekend I am enclosing a tape of some of my work.
>
> The two electronic works are mono transcriptions from stereo and they may suffer a little from this of course, particularly 'Continuum' which I only finished about a week ago. The other piece (Sonata 7) also dates from this year. As a 'fill-up' after Continuum I have put 2 extracts from non-electronic works (@3¾ips) These are not actual performances —only my own synthetic versions which I usually do after completing a work in order to get an idea how they sound. (For this reason I hope you'll forgive my playing and use of 'electric bassoon' and clarinet, but I've only got clavioline & electric piano.)
>
> Let me know what you think when you find time.
>
> Hoping things are well with you
>
> Sincerely
> Donald Henshilwood
>
> V/S

Brian Hodgson (1938)

Born: Liverpool
Earliest Electronic Work: Radiophonic sound productions (1962)
Commitment Factor: 6
Obscurity Quotient: 4
EM recording availability: Excellent

With a childhood background that included some acting for radio, Hodgson carried out his National Service in the RAF in Northern Ireland, where he worked in the sonic detection of submarines. He first owned a tape recorder at this time, and used it for basic sound experiments, while becoming aware of the early musique concrète from Paris. When he left the Air Force he went straight into acting work, and this led to stage managing and theatrical tours around Britain.

He applied for a studio manager job at the BBC around 1960, and secured a position with Central Programme Operations, working on sound effects for radio dramas. Requesting an attachment to the **Radiophonic Workshop** in 1962, the following year he most famously created the TARDIS take off and landing sound for Doctor Who. He did all the special sounds for the series, including the Dalek's ring modulated voices, up until Dick Mills took over in 1972, and has credits for sound on over 300 BBC programmes. In 1971 he masterminded an impressive concert at the Royal Festival Hall for the centenary of the Institute of Electrical Engineers, to showcase the Workshop's output, and demonstrate the recently acquired Synthi 100.

His work outside the Workshop included **Unit Delta Plus** and **White Noise**, both of which involved his close colleague **Delia Derbyshire**. He had made a contribution to the KPM record library during the 1960s, and at the start of the new decade – together with Australian composer Don Harper – Hodgson and Derbyshire recorded tracks for the KPM Electrosonic album, released in 1972. The Kaleidophon studio was established with **David Vorhaus**, and besides a limited input into White Noise, Hodgson made musical contributions for theatre productions, and Peter Logan's Mechanical

Ballet and Square Dance – two works of performance with kinetic sculpture.

In 1972 he left the BBC to focus on his own musical activities full-time, and used money from his pension scheme to buy equipment for the Electrophon studio, based in Covent Garden. Established with John Lewis, and joined briefly by Derbyshire, it picked up on the idea first tried by Unit Delta Plus, for a studio to supply electronic music and effects commercially, free from institutional bureaucracy. The team sometimes worked with regular Doctor Who composer Dudley Simpson, and created music for the feature films Visions of Eight, and The Legend of Hell House (both 1973). For the Olympic Games based documentary Visions of Eight, Hodgson used a computer at **Peter Zinovieff**'s **EMS** studio, to create sounds to accompany a marathon running scene.

He scored several dances for Ballet Rambert, including There Was a Time (1973), Duets (1973-75), and Weekend (1974-76), and worked with choreographer Robert Cohan, for the London Contemporary Dance Theatre, on the piece Forest (1977). Under the names Electrophon and Wavemaker, Hodgson collaborated on several albums in the 70s, among them the feeble 'switched-on' style, In A Covent Garden. In 1977 he returned to the Radiophonic Workshop with a remit to re-equip the studios with up to date technology, and in 1983 he took over as studio head from the retiring **Desmond Briscoe**, remaining until almost the Workshop's demise.

CDs:
Doctor Who at the BBC Radiophonic Workshop Volume 1
    (BBC Music, 2000).
Doctor Who at the BBC Radiophonic Workshop Volume 2
    (BBC Music, 2000).
Doctor Who – The Krotons (Silva Screen, 2013).

John Lewis and Brian Hodgson at the Electrophon studio, mid 1970s

James Ingram (1948)

Born: Sidcup, Kent
Earliest Electronic Work: Pianola Music (1967)
Commitment Factor: 4
Obscurity Quotient: 6
EM recording availability: Poor

Having studied music composition for a time with **David Rowland** during the mid-60s, in 1967 Ingram became a student at the Royal Academy of Music (RAM) in London, and from 1968-71 he was taught by **Harrison Birtwistle**. Also in 67 he acquired from a friend a fresh pianola roll to cut, and access to a player piano to playback the results. He made tape recordings of the completed piece which was composed along serialist lines, and recorded the mechanism and pedals of the instrument as it played through the roll. This became his first tape composition Pianola Music, and around the same time he also made a tape collage, though this he found unsatisfactory and scrapped.

At the dawn of the 1970s he was working on new compositions, including Untitled '70, for wind quartet with automatic conductor. Following its premiere during a student concert at the RAM, a second performance took place at the Cockpit Theatre in London, conducted by a black, four armed 'lantern'. Operated by four unseen human conductors, the 'lantern' featured light bulbs at the end of the arms, and was lowered from the ceiling in darkness just before the performance started. For the Probability of Harmony (1971), for alto-flute, clarinet, conductor and tape, the score was made up of a long roll of paper containing the clarinet part, and a sheet of cardboard with cut-outs for the flute, placed on top of the paper anywhere along its length where the bar lines matched up. It was also performed at the Cockpit with **Howard Davidson** and Marjorie Shansky, and saw Ingram becoming involved with the venue and its resident ensemble **Music Plus**.

While still a student he began as a freelance copyist for music publishers Universal Edition, and worked on a number of scores for composers such as Birtwistle, Earle Brown and Morton Feldman. At one point he was asked to deal with a Karlheinz Stockhausen score, and the two began regular correspondence. In 1974 he was invited to work with Stockhausen full time, and went on to become his principal music copyist. He was initially employed to sort out the notation of parts for the orchestral piece Inori, and worked with a team of copyists including **George Brown** and **Roger Smalley**. He continued his association with Stockhausen on a range of celebrated compositions, staying at his house for half of each year right up until 2000, when the German composer terminated their working arrangement.

Long concerned with theories of musical notation, in recent years Ingram has been developing a computer file format for scores, which encapsulates temporal information inside graphical objects; his Assistant Performer software can use live MIDI input to influence the performance of such a score.

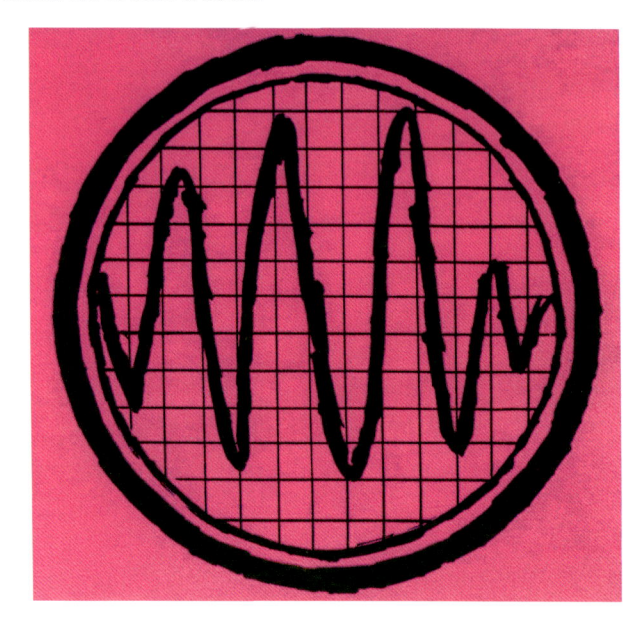

Wilfred Josephs (1927-1997)

Born: Newcastle upon Tyne
Earliest Electronic Work: Catharsis (1967) unconfirmed
Commitment Factor: 1
Obscurity Quotient: 7
EM recording availability: Limited

With his early schooling and piano studies interrupted by wartime evacuation, Josephs was encouraged to pursue education as a medical student, and he qualified as a dentist in 1951. Music and composition were central to his future career however, and an initial scholarship enabled him to become a pupil of Alfred Nieman at the Guildhall School of Music, while a further Leverhulme Scholarship took him to Paris for a year's study with Max Deutsch.

His composing reputation began to build, and he was eventually able to devote his energies to music, with his Requiem, providing great acclaim and his international breakthrough. The piece was conceived in 1961 around the time of the trial of Nazi SS officer Adolf Eichmann, and was a memorial to the victims of the Holocaust. Josephs began receiving a regular string of commissions; among these were 12 symphonies and 22 concertos, and scores for film and television, which included I Claudius, Swallows and Amazons, Cider with Rosie, and All Creatures Great and Small.

The theme he composed for surveillance sci-fi TV show The Prisoner, was rejected in favour of Ron Grainer's, although some of his incidental music was included in the series. His two part Space Time Music, was featured in the Doctor Who episodes The Tomb of the Cybermen (1967), and The Web of Fear (1968). In Five Films (1967), by British director Don Levy, the section titled Catharsis, features a musique concrète piano treatment by Josephs. Also in this period he worked with filmmaker Geoffrey Jones, to compose a soundtrack for terrific short film Rail (1966).

He continued his prolific composing through into the 1990s, and The Wilfred Josephs Society was founded in 1994 to foster interest in his body of work.

> Besides Snow, produced for British Transport Fims, **Daphne Oram** worked for Geoffrey Jones on Trinidad and Tobago (1964), and provided electronic treatments for Rail (1966), as well as assisting with the orchestral recording. **Tristram Cary** created the electronic soundtrack for Don Levy's triple screen film Sources of Power, made for the British Pavilion at Expo 67 in Montreal.

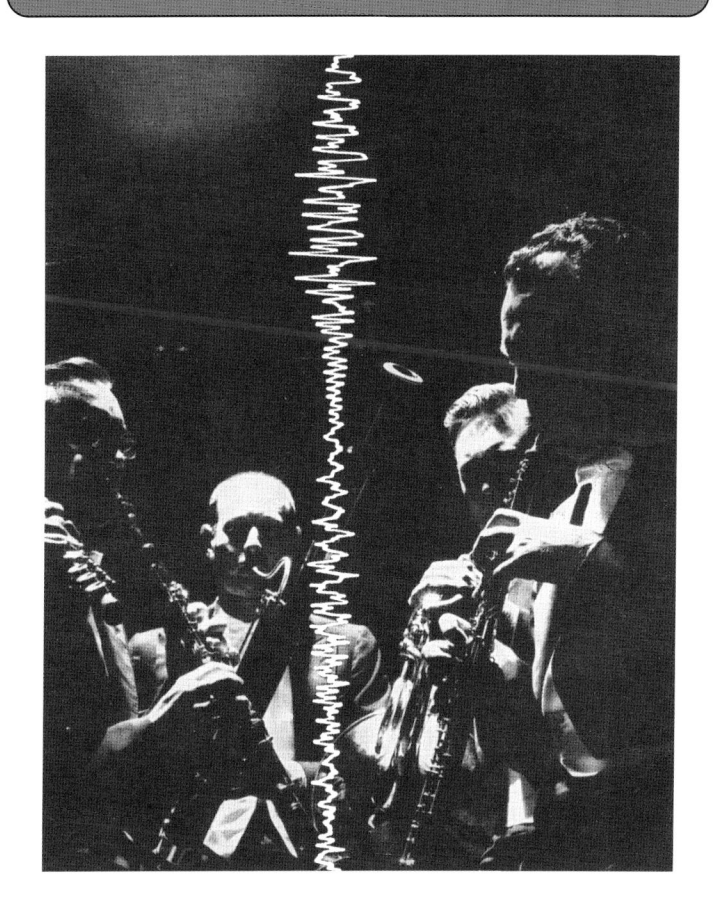

FC Judd (1914-1992)

Born: Woodford, London
Earliest Electronic Work: The Butterfly (1960)
Commitment Factor: 8
Obscurity Quotient: 4
EM recording availability: Excellent

Coming from a radio and engineering background, Fred Judd was drawn to electronic music during the 1950s, and set up a small studio at home in Woodford, East London. Like **Tristram Cary**, whom he would later meet, he had worked with radar during World War II, and left the forces with a solid grounding in electronic engineering. He built his own tape machine in the mid-50s, and his two part article Effects With a Tape Recorder, first appeared in Radio Constructor magazine in June 1956. He had 11 technical books published during his life, including Electronic Music and Musique Concrète, in 1961; one of the first books in the world to tackle the subject from a practical angle, containing a range of circuit designs for readers to build.

From his home at 174 Maybank Road, he established the company Recorded Tuition Limited, under which he co-ran the independent record label Castle, releasing sound effects discs and three EPs of his electronic music from 1963-67. A number of these tracks were later licensed by library music label Studio G, and released as an album, Electronic Age (1970). From the LP his piece Suspended Motion, was used in the 70s children's science fiction series The Tomorrow People, in the stories The Medusa Strain, and The Blue and the Green. A decade earlier, the producers of the tremendous ITV children's sci-fi puppet show Space Patrol, commissioned Fred to create all the sounds and music for each episode, and originally broadcast in early 1963, it is the first British television series to feature a complete electronic score. This was an important milestone in the use of electronics in mainstream TV, and deserves much wider recognition for its adventurous avant-garde approach.

Fred was an inventor as well as engineer, author and musician, and among his innovations was the construction of a simple voltage controlled, keyboard operated synthesizer, which he had operational in the first half of 1963; noteworthy in that no synthesizers were commercially available until more than a year later. He also developed a system for the visualisation of electronic music, using a modified black & white TV with colour scanning disc, into which he fed audio signals from tapes or tone generators. He called the novel assembly Chromasonics, and his integrated Chromatron and Chromascan unit was displayed in London in 1961, and considered for mass production by Austrian tape recorder manufacturer Stuzzi.

Alongside **Daphne Oram**, Fred was a key player in the dissemination of electronic music; they were in regular contact and both served on the judging panels of the 1963 ATR club recording competition, and the British Amateur Tape Recording Contest in 1964. A judge for the BATRC throughout the 60s, he even picked up an award himself in 1965 for his track Tempotune. He had received first prize for his composition The Butterfly, in a competition for new music run by the Tape Recorder magazine six years before, and at the awards ceremony he met fellow electronic enthusiasts **Ralph Broome**, **Stuart Wynn Jones** and **John Harper**. In 1960 he spent three months working on an electronic sound interpretation of the John Dryden poem Alexander's Feast. The resulting 14 minute composition, Power of Music, used the full array of Fred's studio equipment at the time, and featured ring modulation, reverse play, speed changing and envelope shaping.

Lecturing widely throughout the British Isles on experimental music techniques, he wrote for Tape Recording magazine in the late 1950s, and switched to Amateur Tape Recording (ATR) in 1960, becoming editor a few years later. Under his guidance, this regularly featured articles and construction projects for hobbyist electronic music-makers, and encouraged tape clubs to experiment with musique concrète. After ATR folded in 1967 he continued writing for other publications, and the following year he penned a three part article on electronic music for Tape Recording, becoming a regular contributor for his former employer. In 1970 he developed a design for a sound effects synthesizer, published by Practical Wireless in March 71. Although aimed at home organists, the 12 circuit machine,

FC Judd playing his prototype synthesizer

was an early contribution to DIY synth building projects for home constructors. The Centre of Sound established at 12 Archer Street, Soho, London in 1961, was an ambitious but short lived venue housing cinema, hi-fi lounge, restaurant, bar and recording studio. As well as holding the post of technical director, and setting up a Chromasonics monitor in the foyer, Fred gave a lecture and concert of electronic music at the Centre in July of 61, featuring his own tape compositions, plus tracks by Daphne Oram and Toru Takemitsu. Between 1960 and 62 he facilitated electronic music workshops at the Dartington summer school in Devon, alongside leading Italian composers Bruno Maderna and Luciano Berio, and helped set up a multi-speaker sound diffusion system. He worked on his own musique concrète piece incorporating the Dartington grand piano, and gave the lecture Elements of Electronic Music.

Fred's final book on the subject Electronics In Music, was published in 1972, but by that stage he had left serious music-making behind, and was losing touch with avant-garde developments. As time wore on he became much less enamoured with his own early experimental pieces and those of other 1950s pioneers, and effectively renounced his position as a composer, stating that only people with academic training could attain such a position. Disillusionment with the lack of support for electronic sound in Britain contributed to his change of heart, and he concentrated his attention on writing and radio technology for the rest of his life. His master tapes and two of his compositions, The Butterfly, and Power of Music, remain lost, but his surviving work has been salvaged and released, and materials deposited with the British Library Sound Archive.

In November 1960 Fred wrote these words of encouragement for tape activists, "*The composer of electronic music or musique concrète has little need to offer justification of his work. He can regard it as an experiment in an unexplored field, and can supply musical motive by pointing to the fascination of creating new sounds.*"

CD: FC Judd: Electronics Without Tears (Public Information, 2011).

PRACTICAL WIRELESS

MARCH 1971

17½p (3'6)

pw sound effects synthesiser

- SEA ON THE BEACH
- SHIPS SIREN
- CHIME-GONG
- STEAM ENGINE WHISTLE
- TAXI HORN
- TAP BLOCK
- TRIANGLE
- DRUM ROLL
- CYMBAL
- CASTANETS

ALSO INSIDE:
THE 'TROJAN' TOP-BAND TRANSCEIVER
SENSITIVE WIDE-RANGE RF DETECTOR

---

circuits for audio and tape recording

an ATR handbook by F.C. Judd A Inst. E

Images of Juddrabilia

Castle

ELECTRONIC SOUNDS AND MUSIC

amateur TAPE RECORDING

VOL. 4 NO. 4 NOVEMBER 1963 PRICE 5/-

FREE GIFT INSIDE

HOW TO MAKE YOUR OWN HOME CHROMASONICS

BUILD IT YOURSELF BOOKLET NUMBER 1

16 PAGES

RECORDED TUITION LIMITED   Telephone BUCKhurst 9315
174 MAYBANK ROAD, WOODFORD E.17.

Electronic Sounds and Music

Electronic sounds and music are being used to a very considerable extent in radio and television drama. This record introduces sound phenomena that cannot be produced with conventional musical instruments or by simple mechanical or electro-acoustic means.

The electronic music on side 1 is intended for dramatic introduction and background for special documentaries on space travel, etc. The electronic sounds are intended for the creation of short electronic music composition or used purely …

…record were created by F. C. Judd, A.Inst.E., and are free of …

Side One
2. Vortex—composition with mystery element   1 m. 10 secs.
   … 1 m. 13 secs.

Side Two
   18 secs.
   47 secs.
   29 secs.
   10 secs.
   6 secs.
   … (descending)
   … (ascending)
   6 secs.
   … noise (pitch octave low)
   10 secs.

8. Sibilation—white noise (pitch)   10 …
9. Sibilation – white noise (pitch octave high)   1…
10. Three tone ululation
11. Filtered noise
12. Stridor (tonal)
13. Ring modulation and sibilation

extended play 45 rpm

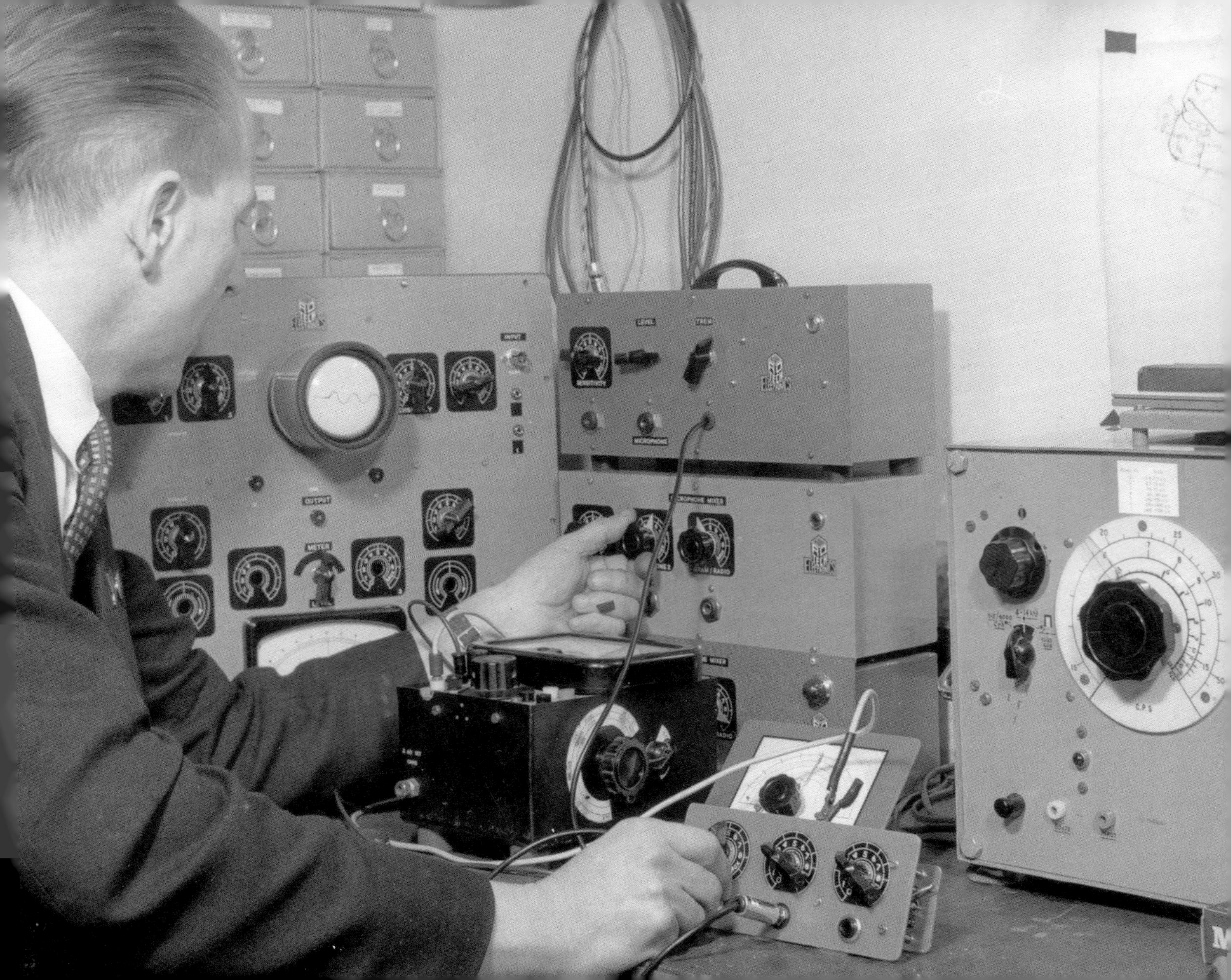
INPUT
LEVEL
TREM
SENSITIVITY
MICROPHONE
OUTPUT
METER
C.P.S

FC Judd in his home studio late 1950s - early 1960s

Peter Keene (1953)

Born: Birmingham
Earliest Electronic Work: Valve radio experiments (1967)
Commitment Factor: 10
Obscurity Quotient: 8
EM recording availability: Limited

Hoping to catch Doctor Who on TV on a Saturday, the schoolboy Keene regularly visited his grandfather, an ardent radio and home electronics experimenter. The elderly man's enthusiasm was passed on to the inquisitive youngster, who developed a life long interest in electronic music and machine building. From his grandad's malfunctioning home-made TV sets, he learnt about using audio to generate abstract patterns, and in 1968 he followed **FC Judd**'s Practical Electronics articles on Chromasonics, and even managed to modify Judd's designs. The previous year the inventive teenager started playing around with radios, and by the end of the 1960s he had developed his own hybrid analogue synthesizer.

He left school at 16 and began repairing, and then building guitar amplifiers and audio mixers, and for a time held a job as a chemist. For three years in the 1970s he worked for a local theatre company in Birmingham, and finished the decade living in Spain, where he continued building audio devices. In the early 80s he was resident in London, and worked for industrial designer Ron Arad, before moving to France in 1985.

Keene has gone on to skillfully build a remarkable collection of ingenious contraptions. These have been exhibited extensively in France, where he has made his permanent home. Finding parallels in his philosophy with maverick artists of the past, such as Leon Theremin, Raymond Scott and Nikola Tesla, he spent many hours at the Science Museum studying **Daphne Oram**'s Oramics apparatus He built his own fully operational version, which was exhibited as part of the Electro exhibition in Paris in 2019. He has also constructed a Minisonic synthesizer from circuit diagrams in Practical Electronics magazine, and in 2017 contributed to Project Symbiosis, with an interpretation of **Malcolm Pointon**'s 1975 graphic score.

Basil Kirchin (1927-2005)

Born: Blackpool
Earliest Electronic Work: ?
Commitment Factor: 5
Obscurity Quotient: 4
EM recording availability: Good

At the tender age of 14, Kirchin made his debut as drummer with his dad's band at a gig in Tottenham Court Road, London. He took the drummer's stool with several other big bands, including the high profile Ted Heath group, earning him recognition in the Melody Maker Readers Poll, for his precocious talent. Nevertheless, after co-leading the popular Kirchin Band with his father, he left drumming on the back burner at the end of the 1950s, opting for a meditation trip to India, and spent the close of the decade living in Sydney, Australia.

His composing career commenced after his return to England in 1961 where he settled in Hull, and for a time wrote music for the De Wolfe library label. His film soundtrack work, often for low budget horror films, thrillers or offbeat documentaries, began with Primitive London (1965), and includes The Shuttered Room (1967), The Strange Affair (1968), I Start Counting (1969), The Abominable Dr. Phibes (1971) and The Mutations (1973). This edgy area of British cinema allowed a certain amount of experimentation, and besides drawing on his connections to London's jazz scene, Kirchin became interested in the manipulation of recorded sound. During 1965-66 he worked with **Ernest Berk** on several pieces, including Jazz I, Jazz II and Beyond Suez; with Kirchin supplying melodies, and Berk adding overdubs at his studio in Camden. In his studio log Berk noted that their collaborative Beirut To Baghdad (1966), had been sold by Kirchin to a Swedish firm for use in a porn film soundtrack.

By 1967 he had bought a Nagra portable tape recorder with an Arts Council grant, and started to make field recordings. He taped the sounds of animals at London Zoo, as well as autistic children at a school in Schurmatt, Switzerland, where his wife was a teacher. Like an audio equivalent of British director David Gladwell's experimental films – shot with high speed cameras for an ultra slow motion effect – Kirchin slowed sounds right down to produce new timbres. In the early 1970s two albums of his Worlds Within Worlds, were issued, with **Brian Eno** contributing sleeve notes to the second volume, released on Island Records in 1974. The instrumentation included horns, woodwind, cello and organ, and sounds from a gorilla, hornbills, flamingos, insects, jet engines and the docks in Hull. Kirchin acknowledged the help of Keith Herd and **Tristram Cary**, as well as his wife Esther, in realising Worlds Within Worlds. Near the end of his life and riddled with cancer, he was still invigorated enough to produce his final work Particles, and died shortly after the recording was completed.

Raymond John Leppard (1927-2019)

Born: London
Earliest Electronic Work: The Tempest (1963)
Commitment Factor: 1
Obscurity Quotient: 7
EM recording availability: Poor

Growing up in Bath and attending the City of Bath Boys School, Leppard went on to study harpsichord and viola at Trinity College, Cambridge. He started conducting and became the music director of the Cambridge Philharmonic Society, and formed and conducted his own Leppard Ensemble. Becoming closely associated with the Goldbrough Orchestra, he also gave recitals as a harpsichordist, and was a fellow of Trinity College and lecturer on music there from 1958-68. His subsequent career has seen him appear with many of the world's leading orchestras, and with 200 recordings to his name, he has published two books and composed several film scores, including Lord of the Flies, in 1963.

During the 60s he played an instrumental role in the rebirth of interest in baroque and early music, and prepared performance versions of several Monteverdi operas. When Peter Hall became director of the RSC in 1960, Leppard was appointed music adviser, and he brought in modernist composers **Humphrey Searle** for Troilus and Cressida in 1960, and **Roberto Gerhard** for Macbeth in 1962. Leppard's tape music for The Tempest, was performed at Stratford in 1963. Between 1987 and 2001, he was the music director of the Indianapolis Symphony Orchestra, and from 2004-06 he served as Music Advisor to The Louisville Orchestra.

Desmond Leslie (1921-2001)

Born: London
Earliest Electronic Work: The Day the Sky Fell In (1957) unconfirmed
Commitment Factor: 6
Obscurity Quotient: 4
EM recording availability: Good

Attending public school at Ampleforth in Yorkshire, the young Leslie was a highly proficient pianist and had a keen interest in drama. He finished at the school in 1939, and the following year joined the RAF and saw action in The Battle of Britain, serving as a Spitfire fighter pilot until being discharged on medical grounds. He met German born actress Agnes Bernelle in 1943, and they married two years later, shortly after VJ day.

Following the end of World War II, he decided to pursue a literary career which had already started to blossom while he was in the RAF, with his first published novel Careless Lives. He also began writing film scripts and formed a production company; co-directing the crime thriller Stranger at My Door (1950), in which his wife had a leading role. His dystopian sci-fi novel Angels Weep, was published in 1948, bearing some comparison to George Orwell's 1984, though not in a commercial sense. Financial struggles were a constant feature of his life, particularly in connection with the ancestral home; Castle Leslie in Monaghan, Ireland.

He was brought up a Catholic and had a great interest in history, religion, spiritualism and a curious belief in alien beings. The co-authored, crackpot book Flying Saucers Have Landed (1953), written with George Adamski, achieved substantial sales and a great deal of publicity. Leslie gave lectures around the British Isles on UFOs, and embarked on a tour of American cities in 1954. He is infamous however, for a brief appearance on the BBC satirical TV programme That Was the Week That Was, in 1963, where he punched weedy, bespectacled Bernard Levin in front of a studio audience, and an estimated 11 million viewers. The story goes that Levin's scathing review of the stage show Savagery and Delight, featuring Agnes Bernelle, was prompted by the poor sound quality from Desmond's custom-built speakers. This inspired the indignant 6'4" writer to interrupt the live transmission, and let fly with a bunch of fives.

His interest in composition had been boosted when he assembled the soundtrack for feature film Stranger at My Door, using tapes of pre-recorded music, and superimposition and editing to create a sound score. In the mid-1950s at his home at 36 South Lodge, Grove End Road, St. John's Wood, London, he put together a small studio, and equipped it with four tape recorders, echo unit and a mixing console designed by Rupert Neve. He had a passion for musique concrète; recording and manipulating all kinds of sounds, and subjecting them to a variety of tape treatments. Showcasing his electronic work, the privately pressed LP Music of the Future, had a limited release in 1960, and the bulk of his experimental recordings were licensed to library music publisher Joseph Weinberger. Some of his tracks occasionally cropped up in TV sci-fi programmes, including early Doctor Who stories The Edge of Destruction (1964), The Space Museum (1965), and The Tomb of the Cybermen (1967).

The Day the Sky Fell In (1959), starred Roger Delgado, who played The Master, the evil nemesis in Doctor Who during the early 70s. This experimental film is a rarely seen anti-nuclear war parable for which Leslie created a musique concrète soundtrack, and which chimed with his involvement in the Campaign for Nuclear Disarmament. Attending a large CND demonstration in Trafalgar Square in 1961, he was arrested and spent a night in police custody, along with Vanessa Redgrave, Shelagh Delaney and George Melly. Nude and Variations (1959), is a documentary written and scored by Leslie, featuring artists and students reflecting on the human form in art, with contributions from sculptor Elisabeth Frink.

A series of Living Shakespeare LP records first issued in 1961, featured plays voiced by well known actors, together with Leslie's musique concrète and sound pattern interludes. He composed a string of pieces during the 1950s, and fellow experimenter **Ernest**

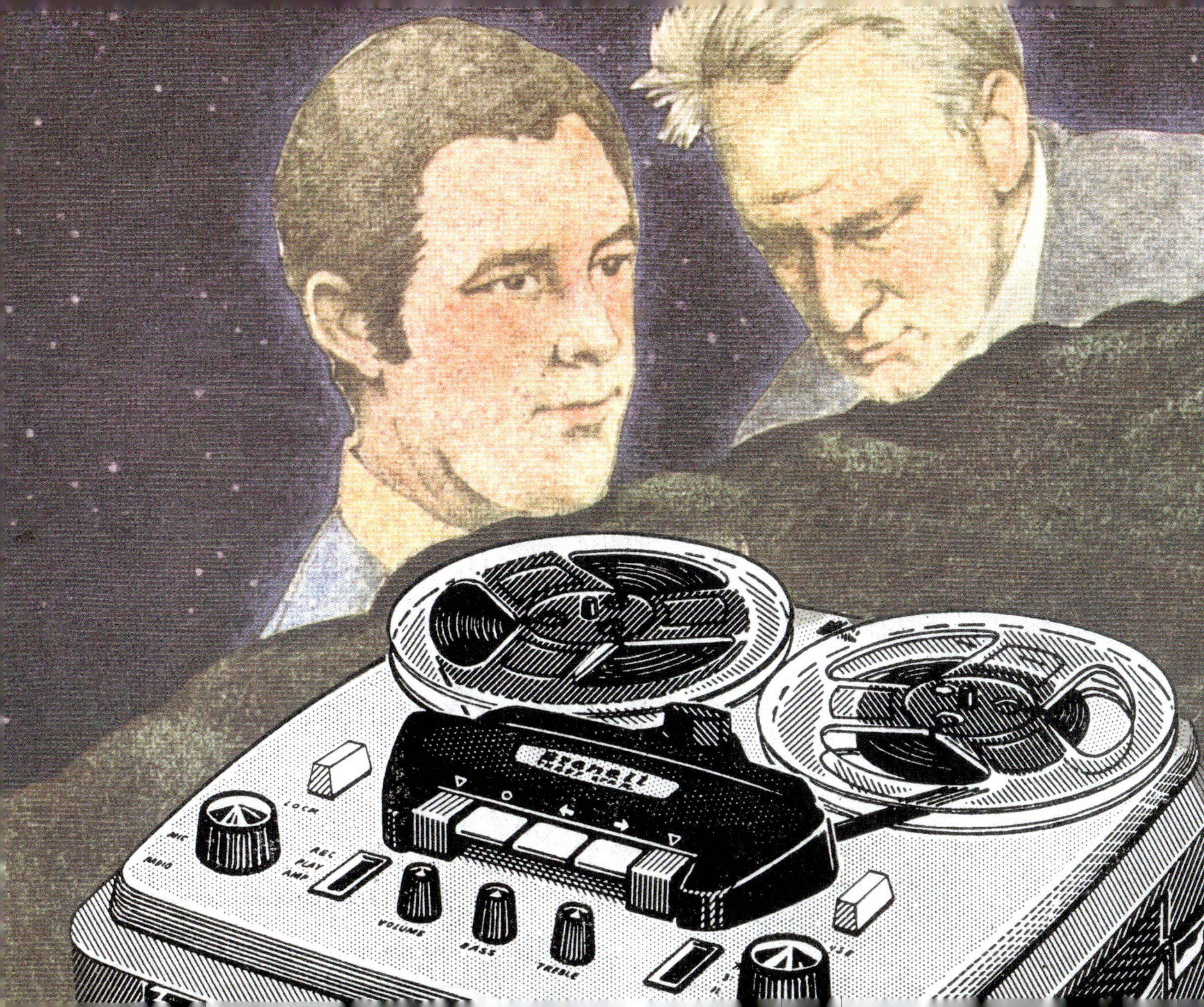

Desmond Leslie and Patrick Moore

Berk also recorded at his studio, and dedicated an electronic composition to him. Desmond left London in 1963 to take over responsibility for Castle Leslie in Ireland, and it was then that his musique concrète composing largely drew to a close. His energies were devoted to the demanding upkeep of the family estate, and he continued to write books; How Britain Won the Space Race, was co-authored with fellow eccentric and Sky At Night stargazer, Patrick Moore, and published in 1972.

Reading like a Hollywood biopic screenplay, the life of Desmond Leslie was punctuated with incident and controversy. While his main electronic music making period ended with his move to Ireland, he was up and running in the formative phase during the 1950s, and thus has an important place; as aside from the colourful headlines, he made some very interesting early electronic contributions, and had an affinity with experimental sound. He died in 2001 aged 79, with Castle Leslie secure for the future, and where his original tapes have been awaiting salvage and release. Robert O'Byrne's book Desmond Leslie 1921-2001: The Biography of an Irish Gentleman, was published in 2010.

CD: Desmond Leslie: Music of the Future (Trunk, 2005).

MORE ROBOTS
Synthetic Animals with "BRAINS" of their own. The LATEST range of projects include: an electronic 'animal' which "LEARNS", an Electro Chemical device capable of "REPRODUCING" itself! Other projects SURE TO INTRIGUE YOU are an audio transmitter/receiver which has quite an amazing range and requires NO LICENCE; also TEN new projects. one of which is an electronic dice machine. HOSTS OF EASY-TO-CONSTRUCT projects, for anyone with a basic knowledge of Electronics. DON'T WAIT. SEND 3/- for your list—NOW!
To: 'BOFFIN PROJECTS'

CYBERNETIC
the computer

A computerised electronic music studio by Peter Zinovieff

WHERE should you seek the most *avant-garde* art exhibition now running in London? Not amidst the glitter and bustle of show biz London, but just a little off from Piccadilly and Leicester Square, in The Mall, just beyond Admiralty Arch. Here in this principal processional route of traditional London, you will find the plain sober-faced terrace which is Nash House. It is now the home of the Institute of Contemporary Arts.
  Step over the threshold, and in a microsecond or so you will be transported from an environment reminiscent of past national glories to another which must be one of the most advanced and outward-looking in a rather different realm—that of art. For here we see exhibited numerous artists' attempts to use modern technology for their creative purpose, just as their predecessors employed brush and palette or pen and ink.

WHAT DOES IT MEAN?
  The title of this exhibition? Well, this is best clarified by quoting the organiser Jasia Reichardt.
  "*CYBERNETICS*—derives from the Greak 'kubernetes' meaning 'steersman'; our word 'governor' comes from a Latin version of the same word.
  "The term cybernetics was first used by Norbert Wiener around 1948. In 1948 his book *Cybernetics* was subtitled 'communication and control in animal and machine'.
  "The term today refers to systems of communication and control in complex electronic devices like computers, which have very definite similarities with the

A creation of American Air Force Data and Boeing Aircraft designers, this man was produced during studies to determine optimum arrangement of cockpit instruments. This 20th Century pilot has been "adopted" by P.E.'s artist and put into the role of an ancient steersman—an appropriate symbol for the subject of this article

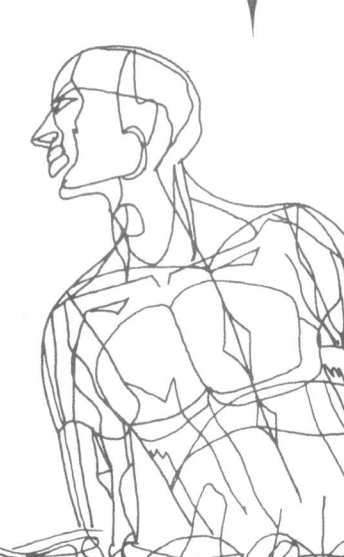

SERENDIPITY
.. and the arts

processes of communication and control in the human nervous system.

"A cybernetic device responds to stimulus from outside and in turn affects external environment, like a thermostat which responds to the coldness of a room by switching on the heating and thereby altering the temperature. This process is called feedback.

"Exhibits in the show are either produced with a cybernetic device (computer) or are cybernetic devices in themselves. They react to something in the environment, either human or machine, and in response produce either sound, light or movement.

"SERENDIPITY—was coined by Horace Walpole in 1754.

"There was a legend about three princes of Serendip (old name for Ceylon) who used to travel throughout the world and whatever was their aim or whatever they looked for, they always found something very much better. Walpole used the term serendipity to describe the faculty of making happy chance discoveries.

"Through the use of cybernetic devices to make graphics, films and poems, as well as other randomising machines which interact with the spectator, many happy chance discoveries were made."

INTERNATIONAL FLAVOUR

That this is truly an international exhibition is clear from the personalities and organisations behind this project. The original idea came from Prof. Max Bense of Stuttgart University; encouragement from the Ministry of Technology, financial help from the Arts Council, and practical assistance in the form of films, exhibits, and technological information, from IBM. British industry was also approached. Their representatives seem to have applied the Nelson touch all right. Telescope to blind eye—they could "see" no need or future in this art business! Perhaps their vision will be restored after a visit to "Cybernetic Serendipity".

The international flavour is also evident from the names of the various artists participating: contributions have come from France, Germany, Israel, Italy, Sweden and U.S.A., as well as the U.K.

The exhibition is divided into three sections:
1. Computer generated graphics, computer animated films, computer composed and played music, and computer verse and texts.
2. Cybernetic devices as works of art, cybernetic environments, remote control robots, and painting machines.
3. Machines demonstrating the uses of computers and environment dealing with the history of cybernetics.

During the course of the exhibition there are lectures on Tuesdays and Thursdays. There are also daily film shows in the auditorium of films either made with the aid of computers, or dealing with the relevance of computer technology to the humanities, the arts, and communications generally.

We now give some impressions arising from our visit on Preview Day.

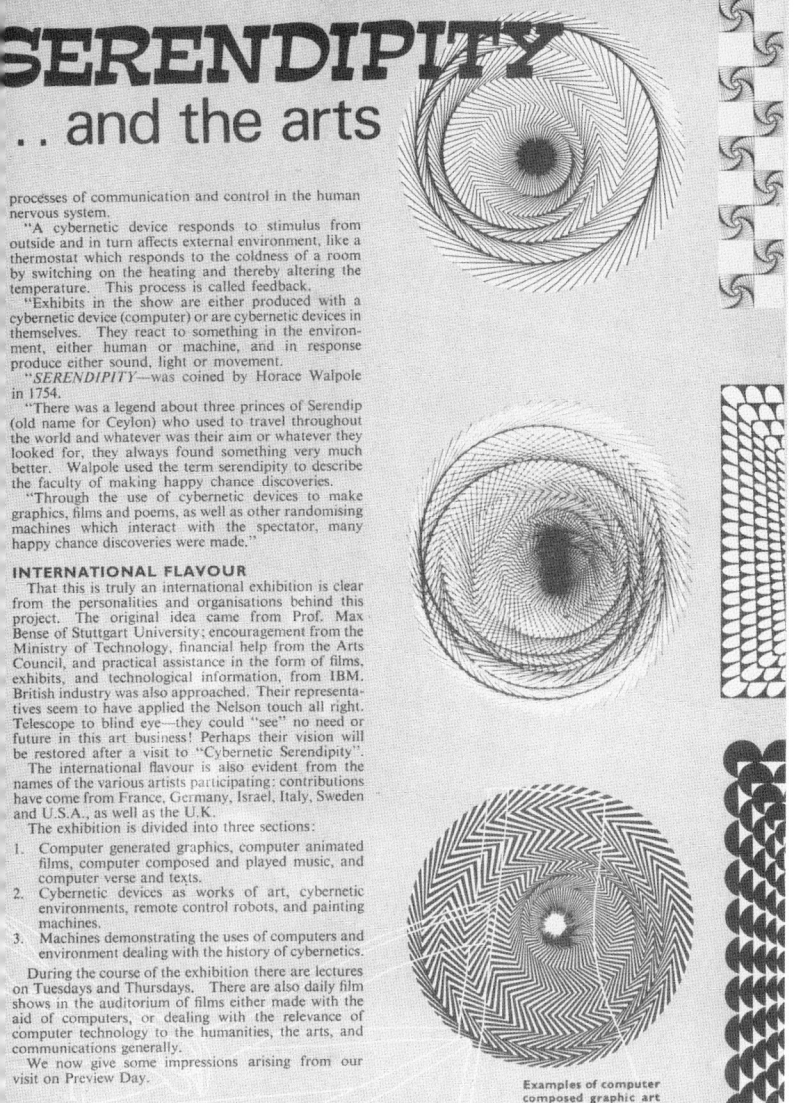

Examples of computer composed graphic art

John Lifton (1944)
Born: Uxbridge, Hertfordshire
Earliest Electronic Work: Interface 3 (1969)
Commitment Factor: 5
Obscurity Quotient: 6
EM recording availability: Poor

Following graduation with a Master's degree in architecture from University College London in 1966, Lifton began to focus his attention on electronics and computerized circuitry. He was most concerned with interlinking sound and kinetic imagery, and his experiments led to his involvement in the Cybernetic Serendipity exhibition at the ICA in London in 1968. His contribution consisted of small walk-in geodesic domes, in which numerous fragments of projected images moved in response to sounds from in and around the display. The following year he exhibited Interface 3, at Event One, organised by the Computer Arts Society (CAS) at the Royal College of Art. Building on his previous work, this involved an array of photocells to detect the movement of visitors near the exhibit, and translate their motion into electronic sound. With its hybrid of analogue and digital computer control, the piece was refined over the next couple of years, and featured in performances and gallery shows.

During 1969, Lifton was a co-founder of the London New Arts Lab, incorporating the Institute for Research in Art and Technology, which offered the first open access computer facilities in Britain, and a base for experimental performance and mixed media work. The following year he collaborated with Carolee Schneemann on Meat Systems, a computer generated 360 degree multiple slide projection, for the exhibition, Happening and Fluxus. This interest in surround and immersive presentations was also evident in the group **Naked Software**, where a 12 cassette recorder system was devised by Lifton and Harvey Matusow for use in performance. For the large scale multi-media ICES-72 festival, Lifton performed with Naked Software, and was in charge of the equipment and technical set up for the event, acting as recording engineer to tape all the performances quadraphonically.

From 1974-77 he taught at the Royal College of Art in London, in both the departments of Environmental Media and Design Research, and carried out a computer project for the Science Research Council of the UK. His Green Music, involved picking up electrical signals from plants, processed by computer and fed to a sound synthesizer. This was shown in 1973 at the CAS 'eventibition', INTERACT: Machine, Man, Society, during a Computers in the Arts conference held in Edinburgh, and it was installed in the Plant Conservatory in San Francisco's Golden Gate Park in 1976. The producers of the Stevie Wonder scored cosmic nature film, The Secret Life of Plants (1979), hired Lifton to work on special sequences for the movie, and his multi-channel audio output, was generated by electrode sensing of plant physiology.

At the end of the 1970s he moved permanently to the USA, where he settled in Telluride, Colorado, with his artist wife Pamela Zoline. Together they founded the Telluride Institute, a non-profit organisation concerned with innovative ideas in the field of environmental sustainability, working with artists, scientists and educators on cultural projects. In 2006 the couple established Lifton Zoline International, and undertook a resort development project in the town of Slavonice in the Czech Republic. To the present day they continue their creative design and research activities, based at their Telluride headquarters.

ELECTRONIC MUSIC

CIRCUIT ASSEMBLIES for all your music projects, ready-to-use modules ideal for Synthesisers, Sound Effects, Organs, Instrument modifiers.

CHOOSE from over 25 circuits, including our new range of I-C designs for Synthesiser work.

OUR CATALOGUE contains full technical details, explanations and definitions, suggestions for projects, and discount price details.

OUR PRICES are the lowest in this field and represent unbeatable value for money.

Send only **20p** for our latest catalogue:

TAYLOR ELECTRONIC MUSIC DEVICES
GREYFRIARS HOUSE ● CHESTER

The New Arts Lab was established by a group of artists, many of whom were associated with London's first Arts Lab in Drury Lane, Covent Garden, founded in 1967 by Jim Haynes. The original space included a cinema as well as a gallery co-curated by Biddy Peppin and Pamela Zoline, and closed in the autumn of 1969. In October that year the New Arts Lab, or alternatively the Institute for Research in Art and Technology (IRAT), opened at 1 Robert Street, Camden Town, in a former chemical factory. Run on a more egalitarian basis, this new lab, housing gallery, and cinema spaces, also provided a base for the London Filmmakers Co-op, along with TVX, a radical video unit formed by John Hopkins and Cliff Evans; a printing workshop led by John Collins; and a music space run by **Hugh Davies. John Lifton** organised the Electronics and Cybernetics Workshop, offering the first open computer access for artists.

Amongst the trustees for the organisation were JG Ballard, Reyner Banham, Dr. Christopher Evans, Richard W. Evans, Cllr. Christine Stewart and artist Joe Tilson. The directors in August 1970 were listed as Lance Blackstone, David Curtis, Hugh Davies, Fred Drummond, John Hopkins, Rosemary Johnson, David Kilburn, Malcolm Le Grice, Diane Lifton, John Lifton, Carla Liss, Joebear Webb, Pamela Zoline and Biddy Peppin.

JG Ballard's Crashed Cars exhibition took place in the gallery during April 1970, with a Pontiac, Mini and Austin Cambridge, hired from a vehicle scrapyard. In operation for less than two years, the New Arts Lab finally closed in March 1971, when Camden Council reclaimed the building. IRAT continued and set up a new space at Prince of Wales Crescent, London, and remained a centre for interdisciplinary work in cinema, video, printing, theatre, music, photography and cybernetics, running operations through the 1970s.

Ronald Lloyd (1929-2008)
Born: Marylebone, London
Earliest Electronic Work: Plane-Tree for tape (1968) unconfirmed
Commitment Factor: 5
Obscurity Quotient: 7
EM recording availability: Poor

Coming from an aristocratic background with his mother related to the British royal family, Lloyd's early life was spent in Canada and India, where his father served in the military. Moving with his parents to London in the 1940s, he studied at the Guildhall School of Music and Drama, and following graduation joined the Halle Orchestra in Manchester as oboist. Becoming interested in serial music, he left the orchestra after three years to travel in North America, where he met composer and instrument builder Harry Partch. He next journeyed through the Middle East, and acquainted himself with the music and culture of countries in the southern Mediterranean region. By the mid-60s he had returned to London, and established his own tape studio where he worked on experimental pieces, in particular for modern dance and work by Hilde Holger. Cell, a dance choreographed by Robert Cohan, featured Lloyd's music; it was premiered in 1969 for the opening season of the London Contemporary Dance Theatre, and in 1983 it was produced by the BBC as a short film for television.

Lloyd scored the films Wild Roses (1966), and The Phantom (1968), and met New Zealand artist Glyn Collins. In 1971 their co-authored Electus Variations, was published as an introduction to an exhibition held at the University of Bradford. It was described as a "*temporal journey through a maze of perceptions*." Together they operated from a North London address as A-VM; which offered "*audio, visual, mutations, structures, murals, sound sources, tapes, abstract films.*" At the end of the 1970s Lloyd moved to Spain and settled in Barcelona, where he continued composing and performed live with Spanish musicians. He left the country in 2001, and two years later returned to Britain, working on his memoirs up until his death in January 2008.

David Lloyd-Howells (1942-2015)
Born: Cardiff
Earliest Electronic Work: Horizons of Man (1957)
Commitment Factor: 9
Obscurity Quotient: 7
EM recording availability: Good

A composer, poet and writer, as a lad Lloyd-Howells joined his school radio club, and had an inspirational encounter with a pair of Grundig tape recorders. The precocious teenager began to work with graphic scores and piano sounds on tape, and incorporated them into his poetry; Horizons of Man being his first completed example. (This was later revised in 1968 as The Promenade, a music theatre electro-acoustic piece.) After playing in a skiffle band, leaving school, and a spell as a gigging jazz musician, he began travelling and made his way to the USA. Here he performed in clubs or busked on the street, reciting his poems accompanied by a portable tape recorder. The young beatnik travelled to Canada in the early 60s, and trekked around Europe, and finally on his return to Britain he took up serious academic study at the University of Wales in 1977. He embarked on a Master's degree at Goldsmiths College from 1981-83, where his tutor was **Stanley Glasser**, and in 1984 he studied computer music with **Richard Orton**.

After his earlier peripatetic lifestyle, in the latter part of the 1980s he was settled enough to put together his own electronic studio, and pursue his interests in sonic art. Since that time he amassed a large body of compositions, writing for children, acoustic ensembles and voice orchestra, as well as electronics. Among his notable tape works are Freakspeak (1991), Molecular Analysis (1998), and Bleak Sleaze (1998). He was a Fellow of the Royal Society by virtue of his commitment to education, and he continued composing at his cottage in Abergavenny, Monmouthshire. His studio contained a modular set-up within a digital system, and before his death he had been working on Aberfan; what he described as a "*satellite based multi media 'acousonic' opera.*"

CD: David Lloyd-Howells: Visions in Sound 1 (1998).

Anna Lockwood (1939)

Born: Christchurch, New Zealand
Earliest Electronic Work: Are Your Children Safe In the Sea
   (with Bob Cobbing, 1966)
Commitment Factor: 7
Obscurity Quotient: 5
EM recording availability: Good

After studying composition at the University of Canterbury in New Zealand, Lockwood came to England in 1961 for further composition studies under Peter Racine Fricker, at the Royal College of Music in London. She also attended summer courses at Darmstadt, Germany, and completed her education in Cologne and Bilthoven, Holland from 1963-64, with electronic music composer Gottfried Michael Koenig. Returning home In 1967, she made the piece Love Field, for the New Zealand Broadcasting Corporation's entry into a Radio Italia competition. This was an electro-acoustic piece based on the John F. Kennedy assassination, recorded at Douglas Lilburn's electronic music studio at Victoria University in Wellington.

Back in Britain during the second half of the 60s, she collaborated with various artists, choreographers and sound poets, and created several tape pieces with **Bob Cobbing**. She worked with modern dance company Strider, led by Richard Alston, who choreographed her piece Tiger Balm. Married to Harvey Matusow, she played with him in both the Jew's Harp Band and **Naked Software**; in the latter group alongside **John Lifton**, **Howard Rees** and **Hugh Davies**. She was heavily involved in organising ICES-72 – the International Carnival of Experimental Sound, where Tiger Balm was performed.

Attending an electronic music workshop at **EMS** during 1970, along with **David Rowland**, **Justin Connolly** and Lifton, she got to know **Peter Grogono** who took quite a shine to her. Grogono visited Lockwood and Matusow at their home in Ingatestone, Essex, and offered to help with a remix of Tiger Balm at the EMS studio; the piece was played at an SPNM concert at the Cockpit Theatre in 1972. Lockwood and Grogono also got together to investigate which elements of sound organisation, were most important for

All ICES-72 images courtesy of Gee Vaucher/Exitstencil Press

trance-inducing ritual music used in various cultures. In the course of a two year project, they conducted audio experiments at the Southampton Institute of Sound and Vibration research.

Exploring the sonic potential of glass, she gave a series of her own concerts assisted by Matusow and **Ron Geesin**; the first one performed at the Middle Earth club in London in 1968. An LP release, Glass World of Anna Lockwood, appeared in 1970 on Tangent Records. She gave 76 glass concerts in total, the last in 1973 in New York. At DIAS – the Destruction In Art Symposium in London in 1966 – she participated in wrecking an old piano, and two years later she worked with Richard Alston on a dance piece titled Heat. With the help of Hugh Davies this included setting fire to a knackered piano, which was ignited and recorded on the Chelsea Embankment. Paying homage to the heart transplant breakthroughs of Dr. Christian Barnard, she started the first of a series of 'Piano Transplants' in 1967, in which broken pianos were set on fire, submerged in the sea or buried in the ground.

From the 1970s her attention focussed on environmental sounds, and narratives with performance elements. Becoming interested in the work of American composers, particularly Pauline Oliveros and the live group, Sonic Arts Union, she moved to the USA in 1973. She split from Matusow, and accepted an invitation to lecture from composer and future partner Ruth Anderson. With her name modified to Annea Lockwood, she continues teaching at Vassar College, NY, and writes vocal, instrumental and electro-acoustic music for solo performers and various ensembles. At the 2013 Festival of the Arts in Harwich on the coast of Essex, her Eastern Exposure: Piano Transplant No. 4, involved a grand piano positioned on the shoreline of The Stour estuary. After a performance on the keyboard with a backdrop of the environment and Felixstowe docks, the instrument was left to be reclaimed by the actions of the waves and weather.

CD: Source Records 1-6, 1968-1971 (Pogus, 2008)
   Compilation includes Lockwood's, Tiger Balm.

ICES-72

At the Roundhouse, Chalk Farm, London;
The Place, Dukes Road, London;
Gallery House London (The German Institute) Exhibition Road;
Riverboat, The Thames, London;
Channel Ferry, The English Channel;
Jet Airplane, Mid-Atlantic;
British Rail Train, London-Edinburgh Festival return;
Swimming Pools, London and the Home Counties;
Woodlands, Essex;
Fire Fighting School, Essex;
Fields, all over;
Streets and Parks,
wherever by composers,
performers,
multi-media artists
and YOU.

FILMS, VIDEO, ENVIRONMENTS,
EVENTS, ELECTRONICS, LASERS,
COMPUTERS, SCULPTURES, DANCE, and SOUNDS,
plus categories yet to be invented.

ICES-72 is a cooperative venture of composers, performers, and multi-media artists. There are no promoters. All money made from ICES is to be shared equally by all groups.
All groups in ICES-72 are united in one thing, and that is that groups be treated equally, and that no stars or inflated artistic ego's dominate the events.
This is the umbrella by which we are drawing together over 300 artists from 21 countries, to share a new kind of energy.

ICES-72 was an ambitious 16 day multi-media avant-garde festival happening, staged in and around London venues the Roundhouse and The Place. Backed by the American Source magazine, it was the brainchild of unpredictable US born go-getter Harvey Matusow, who managed to pull together a fantastic line up of international music, film and dance, with electronic music as a core element. Most of the days between the 13th and 28th August 1972, opened with experimental short films, and a series of tape concerts presented by Swedish outfit Fylkingen. Day 2 of the festival featured dance company Strider performing **Anna Lockwood**'s Tiger Balm, with a concert by **Gentle Fire** in the evening. Day 5 saw a performance by **Ernest Berk**'s Dance Theatre Commune, and Day 9 included concerts by **Intermodulation** and **David Bedford**. The electro-acoustic group **Music Plus**, and work by **Lawrence Casserley**, and **David Rowland**, as well as a forum with the Computer Arts Society, were also featured. Lockwood and **John Lifton** – together with Gee Vaucher and Penny Rimbaud, who appeared in the group Exit, and later founded the vital and influential anarchist multi-media unit Crass – were all closely involved in the organisation of ICES-72.

INTERNATIONAL CARNIVAL OF EXPERIMENTAL SOUND

David Lumsdaine (1931)

Born: Sydney, Australia
Earliest Electronic Work: Babel (1968)
Commitment Factor: 6
Obscurity Quotient: 6
EM recording availability: Good

Lumsdaine attended the New South Wales Conservatorium and the University of Sydney, and emigrated to Britain in 1953. He was strongly affected by the later works of Anton Webern, and developed his own compositional techniques within a framework of serialism. Despite writing music during the 1950s and early 60s, he disowned everything prior to his Annotations of Auschwitz, from 1964. In London he studied at the Royal Academy of Music with Lennox Berkeley, and like close friend **Don Banks**, became interested in electronic sound. He attended evening classes at Goldsmiths College, as well as a week long course at **Peter Zinovieff**'s **EMS** studio. Out of this developed a group of like minded composers, exploring and exchanging information and equipment. Learning how to read circuit diagrams and picking up soldering, Lumsdaine's piece Nursery Rhymes (1969), was created at his home studio in Surrey, using the prototype VCS3 synthesizer. It was first aired at an Arts Council event in London in 1970, organised by **Keith Winter**.

That year Lumsdaine took up a teaching post at Durham University, and established and directed the Electronic Music Studio. During the years that followed, he wrote a number of works that feature tape sounds; these include Looking Glass Music (1970), for brass quintet and tape; Aria for Edward John Eyre (1972), which involves tapes and live electronics; Meridian (1973), for percussion and tape; and Big Meeting (1971-78), a sound collage based on the Durham Miner's Gala. The acoustic Kelly Ground (1966), reflects his staunch opposition to capital punishment, and is based on the final hours of outlaw Ned Kelly.

As a keen and respected ornithologist, he has made field recordings of native Australian birdsong, and his substantial tape collection is stored at the British Library Sound Archive. He is married to composer Nicola LeFanu, and in 1996 announced his retirement from composing. However, in 2011 he was commissioned by the City of London Festival to make a surround sound work with dancers, drawing on some of his recorded soundscapes.

CD: David Lumsdaine: Big Meeting (NMC).

John Herbert McDowell (1926-1985)

Born: Scarsdale, New York, USA
Earliest Electronic Work: Production (1952) Recorded in the USA
Commitment Factor: 8
Obscurity Quotient: 7
EM recording availability: Poor

An American born composer, McDowell studied with electronic music pioneer and teacher Otto Luening at Columbia University in New York, and set up his own studio for recording. He created a number of tape works through the 1950s and 60s, for theatre, dance and film, and it appears he was only temporarily in London in 1965, where he recorded a tape composition for a modern dance titled Escapement. That same year he was back in New York working on six more electro-acoustic tracks, and maintaining an involvement with the Judson Dance Theatre in Manhattan; the film Judson Fragments (1964), by intermedia artist Elaine Summers, features his soundtrack. Working closely with respected choreographer Paul Taylor, McDowell scored a number of dances, which include Insects and Heroes; Public Domain; Music Collage; and Big Bertha. During the 60s he also worked on several Broadway shows, and towards the end of the decade he scored two early Brian de Palma feature films, Murder a la Mod (1968), and The Wedding Party (1969).

McDowell was firmly established with electronic music very early on, and besides his 1952 piece Production, he has credits for over 25 further tape compositions during the 1950s and 60s. These include Landscape (1955); Music for a While (1960); Winter Music (1960); for five instruments and tape; and Tuning Fork (1967).

Joe Meek (1929-1967)

Born: Newent, Gloucestershire
Earliest Electronic Work: Glob Waterfall (1960) unconfirmed
Commitment Factor: 3
Obscurity Quotient: 2
EM recording availability: Good

Maverick and mercurial, Meek is a legendary figure in the annals of popular music, and his tempestuous life and dramatic demise make for a compelling story. Leaving school at 14 with poor academic qualifications, he carried out National Service in the RAF and worked for a spell with the Midlands Electricity Board, before finding employment as a recording engineer at IBC studios in London. His childhood passion for radio and electronics landed him the job, and spurred him on to experiment with new techniques, such as alternative microphone placement, compression and echo. A notable early success was Humphrey Lyttelton's Bad Penny Blues, one of a string of chart hits that Meek would engineer.

In 1960 he co-founded a label, Triumph Records, and before moving to his celebrated studio flat at 304 Holloway Road, Islington, he set about creating his outer space music fantasy album entitled I Hear a New World, in late 1959. This was recorded partly at Lansdowne studio where he was then employed, and at home in Holland Park, and remained unreleased until long after his death. A number of tracks include electronic opening and closing sequences of the type that would feature prominently on Telstar, the number 1 instrumental smash hit he penned and produced for the Tornados in 1962. I Hear a New World, contains instrumental and vocal efforts often sounding naive and clumsy, with Pinky & Perky style sped-up voices designed to evoke alien beings. In stark contrast, the electronic and tape sounds are ominous and convincing, in particular on the extended tape and echo opening of Magnetic Fields, and the complete musique concrète composition Glob Waterfall.

It is not known what contact he had with any other British electronic music makers during the 1950s and 60s, although John Leyton who performed Johnny Remember Me, Meek's first number one single recorded at Holloway Road, attended the 1963 International Audio Festival and Fair at the Hotel Russell in London, where he met **FC Judd**. Invited by Amateur Tape Recording magazine, Leyton visited the Chromasonics demonstration room, and saw his voice fed into Judd's sound visualisation system.

Joe Meek's career took a downward spiral as the 60s progressed and the hits started to dry up. His fragile and explosive temperament alienated colleagues, and in 1967, coinciding with Buddy Holly's birthday on 3rd February, he shot his landlady and turned the gun on himself. The feature film Telstar: The Joe Meek Story, directed by Nick Moran and starring Con O'Neill, vividly dramatises the Holloway Road years, and was released in 2008.

CD: Joe Meek and the Blue Men: I Hear a New World (RPM, 1991).

John Metcalf (1946)

Born: Swansea
Earliest Electronic Work: Sonata for Flute, Percussion and Tape (1969)
Commitment Factor: 0
Obscurity Quotient: 8
EM recording availability: Poor

Attending senior school in Cheltenham and then University College, Cardiff, Metcalf studied with John Carewe, **Don Banks** and **Hugh Davies**. In 1969 he founded the Vale of Glamorgan Festival, and remained its director until 1985, before moving to Canada the following year. After teaching on the Music Theatre course at the Banff Centre in Alberta, he became Artistic Director of the programme and composer-in-residence. His first opera had been composed in 1979, and while at Banff he completed Tomrak, the fourth of six operas he has written.

In 1991 he returned to Britain and picked up where he had left off with the Vale of Glamorgan Festival, while continuing to teach at the annual MusicFest Aberystwyth. He received an MBE for services to music in 2012. His Sonata for Flute, Percussion and Tape, and Notturno (1971), for orchestra and tape, along with most of his other early works prior to the mid-1970s, are now no longer publicly acknowledged by the composer.

JOHN SAYS...
RING MODULATOR by Dewtron is professional, transformerless, 5-transistor, has adjustable F1/F2 rejection. Module £7. Unit £8·90. **WAA-WAA** Pedal kit of all parts, including all mechanics and instructions **ONLY £2·95. AUTO RHYTHM** from Dewtron modules. Simple unit for waltz, fox-trot, etc. Costs under £20 in modules. **SYNTHESISER MODULES** and other miracles! Send 15p for illustrated list. **D.E.W. LTD.,** 254 Ringwood Road, Ferndown, Dorset

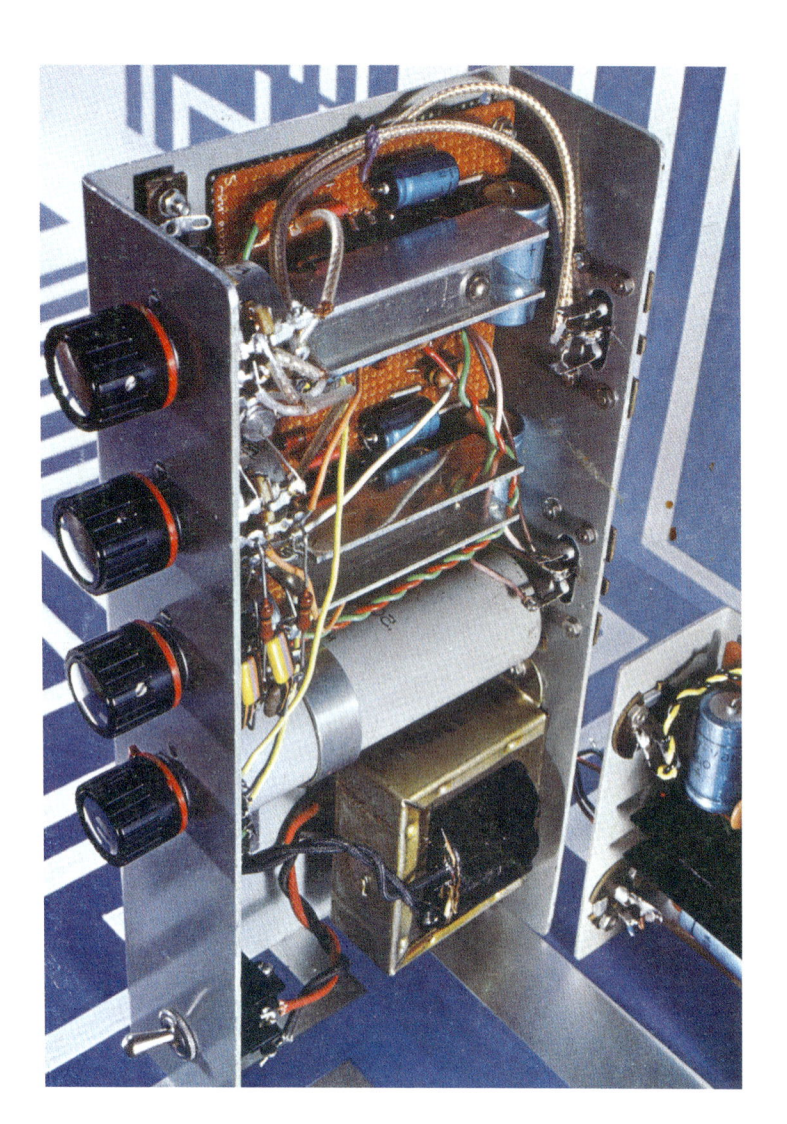

L-R: Rose and Cyril Clouts with Jacob and Patricia Meyerowitz, 1957

Jacob Meyerowitz (1928-1998)
Born: Cape Town, South Africa
Earliest Electronic Work: Synthesis 1 (1961)
Commitment Factor: 6
Obscurity Quotient: 8
EM recording availability: Poor

Graduating from Cape Town University, Jacob Meyerowitz – a veritable Renaissance Man – was a student of medicine, as well as composer, artist, inventor, author, and architect. He came to Britain in the 1950s, and had already become firm friends with **Cyril Clouts** during their early life growing up in South Africa. Once the pair were in London they shared a flat in Belsize Park, and both got married in 1957. Jacob's wife Patricia Meyerowitz, was a respected artist and author, and in 1967 he illustrated her book Jewelry and Sculpture Through Unit Construction.

In the early 1960s he established a tape studio at home, and began experiments with electronic music. He published the book Analog Sounds, and became interested in the work of psychoanalyst Wilhelm Reich, about whom he wrote three books – Before the Beginning of Time; Basic Orgonometry; and Applied Orgonometry. As well as building an Orgone Accumulator as developed by Reich, he constructed his own electronic music making equipment. During the 60s he composed a series of numbered tape pieces under the title Synthesis, and three of them – 8, 9 and 12 – were played at the Queen Elizabeth Hall in a major concert of British electronic music in 1968, alongside work by **Tristram Cary**, **Daphne Oram**, **Delia Derbyshire**, **George Newson** and **Peter Zinovieff**.

His architectural work included the New Hebrew University Synagogue in Jerusalem, and various buildings across the world. In 1970 he left Britain with his wife to live in the USA, first in New York, and in the mid-80s they moved to Easton, Pennsylvania. Continuing their artistic careers, Jacob produced a series of abstract paintings, and furthered the development of 'typewriter graphics', which he had first devised in 1958. An exhibition of his images made with a Smith Corona typewriter was held in Easton in 1992.

Thea Musgrave (1928)

Born: Edinburgh
Earliest Electronic Work: Soliloquy for Guitar and Tape (1969)
Commitment Factor: 4
Obscurity Quotient: 6
EM recording availability: Limited

After graduating from Edinburgh University, Musgrave went on to study for four years with Nadia Boulanger in Paris, and back in London she was composing through the 1950s and 60s and establishing her reputation. Her future lay in America though, and she became visiting professor at the University of California, and moved to the USA permanently in 1972 after her marriage to Peter Mark. Previously, as a member of the Composers' Guild of Great Britain, she visited **Tristram Cary**'s studio in Suffolk in 1966, and gained first hand experience of experimental work with tape.

She directed a workshop programme of contemporary compositions, in a series sponsored by the SPNM in 1971, and two years later she presented a four part BBC radio series on electronic music, discussing the subject with Cary, Bernard Rands and **Daphne Oram**. She had become friendly with Oram, and developed compositions for electronics in combination with acoustic instruments. Tape parts for three of her pieces were created with assistance from Oram at her Tower Folly studio: Soliloquy (1969); the ballet Beauty and the Beast (1969); and From One to Another (1970), for viola and tape. Other instrument and tape works which followed include Orfeo 1 (1975), and Niobe, a composition from 1987 for solo oboe and tape, closely based on the Greek legend of the weeping nymph. The two-act Beauty and the Beast, was premiered at Sadler's Wells in London in 1969, and received a number of performances around England and Scotland in the early 1970s.

Musgrave has received two Guggenheim Fellowships and was Distinguished Professor at the City University of New York from 1987-2002. She continues her prolific composing, fulfilling a steady stream of commissions.

George Newson (1932)

Born: London
Earliest Electronic Work: The Man Who Collected Sounds (1966)
Commitment Factor: 6
Obscurity Quotient: 7
EM recording availability: Limited

Having taught himself to read music and play the piano, Newson was evacuated to Brighton during the Second World War, and back in London aged 14, he received a scholarship to the Blackheath Conservatory of Music. This led to a further scholarship to study composition at the Royal Academy of Music, and during the late 1950s and early 60s he attended classes at Darmstadt and Dartington, studying with renowned Italian composers Luciano Berio, Bruno Maderna and Luigi Nono. The three maestros all lectured at the Dartington summer schools in the early 60s, and conducted electronic music workshops facilitated by **FC Judd**. Like **Tristram Cary**, **Daphne Oram** and a young Jonathan Harvey, Newson visited Expo 58 in Brussels, the first post-war World's Fair. Inside the Philips Pavilion, he experienced the classic tape composition Poeme Electronique, by Edgard Varèse.

For producer Douglas Cleverdon, Newson created music for the BBC radio programme The Man Who Collected Sounds, spending two weeks at the **Radiophonic Workshop** in 1966. He manipulated instrumental recordings on tape with the assistance of **Delia Derbyshire**, who remained a good friend. The following year, with the benefit of a research bursary, he pursued investigations into electronic music in the USA, and visited a number of studios across the country. He spent time with Robert Moog at his Trumansberg factory, and based himself at the University of Illinois, a noted centre for electronic and computer music, where he made his first tape composition, Silent Spring. In 1968 his research led to an invitation to work at the RAI studios in Milan, where singer and composer Cathy Berberian helped him find accommodation for his stay in the city. A year later he worked at the University of Utrecht, in Holland, and using the studio facilities of the Institute of Sonology, he composed two pieces, Oute, and Canto, for clarinet and four track

George Newson in 1967

tape. Silent Spring, which is based on animal and bird sounds, and expresses a drive for conservation, was broadcast on BBC Radio 4 on New Year's Eve, 1967, as part of the Wildlife Review programme. It was played again in a high profile concert of British electronic music at the Queen Elizabeth Hall in London in January 1968, which also included works by Tristram Cary, **Jacob Meyerowitz**, Daphne Oram and **Peter Zinovieff**.

On the recommendation of **Don Banks**, Newson secured a position as lecturer in electronic music at Goldsmiths College from 1970-72, where he created the tape piece Ballet Scene. Following this he became a Research Fellow at Glasgow University until 1977, and composer in residence at Queen's University in Belfast. In the mid-70s he presented a personal overview of his composing career for BBC Radio 3, discussing both his electronic and instrumental music. His final significant foray into electronic sound came in early 1983, with a stay in Paris to work at IRCAM.

Besides being a contemporary composer, Newson is also an established photographer, and has captured many artists, writers and composers featured in the National Portrait Gallery collection. These include photos of **Harrison Birtwistle**, **David Bedford**, Richard Rodney Bennett, Alexander Goehr, Jonathan Harvey, Peter Maxwell Davies and John Woolrich. In recent years much of his distinguished catalogue of compositions has been neglected, and regular performances have dwindled, though he has continued to compose music at his home near Appledore, Kent.

Philips Pavilion at Expo 58

George Newson, BBC RW, 1966

British Pavilion at Expo 58

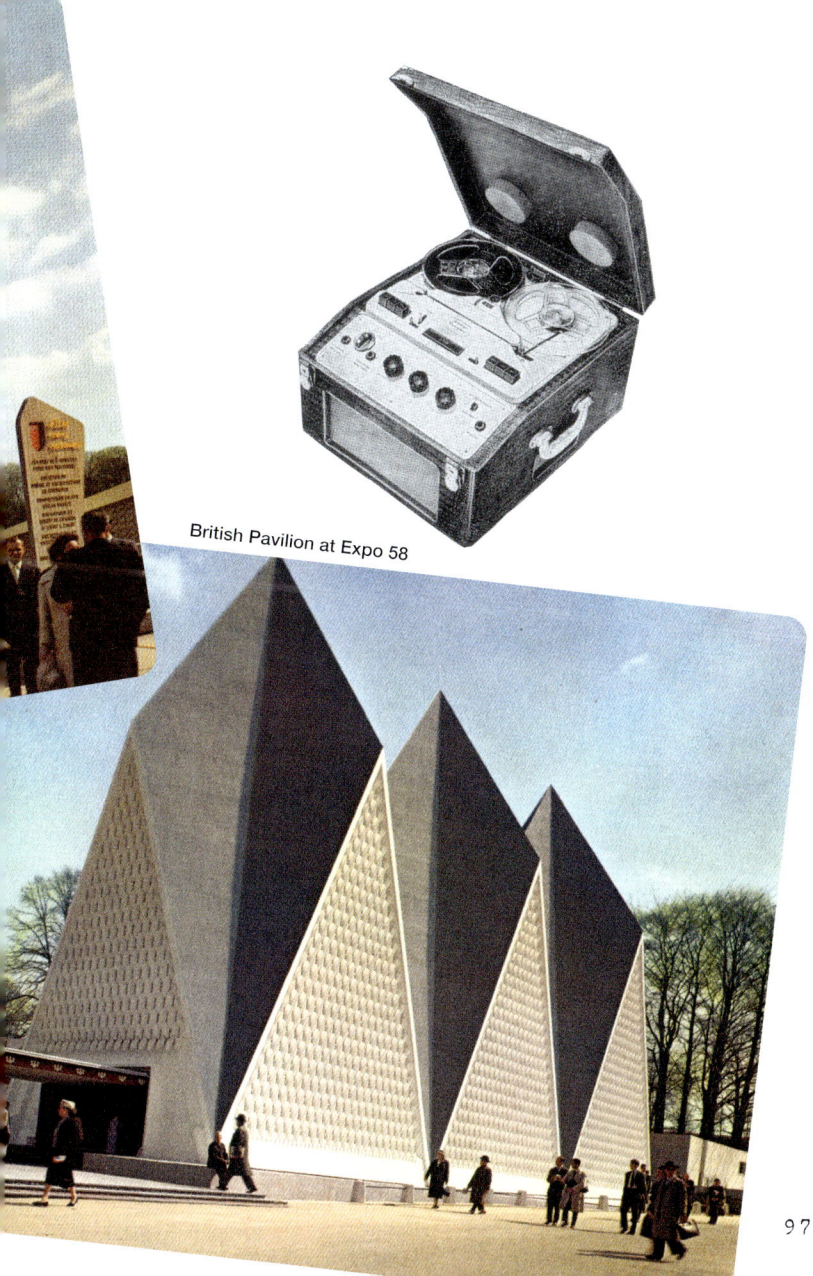

Daphne Oram (1925-2003)
Born: Devizes, Wiltshire
Earliest Electronic Work: Still Point (1949)
Commitment Factor: 10
Obscurity Quotient: 4
EM recording availability: Excellent

One of the true pioneers of early British electronic music, Oram studied piano, organ and composition at the Sherborne School for Girls, and in 1942 turned down an offer of a place at the Royal College of Music. Instead she opted for a job as junior studio engineer at the BBC in London, and by the end of the 1940s was pursuing her own investigations into experimental sound. In 1949 her composition Still Point, was written to fuse a double orchestra with treated sounds on discs, and in the years ahead she was pressing BBC management to create an electronic music studio. With the Music Department suspicious of the need for such a facility, she was forced to carry out recording late into the night on the sixth floor of Broadcasting House, where she could gather up tape recorders and equipment to use in one room, before returning machines back to their original places by the next morning. Working in this manner she created incidental music for the World Theatre play Amphitryon 38, among the first BBC TV programmes to feature a radiophonic soundtrack, broadcast in March 1958.

Through her dedication and the support of **Desmond Briscoe** and sympathetic drama producers, the **Radiophonic Workshop** came into being in April 1958. That same year she visited the Brussels World's Fair, aka Expo 58, and while there she heard electronic music from better supported overseas composers. She became increasingly frustrated at the production line theme tune direction of the Workshop, and in January 1959 she left the BBC and established her own studio at Tower Folly, a converted oast house at Fairseat in Kent. Assistance in equipping her studio came from her brother John Anderson Oram, and engineer Fred Wood, and she began hatching plans for her Oramics drawn sound invention. Crucial contributions to the project came from electronics boffin Graham Wrench, and with his radar experience and knowledge of

IT'S THE CHOICE OF THE PEOPLE WHO KNOW....
Brenell

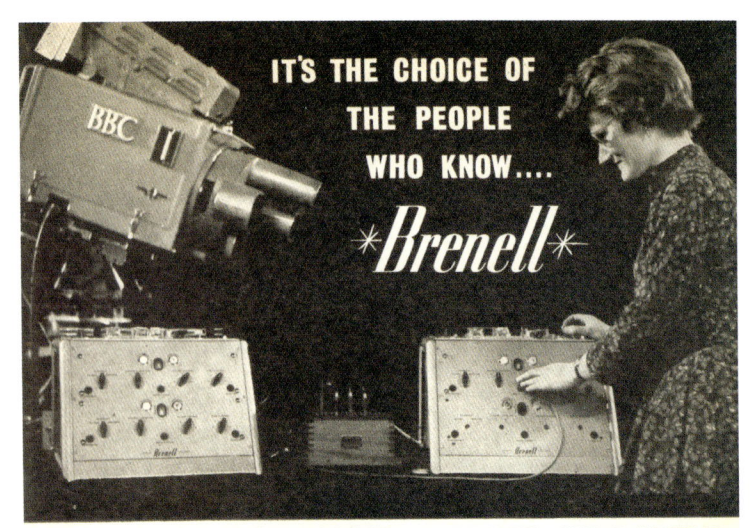

THE MACHINE THAT MAKES ENTHUSIASTS

By THOMAS SHERIDAN

PEOPLE who take up tape recording as a creative pastime as well as an amusement sometimes fall into the error of buying a machine which, they find out later, is not exactly the one which might have fulfilled both their objectives adequately and economically. Those who start off with a Brenell have either made a fortunate choice or, more likely, have been well advised by one who knows.

Among the semi-professional models which not only provide music for critical ears but enable the imaginative recordist to work his minor miracles, those made by Brenell are considered a "best

SEE NEXT PAGE

****

LISTEN, MOVE and DANCE—3   mono

Electronic Sound Patterns
Composed and created by DAPHNE ORAM

HIS MASTER'S VOICE
EXTENDED PLAY 45 r.p.m. RECORD

Electronic Sound Patterns
Composed and created by **Daphne Oram**
in collaboration with Vera Gray

LISTEN MOVE AND DANCE 3

Band 1 and 2   Melodic group shapes
Band 3   Three single sounds taken in canon
Bands 4 and 5   Rhythmic variation
Bands 1 to 6   Ascending and descending sequences of varying nature

45 R.P.M. EXTENDED PLAY RECORD
E.M.I. RECORDS LIMITED
HAYES · MIDDLESEX · ENGLAND

optoelectronics, he helped get it off the drawing board when he accepted a job at Tower Folly in 1965, to work exclusively on the system. Two very large Gulbenkian Foundation grants bankrolled the project, while Daphne pursued commercial recording work. Ironically much of her electronic music output was for adverts, soundtracks and functional purposes, similar to the type she found limiting at the Radiophonic Workshop. As well as providing special sound for the eerie British feature film The Innocents (1961), and electronic treatments for the outstanding Geoffrey Jones short Snow (1963), she made Episode Metallic (1965), the audio for a kinetic sculpture by Andrew Bobrowski at Mullard House in London.

Lecturing on electronic music was another important aspect of her career, and she was in contact with **FC Judd** who was working along similar lines. At Morley College, London, she ran classes from 1959-64, and appeared on the BBC TV programme, Experiment: Sound In Vision, broadcast in March 1960. In January 61 she presented a concert of electronic music entitled The Performer Banished, at the Mermaid Theatre in Blackfriars, London. She was president of the Dartford Tape Recording Society, and in November 62 a contingent of the club's members visited her studio for a demonstration of electronic sounds. She ran workshops and gave advice and assistance to fellow composers, including **Hugh Davies**, **Peter Zinovieff**, **Alan Sutcliffe**, **Janet Beat**, **Thea Musgrave**, **Edward Williams** and **Roy Cooper**. During the latter part of the 60s, she corresponded with Cooper regarding lecturing at Adwick School in Yorkshire, and the provision of equipment for his music classes. Oram and Wrench ran the Electronic Studio Supply Company, abbreviated in 1967 to Essconics Ltd, and she visited Adwick and conducted workshops with the children. A 7" EP record of her Electronic Sound Patterns, was released by EMI in 1962, in the Listen, Move and Dance series. Intended to stimulate movement and imagination in the classroom and beyond, one of the EP tracks was used for a live Soho striptease show, and features briefly in the 1966 short film Strip.

In 1972 her idiosyncratic book, An Individual Note of Music, Sound and Electronics, was published by Galliard, eloquently describing her holistic view of electronic music. Oramics was underpinned with her particular strand of new age thought, yet considering its sophistication and potential, the machine appears to have been relatively little used, and never fully completed despite the large investment of time and money. In a 1972 interview for BBC Radio 3, Oram admitted the machine was still in a developmental stage after almost a decade, and as the number of her serious compositions declined during the later 70s, by 1981 she had switched her attention away from the original Oramics apparatus, to a software version on an Apple II computer.

During most of the 1980s she taught electronic music at Canterbury Christ Church College, but debilitatiing strokes led to her moving to a nursing home, and subsequent break-ins at her Tower Folly studio. After her death in 2003, Hugh Davies did much to secure her archive, though the original Oramics machine was sold and fell into disrepair. Thankfully her tapes and papers have been salvaged and catalogued, and are now housed at Goldsmiths College in London, while the Oramics machine – a unique piece of electronic music history – has been reassembled, and displayed at the Science Museum in London from 2011. With its exhibition came the rarely asked question of how the two substantial Gulbenkian grants were spent. Worth around £5000 in the early 1960s, the sum equates to nothing less than £80,000 by today's standards, and difficult to reconcile with the rough home-made appearance of the equipment. Nonetheless, Daphne Oram made a hugely important and pioneering contribution to British electronic music in its early development and promotion, and it is only in recent years that this has started to be properly acknowledged. For an article in the Composer journal in 1962, she finished with these words: "*This combining of the worlds of music and electronics must come as rather a shock to many people. But to those lucky enough to have had the chance to experiment in the new medium, the fascination of its possibilities seem overwhelming*."

CDs:
Daphne Oram: Oramics (Paradigm, 2007).
Daphne Oram: The Oram Tapes (Young Americans, 2012).

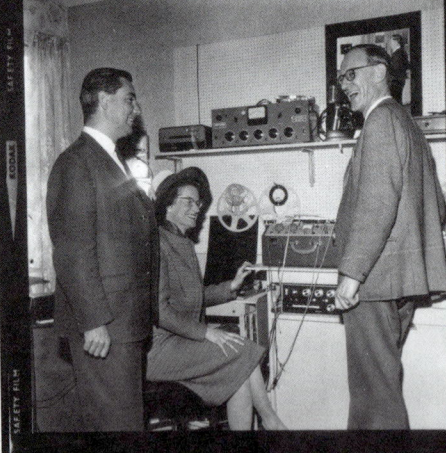

RELAXATION OSCILLATOR

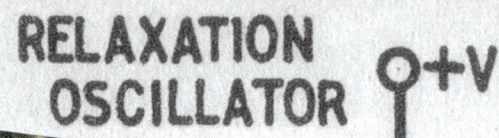

Daphne Oram at Fred Judd's house in London, judging tape competition entries with Fred, John Ratcliff and John Borwick, 1960

a Galliard paperback

AN INDIVIDUAL NOTE

of music
sound
and electronics

by Daphne Oram

99p

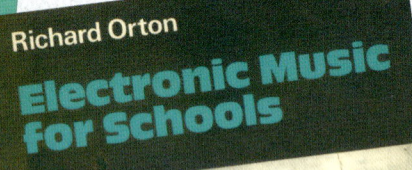

Richard Orton
Electronic Music for Schools

100

York University electronic music studio, early 1970s

Richard Orton (1940-2013)

Born: Derby
Earliest Electronic Work: Kiss (1968)
Commitment Factor: 8
Obscurity Quotient: 6
EM recording availability: Limited

Although he left school at 16 to work in a bank, Orton gained teaching diplomas at the Birmingham School of Music, and won a Choral Scholarship to St. John's College, Cambridge. He sang in the college choir and studied music, and following graduation landed a job as Lecturer in Music at the University of York in 1967. Establishing the University's Electronic Music Studio a year later – not long after EM studios at Manchester University, the Royal College of Music and Goldsmiths College – he completed the tape piece Kiss, premiered at the Harrogate Festival in 1969. **EMS** synthesizers were introduced at York at the start of the 70s, and composers working at the studio included **Trevor Wishart**, Andrew Bentley, Martin Gellhorn, and Richard Pickett. They all had work on the Electronic Music from York album, alongside three tracks by Orton, and this triple LP set was released in 1973. A number of his pieces include electronics, among them Sampling Afield (1969), and Ambience for solo trombone and tape (1975).

Orton was a founder member of **Gentle Fire**, and established the Mediamix series of concerts, which combined performances of electro-acoustic compositions with film, dance and other media. In 1981 his book Electronic Music For Schools, was published, with contributions from Wishart, Bentley, Phil Ellis, Peter Warham and **Hugh Davies**. He also introduced a music technology course at York, and helped to form the Composers Desktop Project, creating a network of like-minded musicians, programmers and designers. He developed music software, and in 1992 he began working on his algorithmic composition language Tabula Vigilans. Designed for real-time performance, it was developed and extended to include Score-Builder and Form-Builder, to assist in composing. After retirement from York University he operated from his home in Willoughby-on-the-Wolds, Leicestershire.

Morris Pert (1947-2010)

Born: Arbroath, Angus, Scotland
Earliest Electronic Work: Omega Centauri (1970)
Commitment Factor: 6
Obscurity Quotient: 6
EM recording availability: Good

Graduating from Edinburgh University in 1969, Pert went on to study composition and percussion under Alan Bush, at the Royal Academy of Music in London. While there his first orchestral work Xumbu-Ata, won the Royal Philharmonic Award in 1970, and his early electro-acoustic compositions Omega Centauri, for six instruments and tape, and Andromeda Link, date from this time. He was unusual in crossing easily between the worlds of classical and rock music, and is known for his work with Japanese percussionist and composer Stomu Yamashta, (another musician straddling both genres).

The early 70s saw Pert playing drums with Yamashta's Red Buddha Theatre, as well as Come to the Edge, alongside **Andrew Powell**. His own group Suntreader, released the fine Zin Zin album in 1973, and performed his piece Chromosphere, for five instrumentalists and tape. At this time he received composition commissions, and during his life wrote three symphonies, and continued to compose works involving tape; The Ultimate Decay, The Book of Love, and Aurora, all feature electronics.

For 18 years he worked as a session musician in top London recording studios, and played with Paul McCartney, Kate Bush, Mike Oldfield, Peter Gabriel and John Williams, amongst many others. He also ventured into composing for theatre and dance, with music for Shakespeare plays, and an electronic ballet score, Continuum, premiered at Sadler's Wells. Moving to the North West of Scotland, he established his own small studio in Balchrick, and at the time of his death he was working on a 4th symphony, and a further electro-acoustic piece.

CD: Morris Pert: Chromosphere (North By North West, 2013).

David Piper (1943)

Born: Truro, Cornwall
Earliest Electronic Work: Mare Crisium (1970)
Commitment Factor: 8
Obscurity Quotient: 7
EM recording availability: Limited

Starting piano studies aged seven, progressing to the organ and taking an organist position at 14 in a church on the Isle of Wight, Piper went on to study at the Royal Manchester College of Music, and the University of Manchester. He was involved with the local new music scene, playing contact miked cello in an improvisation group, and graduated with a music degree in 1965. The following year – at the same time as North American composers R. Murray Schafer, Pauline Oliveros and Reynold Weidenaar – he attended an electronic music summer course at the University of Toronto, organised by Gustav Ciamaga and Hugh le Caine.

His PhD thesis, completed in 1968, compared musique concrète with 'elektronische musik', and during his research, plans were hatched to establish a tape studio at the University of Manchester. Together with his PhD tutor Hans Redlich, they formulated the outline of the studio during 1966, and had it partly operational at the start of 1967. Piper studied electronic engineering part-time, and had been shown around the **BBC Radiophonic Workshop**, and was familiar with basic studio apparatus. With a budget of £800 secured by Redlich, they procured a stereo tape recorder, oscillators, white noise generator, filters and mixer. After further funding, this equipment was followed in 1968 by the acquisition of a modular Moog synthesizer, the first of its type in Britain at that time. Piper recalls, "*the Moog was designed to be idiot-proof... It was simply a case of doing things and listening to the result; analysing those results and hypothesizing other possible approaches. It was all great fun: what a toy! Of course, for the teaching I took a much more strategic approach, examining and analysing the operation(s) of each module individually, and the sonic effect of their inter-connecting.*"

Like **George Newson**, Piper had visited the Moog factory in the USA, and initiated the synthesizer purchase, and by 1969 he was working on his own electronic music. Attending tape concerts in London at the Queen Elizabeth Hall and the Planetarium, he was in touch with **Hugh Davies**, who visited the Manchester studio. Piper's composition Mare Crisium, was inspired by the Apollo 12 moon landing of November 69, and was entirely generated from sounds made with the Moog. In March 1971 he staged an electronic music concert, featuring the experimental work of five of his students plus Mare Crisium. This was played again later that year at a further concert for the Manchester University Music Society, which included his composition for organ and tape, Transcendence.

Upon leaving Manchester, Piper taught for a time at Huddersfield Polytechnic, before emigrating to Canada in 1972 to join the music faculty of Carleton University in Ottawa. Two years later he established the department's electronic studio, and initiated the installation of an **EMS** Synthi 100. In 1991 he became a Canadian citizen, and in 1996, a more fundamental change occured with a new identity as Deirdre. After a distinguished career at Carleton, Dr. Piper retired in 2009.

Malcolm Pointon (1940-2007)

Born: Stoke-on-Trent
Earliest Electronic Work: Radiophonie (1964)
Commitment Factor: 8
Obscurity Quotient: 7
EM recording availability: Excellent

The son of working class Methodist parents, Pointon developed an interest in the sound of the organ via trips to the cinema and church, and his aptitude for music was first recognised at primary school. He learned to play organ and piano, and gained regular performing experience as accompanist for a local singing teacher. Going on to form a modern jazz combo that played gigs in and around the Stoke area, it was apparent that he had a prodigious keyboard talent; being able to play by ear, sight read and improvise. Entering Birmingham University in 1958 to study music, he graduated with a First and was already writing his own compositions, as well as acquainting himself with both traditional and avant-garde musical trends. In 1965 he secured a job at the BBC, working on scripts for music programmes on the Third Network, and in 1969 joined the music department at Homerton College, Cambridge, where he stayed until his retirement in 1992.

Spurred on by hearing Karlheinz Stockhausen's sinewave generated piece Studie II (1954), he made his earliest forays into tape experimentation at home with simple domestic equipment. He used a four waveband radio to generate his sound material, and with a splicing block, blank leader tape and a mono multi-speed tape recorder, he spent two weeks working on his first electronic composition Radiphonie. His composing included chamber music and pieces for piano, alongside experimental tape music, and at Homerton he established the college's electronic music studio in 1970. Beyond academia he was known for his contributions to magazine Practical Electronics, and he communicated with engineer Doug Shaw on designs for the 'P.E. Synthesiser' and Minisonic construction projects from 1973-75. He provided synth playing demonstrations for Shaw's lectures, and his Electromuse column for PE ran during the mid-70s, featuring articles on electronic music, as well as projects for readers to try out. In March 1975 he described the recording of his piece Peloria, derived from short wave radio signals, and in June that year he wrote an extensive feature on his composition Symbiosis. This was generated with the Minisonic synth, and the article included patch settings, and a graphic score for readers to follow and record their own interpretation.

He continued creating tape works through the 1970s and into the 80s, and scored two documentary films, but by 1991 Alzheimer's disease was diagnosed, and he was forced into early retirement. His tragic demise was captured in 2007 in the ITV programme Malcolm and Barbara: Love's Farewell, revealing his deteriorating condition leading to his eventual death. Although the Minisonic did not survive, some of his original self-built equipment and tape machines from the 1970s remain intact. His bookcase in his old studio at the family home is still lined with LPs and tapes, with a section reserved for books about electronic music, including volumes written by **Daphne Oram**, **Terence Dwyer**, and **FC Judd**.

ELECTROMUSE
By Malcolm Pointon

The work of Malcolm Pointon

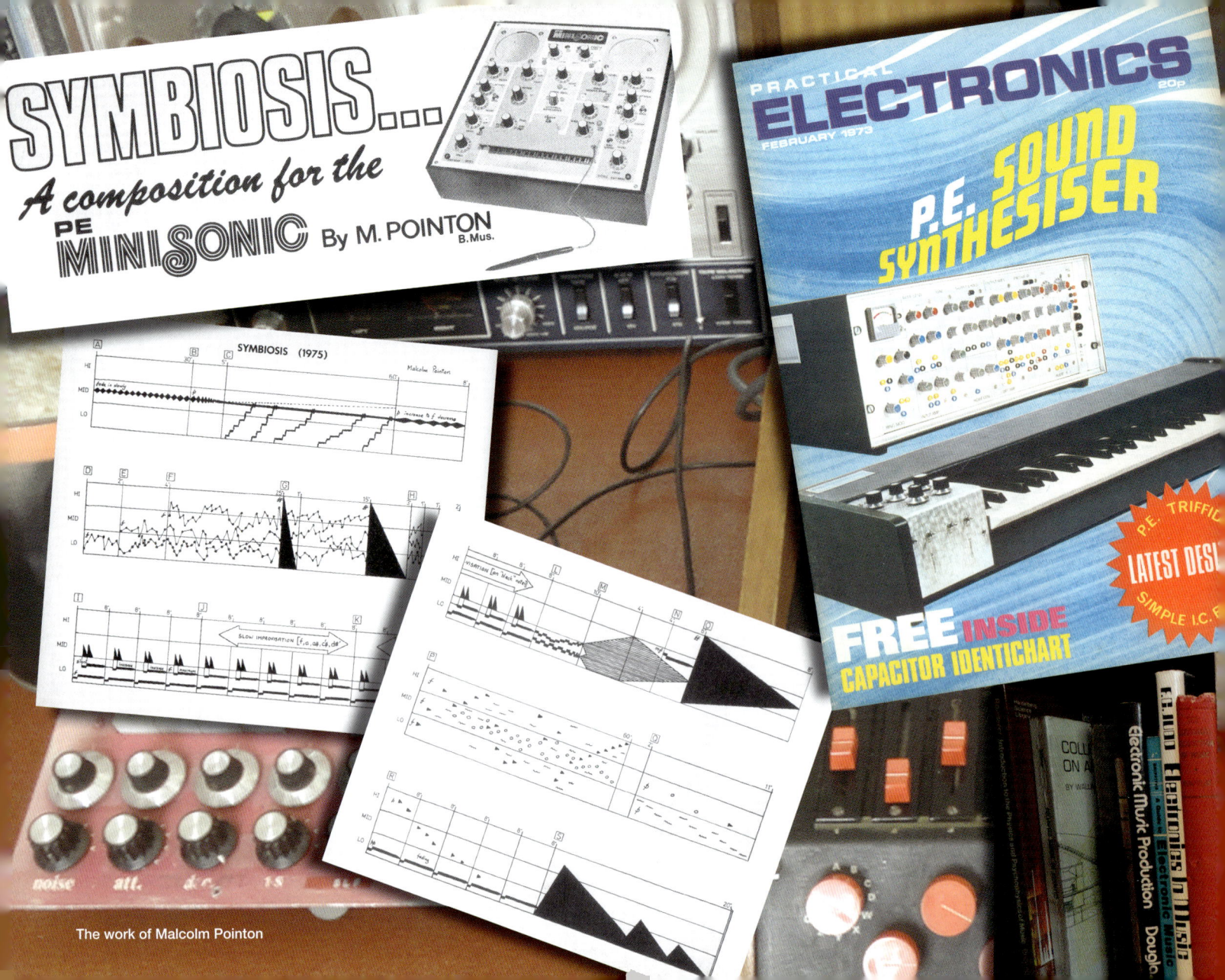

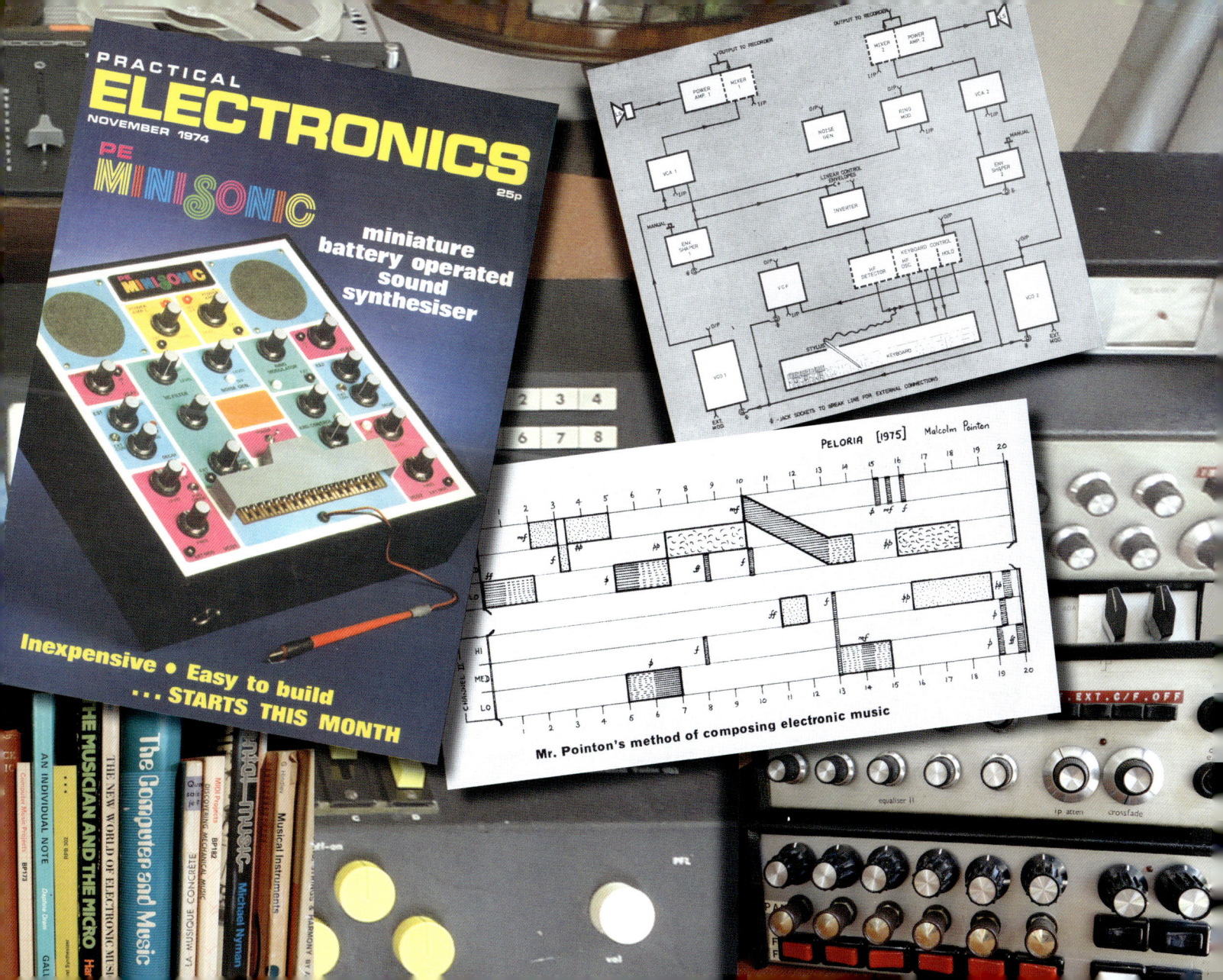

PRACTICAL ELECTRONICS
NOVEMBER 1974
PE MINISONIC
25p

miniature battery operated sound synthesiser

- Inexpensive ● Easy to build
- ...STARTS THIS MONTH

Mr. Pointon's method of composing electronic music

PELORIA (1975) Malcolm Pointon

Andrew Powell (1949)

Born: South London
Earliest Electronic Work: Gamma Ray Absorption (1966) film soundtrack
Commitment Factor: 5
Obscurity Quotient: 6
EM recording availability: Poor

Writing piano pieces at an exceedingly young age, Powell attended King's College School, Wimbledon, studying piano and viola, and created his first tape piece in 1966. This was for a short film, Gamma Ray Absorption, made by Mike Smith, the head of physics at the school, with the electro-acoustic soundtrack recorded by Powell playing sinewave generator and percussion.

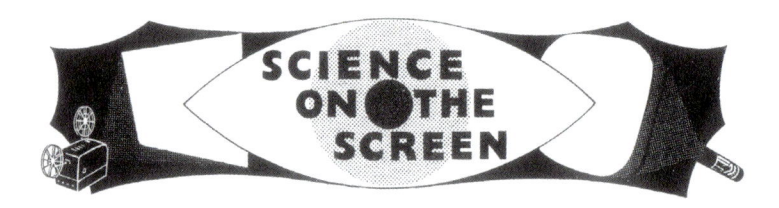

He had lessons with two eminent musicians while still a teenager; James Blades for percussion, and Cornelius Cardew for composition. Before moving up to university, he attended classes in Darmstadt, Germany, with Karlheinz Stockhausen and Gyorgy Ligeti. Entering King's College, Cambridge, he was a founding member of **Intermodulation**, alongside **Tim Souster**, **Roger Smalley** and Robin Thompson. Crossing easily between the worlds of classical, experimental and pop music, he formed part of an early incarnation of Brit-prog group Henry Cow, played with Nick Drake, and established the trio Come To the Edge, together with Thompson and **Morris Pert**. He wrote Dorian Terilament, for the group, featuring organ, electric piano, bass drums, vibraphone, sax and tape delay; this was performed in 1972 at the Queen Elizabeth Hall in London, with regular collaborator Stomu Yamashta.

After graduating from King's College, Powell played Terry Riley's Keyboard Studies, at the Royal Albert Hall Proms, and went on to work with a range of leading orchestras and ensembles, including the BBC Symphony Orchestra. Swinging back to the commercial world he acted as arranger for Cockney Rebel, and worked with all manner of pop acts including Leo Sayer, Donovan, John Miles, Cliff Richard, Al Stewart, The Hollies, Mick Fleetwood, Pilot and David Gilmour from Pink Floyd. Gilmour brought in Powell for his first production assignment on Kate Bush's debut album The Kick Inside, and he began a fruitful collaboration with the Alan Parson's Project, achieving massive global record sales.

Powell has kept up his prolific playing, production, arranging and composition activities through to the present day, and continues to move easily between pop and classical music. He had his Points Upon a Canvas, performed by the BBC National Orchestra of Wales in Cardiff in 2011; in more recent times he has written a piece for contra-bassoon and live electronics, while in 2015 he spent a week working at IRCAM in Paris.

Howard Rees (1945-2011)

Born: Carmarthen, Wales
Earliest Electronic Work: The Cat's Paw Among the Silence of Midnight Goldfish (1969)
Commitment Factor: 6
Obscurity Quotient: 7
EM recording availability: Poor

Attending grammar school in Carmarthen, and going on to study music at the University of Wales from 1962-67, Rees received a Welsh Arts Council bursary for post graduate study with Alun Hoddinott, **Don Banks** and Australian electronic composer Keith Humble, at the Centre de Musique in Paris. In 1969 he gained his first teaching appointment with the Inner London Education Authority, and the following year took on a lecturing post at Falmouth School of Art in Cornwall. While there he ran an electronic music workshop, and directed the New Music Group, which presented concerts of modern works.

During 1969 he worked at the Goldsmiths College electronic studio to make two compositions with tape; The Cat's Paw Among the Silence of Midnight Goldfish, for trombone, six instruments and tape, and Doug's New Flute Thing, for amplified flute, tape and live electronics. For this latter piece, the performers included Douglas Whittaker, Michael Nyman on VCS3 and Rees on electronics. After his spell at Falmouth, he joined the Cockpit Arts Centre in 1972, and became co-director of the Cockpit Ensemble, which also included **Howard Davidson** and **Malcolm Fox**. He played on The Sinking of the Titanic album by Gavin Bryars, the first release on **Brian Eno**'s Obscure Records label. The Cockpit Ensemble's line-up involved two synthesizers alongside regular instruments, and their aim was to introduce the general public to the sounds of contemporary music, with workshops, school visits and concerts.

The 1970s were a particularly active time for Rees – as well as being a member of the groups **Music Plus** and **Naked Software**, and participating in ICES-72 – in 1974 he was appointed head of music at the Cockpit and directed the venue's electronic workshop. He also organised sound and drama sessions at Coventry College; lectured on new music at York University; led workshops with the Rotterdam Philharmonic Orchestra; contributed to BBC radio programmes; composed Jazz Suite, for the London Schools Symphony Orchestra; and created the music video piece Time/Wipe, broadcast on BBC TV in Wales in 1977. This signalled a change of direction in his career; he left the Cockpit Arts Centre and became a producer and director for the ILEA TV Service, originating more than 60 programmes focussed on the arts. When the service closed in 1989, he turned freelance and continued producing, directing and composing, and made programmes for various organisations including Channel 4, the London Symphony Orchestra and the Red Cross. He retired from teaching in July 2010, and sadly that year he slipped and fell, hitting his head causing a severe brain injury, leading to his death in January 2011.

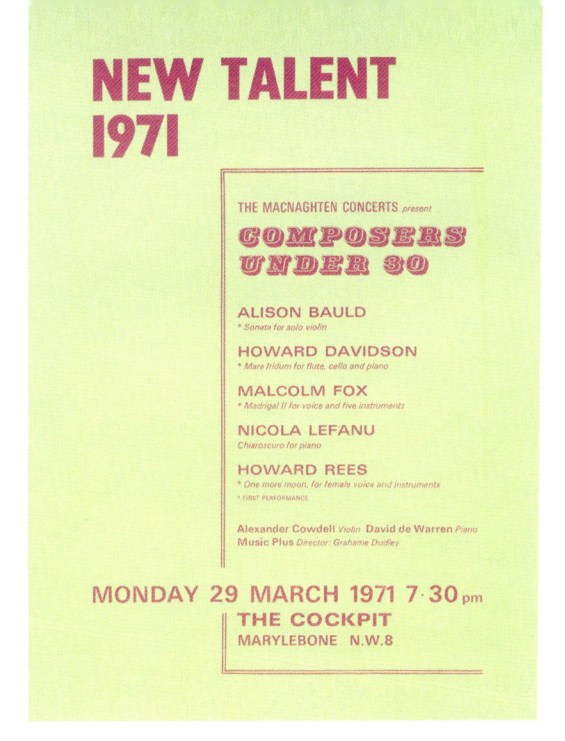

SKIN MUSIC
6th DEC

MUSIC at the COCKPIT THEATRE

GATEFORTH STREET, CHURCH STREET, LONDON NW8 BOX OFFICE 402 5081
THURS 6 DEC 7.30 30p

A multi-media exploration of the mind of the poet Peter Redgrove by musicians, artists, actors and dancers connected with the Cockpit Arts Workshop. Directed by Howard Rees, who composed the music for Redgrove's recent radio play "In the Country of the Skin".

John Marlow Rhys (1935-2011)
Born: Newcastle-under-Lyme, Staffordshire
Earliest Electronic Work: Daidalos (1970)
Commitment Factor: 1
Obscurity Quotient: 8
EM recording availability: Poor

From 1956-59, John Marlow Rhys studied music at Oxford, then spent a year at Dartington in Devon with Richard Hall, and earned a DPhil in composition at York University. In 1970 he became a lecturer at Southwark College, and in the 1980s and 90s taught at Farnham College, Esher College and Brunel University in west London. His compositions were widely performed and he received a number of awards, with Capriccio, premiered in 1978, being one of his best known works. Daidalos, his music-theatre piece first performed in 1970, is scored for three instrumental groups, two track tape and five masked mimes.

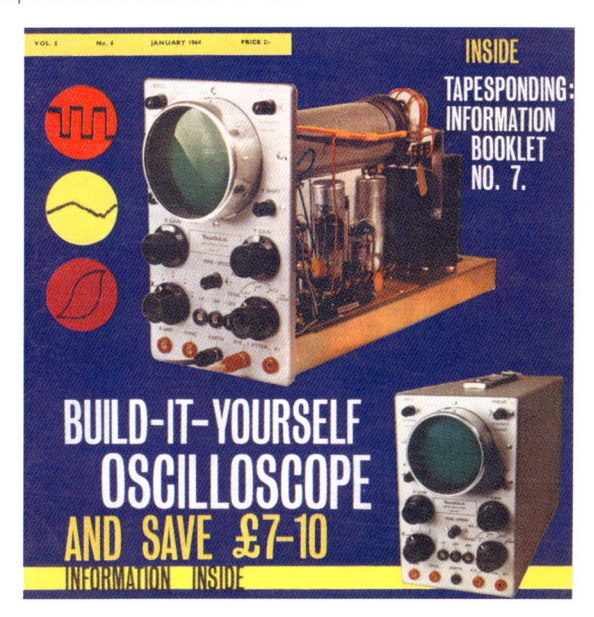

Alan Ridout (1934-1996)
Born: West Wickham, Greater London
Earliest Electronic Work: Psalm for Sinewave Generators (1959)
Commitment Factor: 2
Obscurity Quotient: 7
EM recording availability: Poor

Starting piano lessons at nine years old, and with a body of his own compositions completed by the age of 12, the precocious Ridout went on to study at the Guildhall School of Music, and then at the Royal College of Music under Herbert Howells and Gordon Jacob. Peter Racine Fricker and Michael Tippett gave him further tuition, and with a Netherlands Government Scholarship, he received grounding in electronic and tape techniques from Dutch pioneer of electronic music, Henk Badings.

His musical output was very large and varied, including 15 operas, 8 symphonies and 25 concertos, and his interests encompassed medieval polyphony, serialism, microtonality and electronic music. He was Professor of Theory and Music Composition at the Royal College of Music from 1960-1984, and his autobiography published in 1995, is titled A Composer's Life. So far, his Psalm for Sinewave Generators, is his only identified work in the electronic medium.

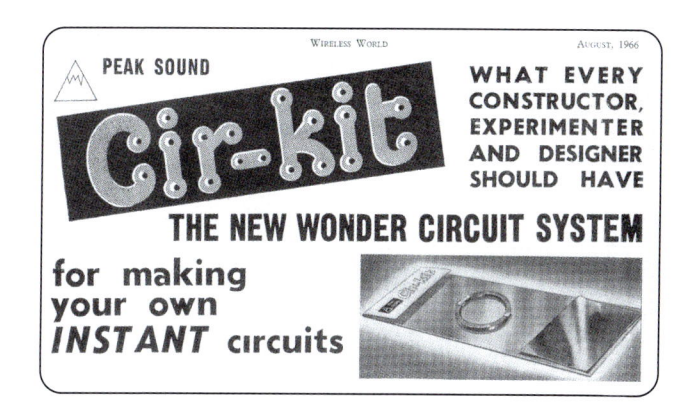

David Rowland (1939-2007)

Born: Exeter, Devon
Earliest Electronic Work: Postil (1968) unconfirmed
Commitment Factor: 6
Obscurity Quotient: 8
EM recording availability: Poor

Studying under Peter Racine Fricker and Arthur Alexander at the Royal College of Music in London, Rowland went on to teach music theory and composition at Trinity College and the RCM, and became musical director for the Royal Shakespeare Company at the Aldwych Theatre. He moved to The Netherlands in 1975, and continued teaching music at the Twents Conservatorium at Enschede, while founding the Arcadia Ensemble, which specialized in performing modern music.

A concert in Great Portland Street in London on 26th January 1969, organised by the Focus Opera Group, included works by Debussy, Satie, **Harrison Birtwistle** and Rowland's Postil. This piece was performed by Jamie Muir, Tony Oxley, Robin Thompson, Gavin Bryars, **Hugh Davies** and Rowland himself on electronics. The score was written on eight separate sheets showing a graphic representation of the inter-relationships of the seven aspects of the music, leaving the instrumentalists free to arrange the sheets in any order. With the players organised in groups, their sounds were amplified, filtered and ring modulated according to a further rearrangement of the score.

Working at **EMS** with assistance from **Peter Grogono**, Rowland created Tetrad, premiered in December 1971 at the Queen Elizabeth Hall, London, and Dreamtime, first aired in April 1972 at Camden's Roundhouse. As well as at EMS, he carried out composition with electronics at the Goldsmiths studio, where he completed Masques, for oboe, cor anglais, percussion and two stereo tapes, in 1973.

Leonard Salzedo (1921-2000)

Born: Leighton Buzzard, Bedfordshire
Earliest Electronic Work: The Travellers (1963)
Commitment Factor: 3
Obscurity Quotient: 6
EM recording availability: Poor

A composer, conductor and violinist of Spanish-Jewish descent, Salzedo studied composition at the Royal College of Music under Herbert Howells, and turned professional in 1944. His first ballet The Fugitive, written that same year, was commissioned by Ballet Rambert, with whom he maintained a close association, becoming their conductor in 1946. To supplement his income, from the following year up until 1966, he played in the London Philharmonic Orchestra, and then the Royal Philharmonic Orchestra. He returned to Ballet Rambert as musical director from 1967-72, and from there he worked with the Scottish Ballet and London City Ballet in the 1980s.

He wrote 18 film scores during his life, and like **Don Banks**, **Tristram Cary** and **Humphrey Searle**, these included works for British horror specialists Hammer. The Revenge of Frankenstein, in 1958 was one of seven he composed for the company, and amongst his most lucrative commissions. A section of his Divertimento for Three Trumpets and Three Trombones (1959), was used as the theme for the BBC's Open University programmes from the 1970s to the 90s. As well as The Travellers, a ballet for small orchestra, he wrote 16 other ballet scores including Agrionia (1964), for six instruments and tape. When approached to write the score for Agrionia, Salzedo explained, "*They could not afford an orchestra so it would have to be a chamber group. The idea appealed to me as, once again, it would be necessary to have some electronic sounds as well as live music.*" A variety of commissions followed, including the concert work Distances, for nine instruments and tape, completed in 1966. After 1986 he devoted his energies full-time to writing music, until ill health in the late 90s concluded his composing career.

Peter Schmidt (1931-1980)

Born: Berlin, Germany
Earliest Electronic Work: A Painter's Use of Sound (1967) unconfirmed
Commitment Factor: 5
Obscurity Quotient: 5
EM recording availability: Poor

Having moved to Britain as a child in 1938 ahead of the outbreak of war, the teenage Schmidt began painting in 1947, going on to study at Goldsmiths College and The Slade. Winning a travelling scholarship he stayed in Sicily, and on returning to England he had his first solo show of his paintings in 1961. The following year he was featured in the BBC TV film Departures: Cubism and Beyond, and he established an art foundation course at Watford School of Art, where he taught for much of his life. During the 60s he moved towards complete abstraction, and began using music as an inspiration; paintings in this abstract style were exhibited in 1966 at London's Curwen Gallery. His interests in robotics and automation and a systems approach to art, extended into electronic music, and at an event entitled A Painter's Use of Sound, at the ICA in 1967, he gave a live performance with electronics. Meeting artists and lightshow exponents Mark Boyle and Joan Hills, he became one of the collaborators in their Sensual Laboratory, taking care of the sound engineering for Son et Lumiere multimedia projection presentations in Bristol; the Cochrane Theatre in London; and the UFO club in Tottenham Court Road.

Schmidt was appointed musical director for the Cybernetic Serendipity exhibition of computer related art at the ICA in 1968, which included audiovisual work by **John Lifton** and **Peter Zinovieff**. He performed Electronic Soup Mix, in 1969 at the Curwen Gallery, and Film Sound Mixes, at the ICA, and created a series of drawings based on the I Ching. Having met **Brian Eno** during the 60s, the pair decided to collaborate on a set of instructions for creative decision making, and in 1975 they produced a set of 113 cards named Oblique Strategies. Schmidt contributed artwork to several Eno albums of the mid-70s, and they worked on a special coloured lightbox in order to illuminate and apparently animate some of Schmidt's abstract paintings.

While maintaining his multi-disciplinary activities throughout the 1970s, Schmidt moved away from abstraction towards a figurative style using watercolours, spending two summers in Iceland painting landscapes. While on a painting vacation in the Canary Islands in January 1980, he died suddenly of a heart attack.

Humphrey Searle (1915-1982)

Born: Oxford
Earliest Electronic Work: Night Thoughts (1955)
Commitment Factor: 4
Obscurity Quotient: 6
EM recording availability: Poor

Searle attended Winchester School in 1928, and while there he took lessons in harmony and received an introduction to serious music. In 1934 he first heard Alban Berg's Wozzeck, and at the urging of composer William Walton, but against his parents wishes, he entered the Royal College of Music, studying with John Ireland. On a scholarship he went to Vienna in 1937, to study with key serialist composer Anton Webern, and returned home ahead of the Nazi occupation of the city the following year. Further study at the RCM in orchestration, conducting and counterpoint, led to a librarian's job with the BBC, and in 1940 he joined the army and entered the Intelligence Corps. At the end of World War II he was posted to Germany, to assist with the investigation into the death of Adolf Hitler, and he was demobbed in March 1946.

Returning to the BBC he took up a job as a music programme producer, until leaving for a post with the ISCM. Struggling financially, a breakthrough for his music came in 1955. The previous year he had penned an article on 'Concrete Music' for Grove's Dictionary of Music and Musicians, and BBC producer Douglas Cleverdon approached him to write the music and special sound, for a long dream sequence in the radio drama Night Thoughts. This required the manipulation of discs rather than tape, and raw sound material was provided by percussionist James Blades. Modified via basic speed changing and reversal, Searle observed that "*in spite of these technical handicaps we produced some very interesting sounds with such meagre resources.*" (Recorded three years before the **Radiophonic Workshop** was established, this was one of the first examples of musique concrète composed for British radio.) He continued providing incidental music for a number of BBC dramas, and wrote scores for the feature films The Abominable Snowman (1957), and ominous chiller The Haunting (1963). In 1958 Hermann Scherchen commissioned him to create a one act chamber opera, with singers, an orchestra and electronic sounds. The result was based on Gogol's The Diary of a Madman, and received its British premiere at Sadler's Wells in 1960, with the electronic part created with studio facilities and help from **Tristram Cary**. Searle provided all the incidental music for the Doctor Who story The Myth Makers (1965), and he made a further foray into electronic sound with a 1963 BBC commission; the three act opera The Photo of the Colonel, based on Ionesco's The Killer. Although his music is not performed so often these days, he maintained a distinguished and prolific composing career, and completed his engaging memoirs, Quadrille with a Raven, shortly before his death aged 66.

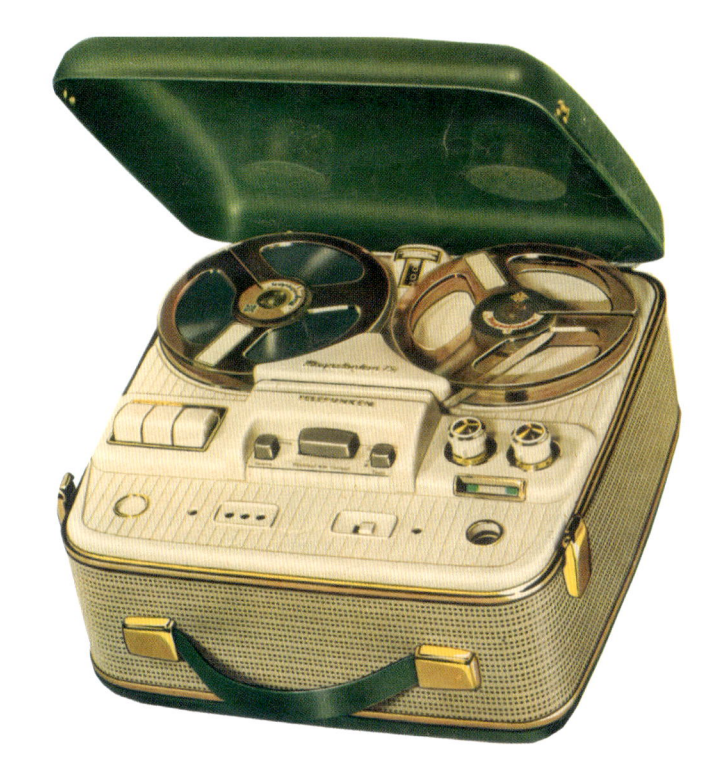

Robert Sherlaw Johnson (1932-2000)

Born: Sunderland
Earliest Electronic Work: The Praises of Heaven & Earth (1969)
Commitment Factor: 5
Obscurity Quotient: 8
EM recording availability: Poor

After attending grammar school in Newcastle upon Tyne, and King's College, Durham, Sherlaw Johnson continued his education at the Royal Academy of Music in London, and from there he travelled to Paris for composition study with Nadia Boulanger, and classes with Olivier Messiaen at the Conservatoire de Paris. His teaching career started at Leeds University in 1961, then Bradford Girls' Grammar School (1963-5), University of York (1965–70), and Oxford University (1970–1999). He became visiting professor of composition at the Eastman School of Music, University of Rochester, in 1985.

He had strong religious convictions and established a considerable reputation as a concert pianist, specialising in performances of piano music by major 20th century composers, most notably Olivier Messiaen. His book on the French composer published in 1974, was the first major study printed in English, and remains an important text. His own music was part of a new modernist impulse in Britain which investigated serialism, extended performance techniques and electronics. While a lecturer at York University, he was involved in the Music Department's presentation in May 1968, of Four Concerts of New and Experimental Music, where he performed with fellow York based composers and future **Gentle Fire** members.

His first piece with tape was created at York, and in 1970 he was made a Fellow of Worcester College, Oxford, where he established an electronic music studio. In the later 1970s he was in discussions with synthesizer company **EMS**, regarding a move to a college building, but this failed to materialise. He retained a firm connection to his north east roots, often playing the Northumbrian pipes, as well as being an enthusiastic campanologist. In November 2000 he collapsed and died while ringing bells in a church near Oxford.

York University concert, 1968

```
John Cage              : Solo for Voice I with Piano Solo
Robert Sherlaw Johnson : Improvisations V
Morton Feldman         : Durations
Richard Orton          : Cycle for Two or Four Players
Toshi Ichiyanagi       : Music for Piano 4

Sunday, 5 May at 8 pm

Inclusive tickets for the four programmes : 18/- (Students 7/6)
Admission to single concerts - by programme : 6/- (Students 2/6)

Tickets and programmes will be available from 8 April from:
Porters' Lodges; Banks and Son (Music) Ltd; Department of Music.
By Post: only from Department of Music, 86 Micklegate, YORK.

Performers to include Keith Abrams; Peter Aston; Christine Ball;
Richard Bernas; David Blake; Hugh Davies; Mike Escreet; Patrick Harrex;
Graham Hearn; Robert Sherlaw Johnson; Stuart Jones; Janet Kemp;
Wilfrid Mellers; Richard Middleton; Richard Orton; Jane Phillips;
Dick Smith; Gillian Stevens; Ruth Stewart; Tim Torry; David Truswell;
Moray Welsh.
```

James Siddons (1948)

Born: Narsarssuaq, Greenland
Earliest Electronic Work: Untitled tape (1966) Recorded in the USA
Commitment Factor: 5
Obscurity Quotient: 8
EM recording availability: Poor

Born on a small US Army base on the southern tip of Greenland, and growing up in Dallas, Texas, Siddons started playing electric keyboards during the mid-1960s, and performed with several pop and beat groups on Farfisa and Hammond B-3 organs. In 1966 he submitted a tape to the BMI Student Composers Competition, made with sounds from a Solovox keyboard and modified piano. In early 1967 he attended a performance of Kaleidoscope, by Merrill Ellis, for female voice, orchestra and live Moog synthesizer. Ellis himself had been stimulated by US pioneer of electronic music, Vladimir Ussachevsky, and established the Electronic Music Composition Laboratory at North Texas State University (NTSU) in 1963. Siddons studied under Ellis from 1967-70, and created several experimental works in the university's sound lab. Texas Whistler, was realised in July 1968 with the lab's first Moog synthesizer, and the same year he produced Happenings in a Socio-electronic Environment; a music-theatre piece with tape sounds, singer, announcer, mobile mannequin and projections. Vashti's Revealing: A Dance Experience, further explored the multi-media presentation of electronic music, and was produced and videotaped in the NTSU television studio in 1969.

In 1970 Siddons came to Britain for study in musical analysis at the University of London King's College, and one day a week he frequented the Goldsmiths College electronic music studio, under the guidance of **Hugh Davies**. Starting in September that year he worked on his piece Guy Fawkes, scored for actors, melodic instruments, percussionists and electronic sounds generated with a VCS3. He attended a music fair at Earl's Court in October, where he met Robert Moog, and around that time visited Dutch centre of electronic music, the Institute of Sonology in Utrecht. Along with fellow King's students, he toured the **BBC Radiophonic Workshop** studios at Maida Vale the following year. His final thesis at King's examined Hyperprism, by Edgard Varèse, and from 1972-74 he studied in Japan; partly in Osaka and primarily at the Tokyo University of the Arts. With his official status as a research student in ethnomusicology, he explored the work of Japanese composers in the electronic music studios at the Sogetsu Hall, and the NHK broadcasting corporation. His bio-bibliography of Toru Takemitsu, (one of the early exponents of electronic music in Japan), was published in 2001, and provides information and a list of concert, film and tape music from 1954-75.

Since 2013, Siddons has been re-evaluating his early work, making available music by his 1960s beat group Searchin` 5, and rediscovering a series of broadsheet bulletins he published in the late 60s as Musical Happening. The February 1969 issue came as a quarter inch tape, and included a Moog synthesizer improvisation from Merrill Ellis.

James Siddons next to a bearded Merrill Ellis, at NTSU late 1960s

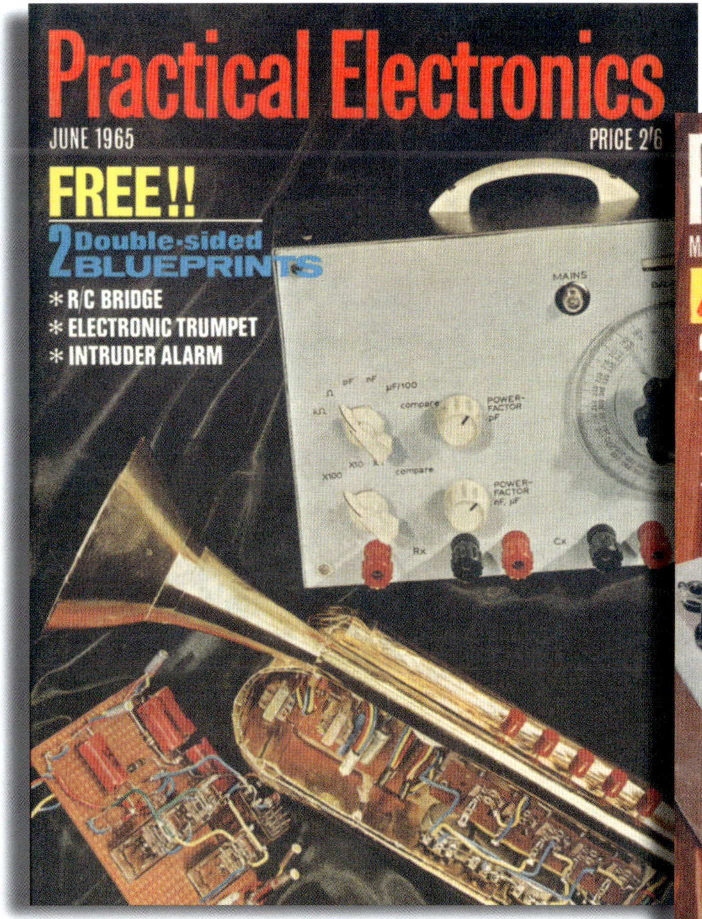
Practical Electronics
JUNE 1965
PRICE 2/6
FREE!!
2 Double-sided BLUEPRINTS
* R/C BRIDGE
* ELECTRONIC TRUMPET
* INTRUDER ALARM
MAINS
compare
POWER-FACTOR pF
POWER-FACTOR nF, µF
Rx
Cx

Practical Electronics
MAY 1965
PRICE 2/6
FREE inside
2 BLUEPRINTS
* AUDIO OSCILLATOR AND OUTPUT METER
* MICROPHONE MIXER
* SIMPLE SHORT WAVE RECEIVER
off
on
tuning
VOLUME
OUTPUT
ON
GAIN

Roger Smalley (1943-2015)

Born: Swinton, Salford
Earliest Electronic Work: A Round of Silence (1963)
Commitment Factor: 7
Obscurity Quotient: 6
EM recording availability: Good

Smalley's early interest in music was ignited at Sunday school, where the church organ provided a welcome distraction from dreary bible studies and singing hymns. Expressing the desire to play the organ himself, his parents arranged keyboard lessons with a piano teaching neighbour when he was around eight years old, and by his mid-teens he had developed beyond his teacher's abilities. After attending Lee Grammar School, he went to the Royal College of Music in London in 1961, studying composition under Peter Racine Fricker and then John White. He heard the orchestral piece Gruppen, by Karlheinz Stockhausen, and one of his earliest vinyl record purchases included Stockhausen's two electronic studies. His interest in composing with tape led to the opportunity to work at the **BBC Radiophonic Workshop** on A Round of Silence, a radio play by Christine Brooke-Rose. He attended the Dartington summer schools in this period, and in 1965 he and **Brian Dennis** went to Germany for classes given by Stockhausen in Cologne, while also visiting the influential summer school at Darmstadt.

From 1967 he lived in Cambridge, and the following year he was appointed the first Artist-in-Residence at King's College, where he pursued a three year research fellowship, and set up a small electronic studio. As a pianist he won acclaim for performances of contemporary music, and in January 1969, a Macnaghten Concert which featured Stockhausen's Mikrophonie II, included Smalley on Hammond organ, with **Gentle Fire** members **Hugh Davies** on ring modulators, and **Richard Orton** operating the tape recorder. That same year he composed Pulses, which reflected many of his preoccupations at the time; electronics, improvisation and sound spatialisation. It was commissioned and first performed by the London Sinfonietta, and dedicated to Karlheinz Stockhausen. The piece involves five groups of four players stationed in different parts of a concert hall, with all the instrumental sounds being fed into a ring modulator.

Together with **Tim Souster**, **Andrew Powell** and Robin Thompson, Smalley formed the electronic performance group **Intermodulation**, which played throughout England and Europe until 1976. He travelled to Australia initially for a three month composer residency at the University of Western Australia in 1974, and returned permanently two years later to become a research fellow, and subsequently Associate Professor of Music. For his contribution to Australian music, he was awarded the Australia Council's prestigious **Don Banks** Fellowship in 1994. He was Emeritus Professor and Honorary Senior Research Fellow at The University of Western Australia, and Honorary Research Associate at the Sydney Conservatorium of Music. Unfortunately in his final years the onset of debilitating illness curtailed his music and research activities.

CD: Roger Smalley: Pulses (NMC, 1994).

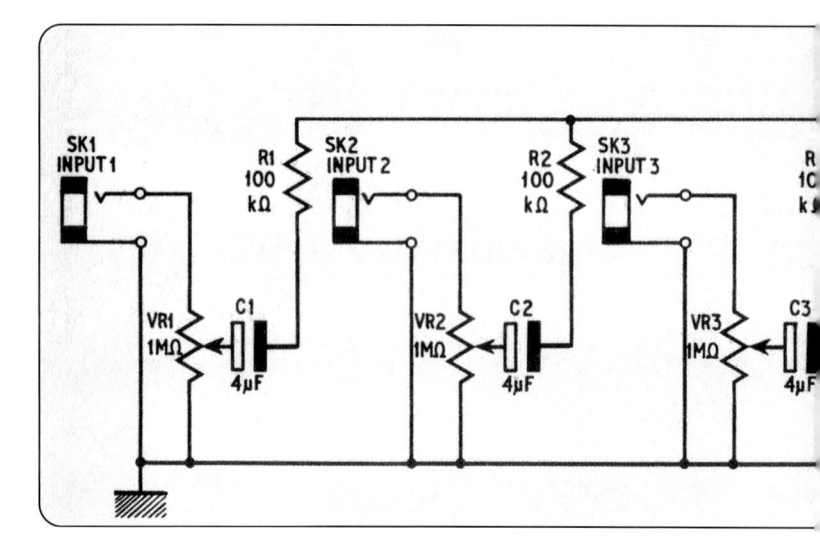

Tim Souster (1943-1994)

Born: Bletchley, Buckinghamshire
Earliest Electronic Work: Titus Groan Music (1969)
Commitment Factor: 8
Obscurity Quotient: 5
EM recording availability: Limited

Reading music at New College, Oxford, from 1961-64, in his final year Souster attended the summer music courses at Darmstadt, Germany, going to lectures by Karlheinz Stockhausen. In London he took composition lessons with Richard Rodney Bennett, and in 1965 joined the BBC Third Network as a producer of contemporary music programmes. Two years later he left the BBC to focus on composing and writing music criticism for various publications, including The Listener and the London Review of Books. His interest in electronic sounds stimulated at Darmstadt, led to his writing Titus Groan Music, in 1969, scored for wind quintet, ring modulator, amplifier and tape. In August that year he became composer-in-residence at King's College, Cambridge, and he formed the live electronic group **Intermodulation**, with Cambridge alumni **Andrew Powell** and **Roger Smalley**. In 1971 Souster renewed his link with Stockhausen by becoming his teaching assistant, at the State Music High School in Cologne. After two years he moved to Berlin for a further residency, finally returning to Britain for a Research Fellowship at Keele University in 1975. While there he established the university electronic music studio, and formed a new live electronic group 0dB, with Peter Britton and rock drummer Tony Greenwood. His LP, Swit Drimz, featuring five compositions and contributions from Britton and Greenwood, was released in 1977.

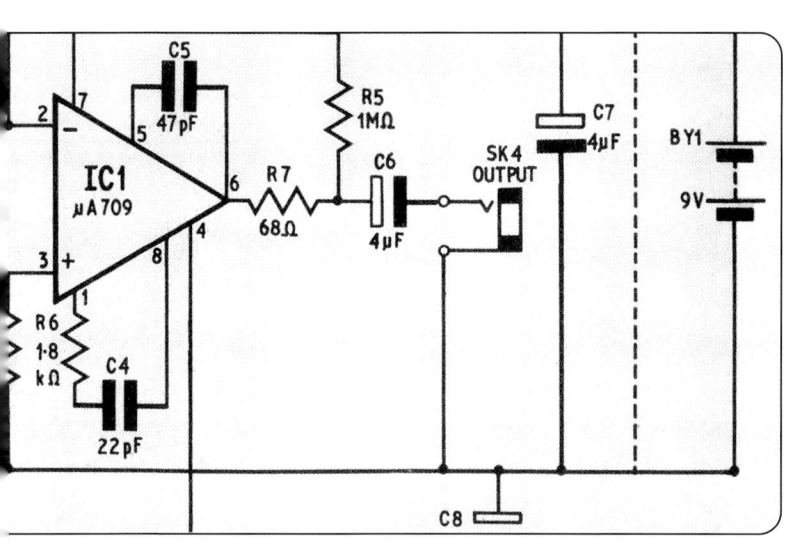

A travelling fellowship gave Souster another spell abroad, and he went to Stanford University in California, where the advanced facilities allowed him to create the computer music piece Driftwood Cortege (1978). Back in Britain he settled again in Cambridge, and by 1980 was established as a freelance composer, and presented a two part programme for the Music In Our Time series on BBC Radio 3, surveying developments in computer music. The previous year he played electric viola on A Touching Display, from the excellent 154 album by British group Wire. His commercial work saw him increasingly involved in writing scores for films and television, and he arranged and performed a version of The Hitchhiker's Guide to the Galaxy, signature tune. An adaptation of Kingsley Amis's The Green Man, starring Albert Finney, won Souster a Bafta award for Best Television Music in 1990. He had started work on a vocal and instrumental piece at the time of his early death in 1994.

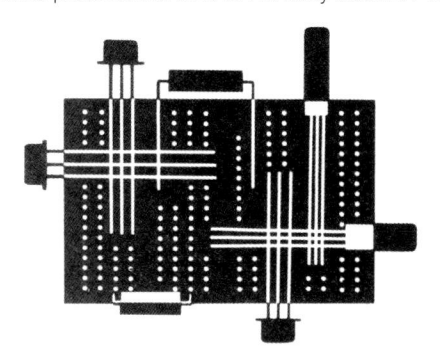

Alan Sutcliffe (1930-2014)

Born: Todmorden, West Yorkshire
Earliest Electronic Work: Icarus (1960)
Commitment Factor: 6
Obscurity Quotient: 6
EM recording availability: Limited

Early musical experience for Sutcliffe came via lessons on the French horn, and after attending Bristol University from 1949-51, he was called up for National Service. Following his spell in the military, he worked for the Metal Box company until 1960, and that year visited Darmstadt, Germany, for the renowned modern music courses. His interest in electronic sound prompted a visit to **Daphne Oram**'s Tower Folly studio in Kent, for a weekend tape workshop with four other students. Their goal was to create a piece based on the Greek legend of Icarus, using three tape recorders, tape loops and tone generators. After the workshop, Sutcliffe wrote an article for Tape Recording magazine in May 1960, detailing his first exposure to electronic composition, and subsequently equipped himself with three interlinked Brenell tape recorders to continue his experiments. In 1963 he contributed again to Tape Recording, where in two parts he described his soundtrack made for a stage production of Macbeth, by the Leeds Arts Centre. In the first instalment he explained the creation of effects using French horn mouthpiece and rubber tubing, treble recorder and banjo. The next month he followed up by describing his manipulation of piano sounds, for accompaniment to the play's main characters.

During 1963 he secured a job with English Electric in Staffordshire, and around this time became intimately involved with **Delia Derbyshire**. They remained friends after their affair finished, and she introduced him to **Peter Zinovieff** during 1966. Over the years, Sutcliffe's connection to computing had been increasing, and with International Computers and Tabulators (ICT) he became head of a new systems development department in Bracknell, Berkshire. ICT had its headquarters close to Deodar Road in Putney, and on his visits there he was able to nip across to Zinovieff's house, and discuss their shared interest in computer music. In 1968 Sutcliffe wrote a program on the mainframe at the recently formed International Computers Limited, and with output to punched paper tape, it was run on the PDP-8/S computer in Zinovieff's **EMS** studio. The collaboration resulted in the composition ZASP – the title an anagram of their initials – which won a prize in a computing competition in Edinburgh, at the International Federation for Information Processing Congress. During the event Sutcliffe instigated the formation of the influential Computer Arts Society, alongside George Mallen and John Lansdown, in order to bring together people working across different computing fields.

Sutcliffe and Zinovieff created a further collaborative piece, March Probabilistic, in 1968, which was played at the Queen Elizabeth Hall. A major concert of British electronic music in February 1969, again at London's QEH, included Sutcliffe's multi-media piece Spasmo, alongside work by **Harrison Birtwistle**, **Don Banks**, **Lawrence Casserley**, **Tristram Cary**, **Donald Henshilwood** and Peter Zinovieff. The performance addressed the problem of a lack of visual focus for tape music playback, by incorporating lights, a film, a selection of slides, a piano improvisation played by Sutcliffe, plus a computer printout of a poem included in the concert programme. At the projection of a slide of the moon, audience members were instructed to read out the computer composed text, based on a few words from Samuel Beckett's play Waiting for Godot.

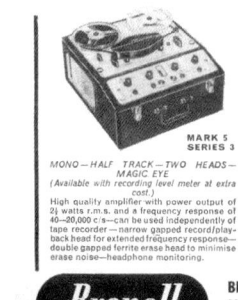

The Computer Arts Society organised Event One, at the Royal College of Art in March 1969, which included Sutcliffe's computer poem Likeness, and a collaboration with filmmaker Malcolm Le Grice, on a piece entitled Typodrama. Sutcliffe became a director of EMS in 1973, and carried on working with Zinovieff until 1979 when the company folded. With System Simulation Limited he developed computer animated sequences for the feature film Alien (1979), and he remained with the Computer Arts Society through to the mid-1980s, when the organisation wound down. It was regenerated in 2003, and right up until his death he continued his close involvement, editing the CAS bulletin PAGE.

In 1946 English Electric took over the Marconi Company, and in 1963 English Electric and J. Lyons and Co. combined to form English Electric LEO Company, which manufactured the LEO Computer developed by Lyons. English Electric took over Lyons' half-stake in 1964, and merged it with Marconi's computer interests to form English Electric Leo Marconi. A further merger with Elliott Automation and International Computers and Tabulators, formed International Computers Limited (ICL) in 1968, with the company operational until 2002.

```
POEM 2413               FOR SPASMO               ALAN SUTCLIFFE
COMPOSED USING ICL 1904    INTERNATIONAL COMPUTERS LIMITED

WHEN YOU SEE THE MOON PLEASE SAY THIS POEM BEGINNING QUIETLY



PLANETS                                                          LIKETWIGS
HAIL                                                             LIKEFLESH
                             LIKES                          LIKE GRASS
                             LIKESC                              LIKETWIGS



     LIKEWARP      LIKEWAVES      LIKECOPPER     LIKECARNAGE    LIKERAINBOWS       LIKE
     LIKESNOW      LIKEGRASS      LIKESTICKS     LIKESILENCE    LIKE               LIKE
     LIKESOIL      LIKEFLESH      LIKEGRAVEL     LIKEFREEDOM    LIKECIRCUITS       LIKE
                   LIKE  BRASS    LIKE  BRICKS                                     TWIGS
                   LIKE  TWIGS    LIKE  LOAVES                                     STARS
                   LIKE  STARS    LIKE  LEAVES                                     WAVES
                   LIKE  WAVES    LIKE  COPPER                                     FLESH
                   LIKE  FLESH    LIKE  GRAVEL                                     GRASS
                   LIKE  GRASS    LIKE  STICKS                                     BLOOD
                   LIKE  BLOOD    LIKE  BRAINS                                     TEARS



     LIKEHAIL      LIKEFLESH      LIKEGRAVEL     LIKEFREEDOM    LIKECIRCUITS
     LIKESOIL      LIKEWAVES      LIKECOPPER     LIKECARNAGE    LIKERAINBOWS
     LIKERAIN      LIKEGRASS      LIKESTICKS     LIKESILENCE    LIKE



     LIKEHAIL      LIKEWAVES      LIKECOPPER     LIKECARNAGE    LIKERAINBOWS
     LIKEDARK      LIKEGRASS      LIKESTICKS     LIKESILENCE    LIKE
     LIKERAIN      LIKEFLESH      LIKEGRAVEL     LIKEFREEDOM    LIKECIRCUITS
```

Robert Swain (1947)

Born: Cardiff
Earliest Electronic Work: Skyline for Chamber Group and Tape (1969)
Commitment Factor: 2
Obscurity Quotient: 9
EM recording availability: Poor

Studying at the University College of Wales in Cardiff, with Alun Hoddinott and Arnold Whittall, Swain has spent the bulk of his professional career holding posts in music education, and in 1989 he became HM Inspector for Education and Training in Wales. His own musical work involving composition, arranging and performing, has seen regular commissions and performances, as well as broadcasts on BBC radio.

John Tavener (1944-2013)

Born: Wembley, London
Earliest Electronic Work: The Whale (1966)
Commitment Factor: 4
Obscurity Quotient: 2
EM recording availability: Good

Educated at Highgate School in London, Tavener displayed an early liking for hymns, and began conducting and playing organ at St. John's church in Kensington. He won a place at the Royal Academy of Music where his teachers included Lennox Berkeley: he also received tuition from fellow composer **David Lumsdaine**, who shared his interest in contemporary music. Despite his traditional, religious leanings, Tavener was drawn to the experimentation of the 1960s, and by the time he left the Academy, he already had several compositions under his belt. He felt that contemporary music was in a cul-de-sac, and in 1965 he set about writing a biblical based cantata, and finished The Whale, the following year. It was premiered in 1968 at the inaugural concert of the London Sinfonietta, and included tape, amplified percussion, loudhailers and an improvising section. The piece was a sensation and catapulted the flamboyant young composer into the spotlight, and the attention of **The Beatles**.

Both Ringo Starr and John Lennon were impressed with The Whale, and it was issued on the Apple label in 1970, with Ringo attending rehearsals and appearing on the recording.

In 1967 Tavener completed his unpublished opera Notre Dame Des Fleurs, based on a book by Jean Genet, and created using Revox tape recorder and basic electronic equipment. A recording session featured David Lumsdaine at the Revox, Edward Lucie-Smith chanting a blasphemous litany, and Tavener assailing the organ. His Celtic Requiem (1968), was also released on Apple, and he composed other pieces with tape parts, including In Alium (1968), for an ensemble with strings, Hammond organ, gongs and four track tape. This composition was premiered at the 68 Proms season, and won an audience voting system to choose a replay of one piece in the programme. For both performances the tape recorder was operated by **BBC Radiophonic Workshop** soundman and engineer, Richard Yeoman-Clark.

In 1977, Tavener joined the Russian Orthodox Church, and his music moved into a spiritual phase after his earlier experimentation, gaining wide mainstream acceptance. His piece Song for Athene, was performed at the funeral of Princess Diana in 1997, and three years later he received a knighthood for services to music. His own funeral took place at Winchester Cathedral in November 2013, where several of his spiritual works were played during the service.

CD: John Tavener: The Whale + Celtic Requiem (Apple, 2010 reissue).

35mm slide montage by Ian Helliwell

Stephen Trowell (1948)

Born: Hertford
Earliest Electronic Work: Gabriel, Piano and Forte (1968)
Commitment Factor: 2
Obscurity Quotient: 9
EM recording availability: Poor

As a youngster in the late 1950s, Trowell was made aware of modern European composers through picking up German radio broadcasts, and recalled hearing music from the Proms and the Cheltenham Music Festival, while studying for his school exams. Although his professional career took him into the world of banking where he worked until retirement in 1996, he carried on some private studies in piano and music theory until 1970. He became firm friends with **Hugh Davies**, and experimented with electronics in several pieces, while remaining mainly outside the contemporary music establishment. Nonetheless, his Gabriel, Piano and Forte, was performed at the Arts Lab in London in August 1968, alongside a tape work by fellow outsider **Cyril Clouts**. Trowell's composition was scored for piano, monochord, ring modulator, tape and live electronics, which Guardian reviewer Meirion Bowen described as "*pleasurable without being overtly sadistic.*"

He worked on two other experimental tape pieces; Radio Music I (1971), which was assembled from short wave sounds, and the unfinished Radio Music II (1972), realised at the Goldsmiths electronic music studio, using manipulated acoustic sources. The recording at Goldsmiths was part of an initiative run by Davies with a grant from the SPNM, to originate a number of new tape works. In March 1968 Trowell was one of four performers at the London Planetarium, in the premiere of Galactic Interfaces, by Davies.

Trowell has tended to work slowly on his music, and consequently has only a small number of compositions to his name; most often credited to his alter-ego, Stephen Peter Lawson. He has had performances internationally, while much of his time has been taken up with administering the British Music Society, which sets out to champion the work of lesser known traditional classical composers.

Edgar Vetter (1913-1988)

Born: London
Earliest Electronic Work: ?
Commitment Factor: 4
Obscurity Quotient: 8
EM recording availability: Limited

In his early life, Edgar Alfred James Vetter found work in the film industry in Wardour Street, Soho, London. He served as a war correspondent during World War II, and the rest of his career was focussed on sound engineering and recording. His expertise saw him involved with a number of British companies, including Jupiter Recordings, Poetic Films Ltd. and Leomark Recordings. In 1960 he contributed to ATR magazine, detailing the complex stereo recording operation of a staging of Der Rosenkavalier, at the Salzburg Opera House. Two years later he co-founded Edgar Vetter-John Cape Ltd, a recording studio based at 27 Soho Square, London. The company offered mixing, dubbing, editing, mastering, a mobile recording service and a library of tape music and sound effects. Studio equipment included echo units, noise gates, compressors and a customised modular synthesizer.

In 1971 Vetter teamed up with composer, conductor, violinist and good friend William Merrick Farran (1912-1987), to produce an album of electronic tracks for library label KPM. Titled simply Electronic Music, it featured tape manipulation and sounds presumably generated with the custom synth at the Soho Square studio. Farran was a classical music veteran, able to compose in various styles, and known for his piece Symphonic Variations on a Rock 'n' Roll Theme, premiered in London in 1957. The pair collaborated again in 1972 to record Electronia, a second LP of library electronic tracks, this time for the Josef Weinberger label, and including the sounds of synthesizer, beating heart, coiled springs and tape loops. Farran featured on several more library labels, with releases on KPM and Bruton Music, while Vetter contributed a chapter on film music to the book Sound Recording Practice. First published in 1976, it was edited by John Borwick, and also contained articles by **Tristram Cary** and John Keating.

David Vorhaus (1943)

Born: Hollywood, California, USA
Earliest Electronic Work: Tapes for Oedipus (1967)
Commitment Factor: 10
Obscurity Quotient: 5
EM recording availability: Excellent

With his film directing father blacklisted, and facing persecution from the anti-communist backlash and witch-hunts of the McCarthy era, David Vorhaus and family left America and moved to mainland Europe. After stays in France, Switzerland and Italy, and with his father still undergoing surveillance from CIA agents, by 1953 they had finally settled in England. Vorhaus had piano lessons as a child and attended Holloway Comprehensive in London, with formative lessons in physics and music proving to be significant for the young student. A great influence was his music teacher George Self, who, like **Roy Cooper** and **Brian Dennis**, was a leading proponent of progressive teaching initiatives in British schools.

Completing a physics degree at Aberdeen University from 1962-66, and with post graduate study at North London Polytechnic in 1967, Vorhaus gained British citizenship, excusing him from the US military and conscription to Vietnam. He was playing double bass at this stage with the Morley College orchestra, but was only roughly acquainted with electronic music from Europe, and yet to experiment himself. This was to change however, following attendance of an inspirational college lecture by **Unit Delta Plus** during 1967. Afterwards he approached members **Delia Derbyshire** and **Brian Hodgson**, and as their group with **Peter Zinovieff** dissolved, a new collaboration was forged between Vorhaus and the two Radiophonic experimenters.

To begin with they set up in a London bedsit with three Revox tape recorders, subjecting natural sounds to various musique concrète tape treatments. Their first music commission later in 1967, was for a production of Oedipus, by British director Philip Saville, realised by Derbyshire and Vorhaus. A later commission from Ballet Rambert, required the recording of actresses' voices at the bedsit, leading

The Magnificent 70

Above, you see our new Arborite 70 range. The laminates for the seventies. It is made of all the best and most popular Arborite effects. Authentic woodgrains and marbles, subtle patterns and fresh plain colours.
Which is no news at all.
What is news, is the way we've organised

to sensitive neighbours calling the police, and an eviction notice being issued. This spurred on a move to 281-283 Camden High Street in North London, and the establishing of the Kaleidophon studio. Here recording for the **White Noise** An Electric Storm LP began, and during this period Vorhaus became more than just good friends with Derbyshire.

His electronic engineering skills and inventiveness, are displayed in both his Multiphasic ANalog Inter-Active Chromataphonic sequencer or MANIAC, and the Kaleidophon electronic double bass type instrument. MANIAC is a 64 step sequencer, and one of the first machines he co-constructed in the late 60s; a highly versatile and advanced design for its time. The Kaleidophon has a long upright neck with four ribbon controllers, and is played with one hand, while the other operates switches and a joystick to simulate a string action. Vorhaus is featured demonstrating and discussing his equipment, in the first-rate 1979 BBC TV documentary The New Sound of Music, presented by Screen Test compere and Tomorrow's World reporter Michael Rodd.

In 1974 Vorhaus provided sounds and effects for intelligent creepy-crawly, sci-fi shocker Phase IV, and during the 70s and 80s he composed library music principally for the label KPM. He supplied electronic sounds for a range of adverts, promotional films and documentaries, and his clients included manufacturers of Andrex and Alka Seltzer, and the nationalised industries for coal, gas and steel. He created music for the BBC Horizon series, and wrote the theme tune for Channel 4's Equinox science programmes, which aired from 1986-2001. In more recent years he has fully embraced digital technology, and remains committed to making electronic music, playing concerts in Europe and the Far East during 2013.

CDs:
White Noise: An Electric Storm (Island, 2007 reissue).
White Noise 2 (Virgin, 1975).

Margaret Lucy Wilkins (1939)

Born: Kingston Upon Thames, Greater London
Earliest Electronic Work: Music for an Exhibition (1970)
Commitment Factor: 5
Obscurity Quotient: 8
EM recording availability: Poor

As a talented youngster composing from the age of 12, Wilkins won a place at Trinity College of Music in London, and later studied at the University of Nottingham. Her teaching career began in 1964 as lecturer in music theory and piano, at the University of St. Andrews in Scotland, and from 1976-2003 she taught at the University of Huddersfield. She has received various awards and commissions, and her compositions have been widely performed. Heavily involved with contemporary music, she has served on the committees of the Composers' Guild of Great Britain, and the Society for the Promotion of New Music. In 1989 she founded the ensemble Polyphonia, to perform modern works.

In 1970 she was commissioned to create a musique concrète sound installation, for the Exhibition of Modern Sculpture show at Ledlanet in Scotland. A further installation piece, Sci-fi, came in 1973, commissioned by the Fine Art department of St. Andrews University, for a science fiction exhibition; the sound was put together in London at the Goldsmiths College electronic studio. Her large scale work Kanal, for 75 musicians, actors, dancers and electronic tapes, is a multi-media environmental experience, conceived for outdoor performance. It was first presented in 1990, incorporating words, music, light and a mobile oboe soloist.

Marc Wilkinson (1929)

Born: Paris, France
Earliest Electronic Work: Improvisation K (1957) Recorded in Italy
Commitment Factor: 4
Obscurity Quotient: 6
EM recording availability: Limited

Having studied composition at Columbia and Princeton Universities, and taken some private lessons with Edgard Varèse at his home in New York, Wilkinson's earliest known tape work Improvisation K, is from the time he was living in Italy and working at the RAI studio in Milan. Here he also made a recording of Henri Pousseur's Scambi (Exchanges) – a tape piece designed to be assembled in various ways with the realisation of several different versions – two by Pousseur, two by Luciano Berio and another by Wilkinson. Back in Britain, he kept up his Italian connection at the 1960 Dartington Summer School, where he gave a demonstration of electronic music alongside Bruno Maderna.

The BBC Third programme production of Anathema, featuring Wilkinson's electronic score, was produced by Douglas Cleverdon in 1962, and created at the **Radiophonic Workshop**. He met British director Lindsay Anderson at the Royal Court Theatre, and scored Anderson's version of Julius Caesar, and his superb British feature If.... (1968); Wilkinson's film soundtrack breakthrough. For a spell he was resident composer and musical director of the RSC, and then musical director at the National Theatre up until 1974. The score for Peter Shaffer's The Royal Hunt of the Sun, was one of the first he composed in his post at the National, and he also wrote incidental music for Shaffer's play Equus (1973).

He composed music for Shakespeare plays and other stage productions, including Tom Stoppard's Rosencrantz and Guildenstern Are Dead (1967), and Jumpers (1972), and met aspiring director Piers Haggard. The two had collaborated on a production of The Dutch Courtesan, in 1964, and Wilkinson was invited to score Haggard's first feature film Blood On Satan's Claw (1971). To create the atmospheric soundtrack he employed a classical orchestra,

VCS3 owned by Edward Williams

Edward Williams (1921-2013)

Born: Hindhead, Surrey
Earliest Electronic Work: Between the Tides (1958)
Commitment Factor: 8
Obscurity Quotient: 6
EM recording availability: Limited

Educated at Rugby School, Williams served in the Royal Navy during World War II. Back in civvy street in 1946, he became assistant to renowned film music conductor Muir Mathieson, and his career as a composer of soundtracks began in earnest two years later with his first commission. He formed a particularly fruitful relationship with British Transport Films, for which he scored 24 shorts. Among them was his first work with tape in 1958 for Between the Tides; an evocative documentary of coastal marine life around Britain at low tide. The film is a notable early example of electronic sound for a sponsored production, realised with the facilities and help of **Daphne Oram**. At that stage Williams had little equipment of his own, though after moving to Bristol in 1968, he purchased the first of several **EMS** VCS3 synthesizers a year or two later, and set up his studio in the family home.

His link with the synthesizer manufacturer EMS became much greater after the company went bankrupt in 1979, and Williams stepped in and took control in 1984. That year he worked with EMS designer Richard Monkhouse, and commissioned the ultrasonic movement reactive device, Soundbeam; initially developed for use by modern dancers to generate electronic sounds in live performance. Williams handed over the reins of EMS to current owner Robin Wood in 1995, and Soundbeam carried on as a separate company, which continues to manufacture and refine the system. Besides Soundbeam, Williams and his wife Judy, set up Elektrodome, to commission new performance works, and these interests as well as composing, carried on until his death. Although best known for his television scores including Life On Earth, and Excalibur: The Search for Arthur, he had an enthusiasm for experimental sound, as exemplified in his 1972 soundtrack for the documentary This Land, made for the Shell Film Unit.

augmented by cimbalom and the electronic keyboard instrument the Ondes Martenot. In his subsequent musical career he worked on various TV and film productions, including Quatermass, The Fiendish Plot of Dr. Fu Manchu, Play for Today, and Tales of the Unexpected. For the Hammer House of Horror series, he devised an electro-acoustic score for the episode Visitor from the Grave. Since retiring from composition he has settled in France, and his activities include writing and gardening.

Keith Winter (1940)

Born: London
Earliest Electronic Work: ?
Commitment Factor: 6
Obscurity Quotient: 8
EM recording availability: Poor

Having studied with Bernard Rands and Reginald Smith Brindle, Winter went on to work for the Arts Council from 1967-69. During his time there he compiled a British electronic music studio list published in 1969, which identified 40 studios, and contributed to the founding of the British Society for Electronic Music. He was also instrumental in securing grants for jazz and improvising musicians, including Evan Parker and Ian Carr. After leaving the Arts Council he took up a post at Cardiff University, and developed and directed the electronic music studio, established in 1971 as part of the Department of Physics. It was constructed around an **EMS** Synthi 100, a mainframe computer and smaller PDP-8; operating at the intersection of music, physics and psychoacoustics. While at Cardiff, Winter was actively involved in organising the publication of a twice yearly electronic music magazine, though the project was apparently short lived.

Among his compositions are Act Without Words, and The Time Flowers (1971), written with Neil Ardley for jazz soloists, orchestra and tape. For The Sinking of the Titanic album by Gavin Bryars, released in 1975, Winter gave technical assistance in the compiling of tapes, and played VCS3 synthesizer for progressive jazz fusion group Nucleus, on their fine album Solar Plexus (1971).

During 1977 he left Cardiff and relocated to Australia, and became a lecturer in the Music Department of La Trobe University in Melbourne. (This had been established in 1974 by electronic composer Keith Humble.) Winter taught there throughout the 1980s, for a time specialising in music programmes for the BBC microcomputer. He continued lecturing until the early 90s, by which time he was back in Britain and living in Devon, though more recently he is said to have returned to Australia.

The British Society for Electronic Music (BSEM) was an offshoot of the Society for the Promotion of New Music (SPNM). With a committee consisting of chairman Peter Maxwell Davies, plus **Peter Zinovieff**, **Don Banks**, **Tristram Cary**, **Hugh Davies** and James Murdoch, it was launched in 1969 with a concert at the Royal Festival Hall. Its main aim was the founding of a National Studio for Electronic Music, and as well as the studio facilities, the plan was to create an acoustic research laboratory, lecture and concert hall, and an audiovisual library. The dream unfortunately went unrealised, even though by the close of the 1980s the prospect was ostensibly very much alive. Before the BSEM could really get anywhere, the organisation was subsumed back into the SPNM, which in turn evolved into Sonic Arts Network and eventually Sound and Music.

The BSEM concert at the RFH on 30th June 1969, was titled Project: Electronic Music, and was presented by the SPNM in conjunction with The Pierrot Players, with an introduction by Milton Babbitt. It featured an Anglo-American, electro-acoustic programme of works by Babbitt, **Justin Connolly** & Peter Zinovieff, Mario Davidovsky, **Roberto Gerhard**, JK Randall, **Richard Orton** and Vladimir Ussachevsky.

Electronic music studio survey

Sir—I am conducting a survey of electronic music studios in Great Britain.

Perhaps some of your readers will know of studios either privately or collectively owned with which they could put me in touch. Some may even have their own equipment. In any case I would be grateful if they would contact me with any relevant information.

K. Winter,
The Arts Council of Great Britain,
105 Piccadilly, London, W.1.

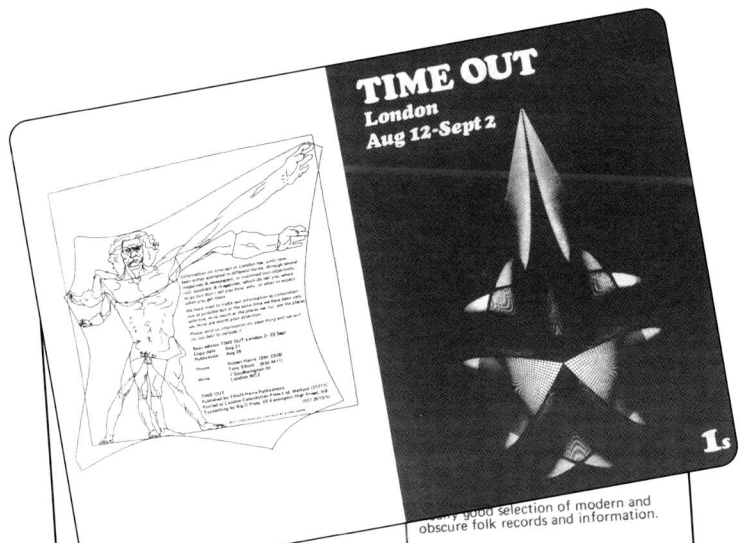

TIME OUT
London
Aug 12–Sept 2

FREE BOOKSHOP, Colherne Mews, Wharfedale Street SW10 (PAD 2409) for Free books! (Open 6pm–9pm 10am–6pm Sat & Sun)

DOBELLS JAZZ RECORD SHOP, 77 Charing Cross Road WC2 (437 3075) Widest selection of Jazz in London. Also comprehensive choice of folk LP's.

Ballet

ROYAL FESTIVAL HALL, South Bank (928 3191) London's Festival Ballet in 'The Sleeping Beauty' by Tchaikovsky. Seats 28/- to 7/6d Mon—Fri 7.30pm Sat 4 and 8pm. Until 31 Aug.

Electronic Music

COMPUTER MUSIC
29 Aug 'Music composed with and played by Computer'. Concert of taped computer music from the Experimental Music Studio at the University of Illinois, with works by Lejaren A. Hiller, Herbert Brun, Gary Grossman, James Cuomo etc.
ICA, Nash House, The Mall W1 (WHI 6393) 8pm Members 5/-, others 7/6d

ELECTRONIC MUSIC STUDIO SURVEY
The Arts Council is undertaking research into the present state of electronic music facilities in Great Britain. Certain studios are known of, but if readers know of studios either privately or collectively owned, could they please contact Keith Winter, Music Assistant, 105 Piccadilly W1.

This publication would like to list performances and performers of Electronic music in future editions. Would anyone with any information please contact us.

Trevor Wishart (1946)

Born: Leeds
Earliest Electronic Work: Machine (1969-71)
Commitment Factor: 7
Obscurity Quotient: 5
EM recording availability: Excellent

Although originally a student of chemistry, Wishart studied music at the Universities of Oxford (BA, 1968), Nottingham (MA, 1969) and York (PhD, 1973), and he is a composer, performer and writer on music and technology. Owning a tape recorder as a teenager, all his early composing was nevertheless in an orthodox form, though he was fascinated by the work of Greek composer Iannis Xenakis. He first came across electronic music by Karlheinz Stockhausen while a student at Oxford, and subsequently his tutor at York, **Richard Orton**, encouraged listening to American experimental music, involving improvisation and electro-acoustic composition.

Triggered by the death of his father, he began working with tape in 1969, and collected sounds with a portable recorder from power stations, factories and bottling plants around Leeds and Nottingham; environments which had a direct relevance to his dad's working life. This became the basis for his first large scale tape composition Machine – An electronically preserved dream, which was first issued in 1973 on the triple LP set Electronic Music from York.

Interested in devising studio tools and techniques for sound transformation, from 1973-77 he composed Red Bird, created in the form of a political prisoner's dream. It was intended as music and mythic narrative, structured around the morphing of voices, machines, animals and birds, using analogue studio processes, and directed improvisation.

For the BBC Sounds Different series, he was featured preparing a concert called Auto Music, in a Bristol scrap yard, involving an array of professional and student players improvising against a tape collage; this was one of several audio-visual environmental music events he created in the 1970s. He has written a number of books, including Whose Music? (1977), On Sonic Art (1985), and Audible Design (1994). His volume Sound Composition, discussing specific compositional projects, was published in 2012.

Various composer-in-residence positions have taken him to countries around the world, including Australia, USA, Canada, Sweden, Germany and Holland, and between 2006 and 2010, his base was at the University of Durham. He continues his research into speech and vocal sounds which he started in the mid-1970s, and while at Durham he worked on the electro-acoustic opera Encounters in the Republic of Heaven, centred on the dialect and speech of north east England, and premiered in 2011.

CD: Trevor Wishart: Machine (Paradigm, 2008).

Geoffrey Wright (1912-2010)

Born: Kingston upon Thames, Greater London
Earliest Electronic Work: Catharsis (1961)
Commitment Factor: 1
Obscurity Quotient: 9
EM recording availability: Poor

At Stowe school in Buckingham, Wright was able to study piano and set design, and in 1931 he won an organ scholarship to Corpus Christi College, Cambridge. He joined the Footlights drama club, and wrote music and designed sets for several stage productions. In 1935 he received his first break into the theatrical world of London's West End, and this set the scene for much of his later career. After military service during World War II as a Royal Navy signaller, he returned to composing for the stage, with pieces for mime and ballet. He worked on soundtracks for a number of films before and after the war, including A Ship in the Bay (1939), Peril for the Guy (1956) and How to Undress in Public Without Undue Embarrassment (1965).

In 1961 at his own ad hoc studio, he composed a score which included a tape part for Catharsis, a ballet staged at Morley College, London. This appears to be his only work with electronics during his varied musical life, which lasted until retirement to Suffolk in 1975.

Peter Zinovieff (1933-2021)

Born: London
Earliest Electronic Work: Chorus from the Bacchae (1962)
Commitment Factor: 8
Obscurity Quotient: 4
EM recording availability: Excellent

Born to aristocratic Russian parents who had met in London after emigrating to escape the Russian Revolution, Zinovieff was educated at Guildford Royal Grammar School, Gordonstoun School, and Oxford University, earning a doctorate in geology. Following this he worked for a time as a mathematician for the MOD, and married into a wealthy family, allowing him to give up everyday work and focus on his childhood passion for electronics. Like **Tristram Cary** and many other British experimenters, he scoured second hand shops in Lisle Street in London for war surplus equipment to cannibalise for parts, and began to assemble a collection of waveform generators. With an inventive streak and interested in music, he set up his first home studio in Ebury Street in Belgravia, London, in 1962, and was shown tape cutting rudiments by **Daphne Oram**. He made sound recordings, but was dissatisfied with the fiddly and time consuming nature of tape splicing, inspiring him to build an elementary electromechanical sequencer out of telephone relays, to circumvent the process.

Establishing a well equipped studio in his back garden in Putney overlooking the Thames in 1965, he met **Delia Derbyshire** and **Brian Hodgson**, and formed **Unit Delta Plus**. He worked with Mark Dowson until 1966, and was introduced to NHS technician and electronics engineer David Cockerell, who designed and built various oscillators and voltage controlled circuits, until it was decided to harness the capabilities of computer process control. By 1967 Zinovieff had purchased his first DEC PDP-8/S computer costing around £4800, and the only one to be privately owned in Britain. (His first two computers were christened Leo and Sofka after two of his children.) During this period Unit Delta Plus dissolved, and **EMS** was formed; Zinovieff and Cockerell were joined by Tristram Cary, who brought in his experience of electronic engineering and tape music composition. Besides heading the company, Zinovieff undertook a series of musical collaborations which enabled **Alan Sutcliffe**, **Justin Connolly** and **Harrison Birtwistle**, to realise electronic pieces with him in the EMS studio. In 1968 he contributed to the Cybernetic Serendipity exhibition at the ICA in London, which included his computer system installation with interactive microphone input, inviting visitors to whistle a tune for the computer to analyse and play back with electronic variations. Being a trailblazer in the development of British computer music, he had discussions with his counterparts in the USA, including Max Matthews, one of the founders of creative music computing at Bell Labs in New Jersey.

Zinovieff worked on the soundtracks for two excellent British feature films, The Executioner (1970) and The Offence (1972). For the latter film score by Birtwistle, played by the London Sinfonietta, he created the electronic realisation. Although he did not produce the synthesized parts, he further collaborated with Birtwistle by writing the libretto for the epic opera The Mask of Orpheus, which included inventing a language to be heard in Act 3. A complex and time consuming project running over several years, it was finally premiered in 1986. Involved with German composer Hans Werner Henze in the early 70s, he worked on another large scale work; the six movement Tristan, for piano, tape and orchestra, from 1973.

By the mid-1970s EMS was running into financial difficulties, and Zinovieff's first marriage was on the rocks. The house in Deodar Road was sold and he moved from Putney to Great Milton in Oxfordshire, and subsequently to the remote island of Raasay in Scotland. His cottage had no mains electricity supply, and his surviving EMS filter bank was run from a series of car batteries charged up by a windmill. Before long he moved back to England and settled in Cambridge, and during the 1980s received two commissions from Cambridge based electronics mastermind Clive Sinclair. One of them was for a ZX Spectrum home computer music demonstration, but after that Zinovieff left electronic sound behind for the next couple of decades, while picking up on his early interest in geology.

As a key figure in early British electronic music, he features in the documentaries The Same Trade As Mozart (1969), The New Sound of Music (1979), and What the Future Sounded Like (2007). With a renewed compositional zeal, and characteristically still working in collaboration, he had in recent years fully embraced modern music-making software to realise his ideas. The album RFG Inventions for Cello and Computer, by Zinovieff and cellist Lucy Railton, was released in 2020.

CD: Peter Zinovieff: Electronic Calendar The EMS Tapes (Space Age Recordings, 2014).

PDP-8/s*

THE SOURCE OF MUSIC

digital

DIGITAL EQUIPMENT CORP. (U.K.) LTD., Arkwright Road, Reading, Berks.
Tel: Reading 85131

* Basic PDP-8/S digital computer — used with music, FORTRAN, or equipment control programmes.   £4,800 complete

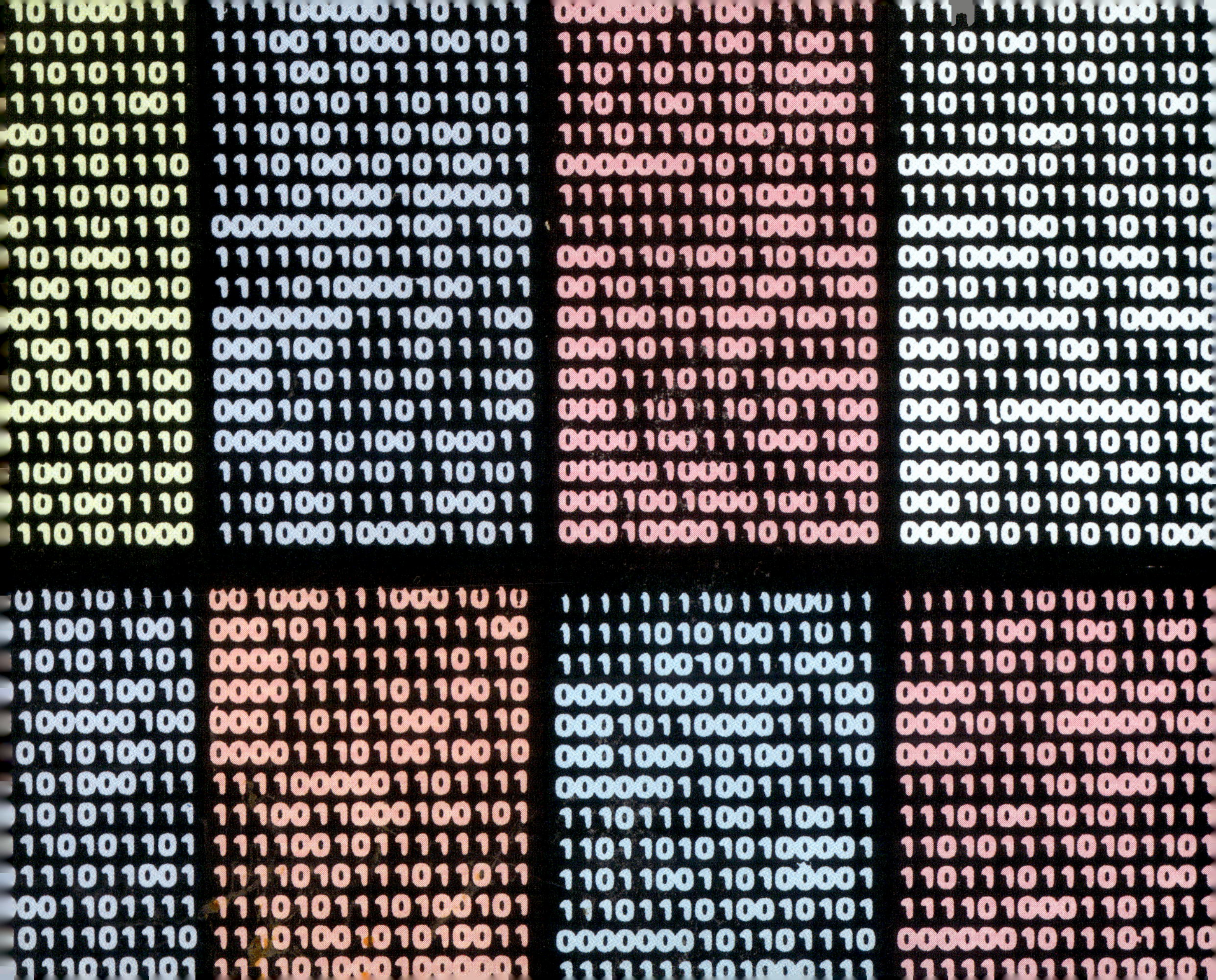

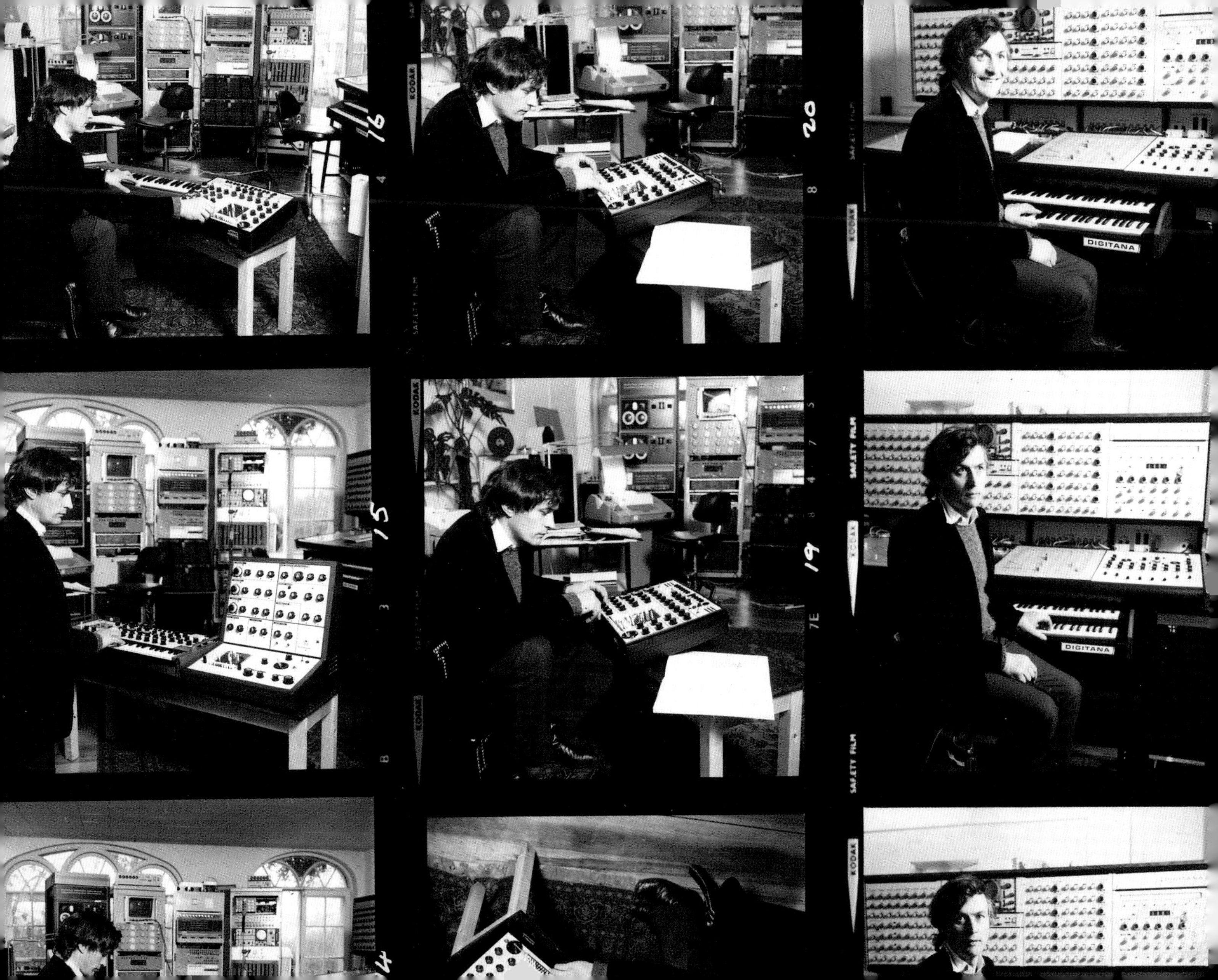
KODAK
SAFETY FILM
16
20
15
19
DIGITANA
DIGITANA

② EXPERIMENTAL AMATEURS

EXPERIMENTAL AMATEURS - OVERVIEW

The British amateur tape recording scene flourished from the late 1950s, with dozens of clubs springing up right across the country. For the most part members' interests were conventional and straightforward, with much activity based around actuality recordings, hospital radio broadcasts, recordings for the blind and tapespondence; the communication via tapes sent through the post, between clubs, relatives and friends. To a much lesser degree, but significant nonetheless, there was a small but strong interest in musique concrète and electronic music, with lectures and demonstrations a reasonably common feature of club meetings, particularly in the first half of the 1960s.

The term musique concrète seems most appropriate here, as experimentation with extremely limited equipment was often centred on the manipulation of taped sounds recorded with a simple microphone, before dedicated and versatile electronic instruments became available and affordable for the amateur. As time wore on and tastes and interests changed amongst tape club members, musique concrète and the excitement of experimentation evidently dwindled, and the term dropped out of fashion. Seeing as the techniques were rather interchangeable anyway, electronic music became the catch-all description, and by the 1970s encompassed work with synthesizers, an area that the older generation of tape club members had much less interest in. During 1973, Practical Electronics magazine introduced the 'P.E. Sound Synthesiser'; designed by G.D. Shaw, it was one of the first synth construction projects available for hobbyists, and as tape clubs began to wane, it signalled a new wave of amateur electronic music-making.

Back in the 1950s and 60s, many households in Britain still had an upright piano, and the instrument was an obvious starting point for musique concrète experiments. Often ignoring the keyboard and playing the open strings – then recording, splicing, reversing, looping and playing back at different speeds – opened up a wealth of possibilities for generating sound material with very limited resources. **FC Judd** appeared on the BBC radio programme, Sound, in June 1962, discussing and demonstrating musique concrète. He played an extract of an ingenious composition he had created with the single sound from tapping a china bowl, and the piece expertly revealed what could be done with such a restricted starting point. Presenter Douglas Brown thanked Mr. Judd for his demonstration, yet ungraciously warned that listeners might wish to pursue activities that required less effort.

Circuit diagrams useful for tape experimenters had appeared in 1961 with Fred Judd's book Electronic Music and Musique Concrète, and the construction of homemade equipment represented another important strand of amateur activity. Mixers, oscillators, ring modulators and even complete tape recorders were built by enthusiasts, and the more seriously

Views of the Audio Fair at the Hotel Russell, London, in 1963. Bottom photo shows John Leyton, FC Judd and Julie Grant.

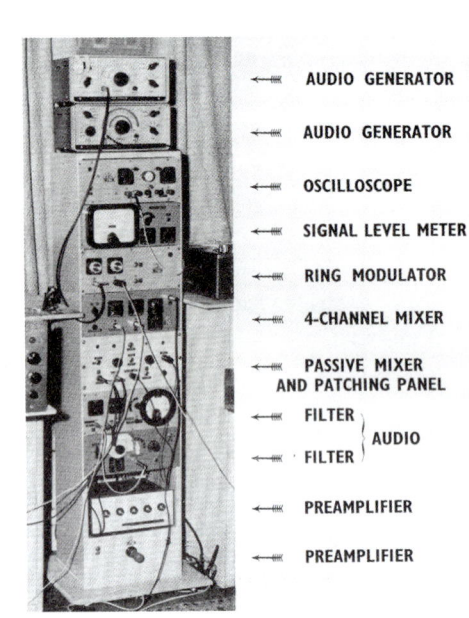

Studio equipment of FC Judd, early 1960s

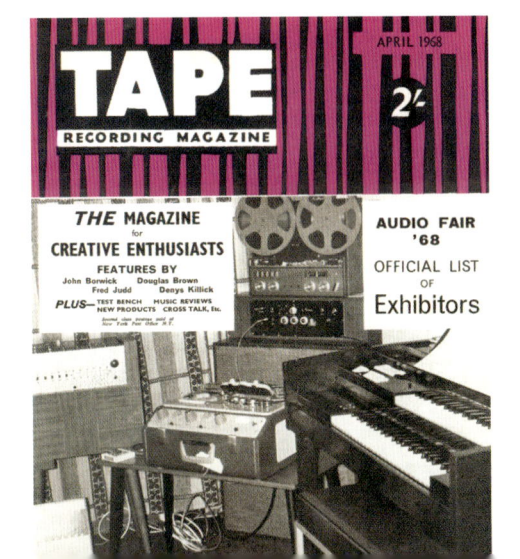

committed constructed their own recording dens at home; in spare rooms, garages, sheds, under the stairs or even in the lounge. With typical make-do-and-mend initiative, tape clubs with premises would often pool their resources and equipment, and kit out and sound proof their own recording spaces.

A remarkable range of magazines published from the 1950s through to the 1970s, catered for the widespread interest in tape and electronics. These included Tape Recording, Amateur Tape Recording, The Tape Recorder, Practical Wireless, Practical Electronics, Wireless World, Radio Constructor, Everyday Electronics, Hi-Fi News, Electronics Today International and Elektor. The merged Everyday Practical Electronics is the sole magazine that still exists for hobbyist electronics enthusiasts.

The British Amateur Tape Recording Contest (BATRC) was established in 1957 as an annual competition for hobbyists to submit their work, and allowed entries in several different categories, including Compositions, Music and Speech, and Documentary and Reportage. The Technical Experiment class was reserved mainly for recordings of musique concrète and electronic music. The BATRC was affiliated to a European network of tape clubs, organised by the International Federation of Sound Hunters, and the best of the winning British entries went forward into a continental championship. The British Sound Recording Association, who continued to administer the amateur contest into the 21st century, only voted to wind up operations in 2014.

The BBC radio programme, Sound, dedicated to audio production, aired a number of the winning entries in the early 1960s, and for the 1963 competition, presenter Douglas Brown – in his role as editor of Tape Recording magazine – reported on that year's results. In his analysis of the contest he wrote that "*disappointingly few tapes (were) submitted in the Technical Experiment class.*" He went on to comment, "*British recording enthusiasts, I can report, are trailing a long way behind their Continental friends in this field of technical experiment. Potentially, it is one of the most fascinating fields for activity; but we have barely scratched the surface yet.*" Considering his previous comments regarding Fred Judd's china bowl composition on the programme Sound, his position was emblematic of an ambivalent and unsupportive attitude towards amateur electronic music making in Britain, and it comes as no surprise that many people at the time regarded it as a peculiar or pointless pursuit.

Running parallel to the electronics and tape recording scene, was a very similar world of amateur filmmaking, which shared much of the same hobbyist initiative and local organisation. The formation of dozens of cine clubs across the British Isles had started much earlier, and

TOP OF THE TAPES

while they operated on more or less the same basis, there appears to have been a limited crossover and exchange in tape clubs providing soundtracks for amateur film productions. Published since the 1930s, Amateur Cine World was the foremost magazine in the filmmaking field, and organised the Ten Best competition for amateur movies; similar in spirit to the BATRC.

One niche area quite particular to the cine experimenters, but relevant to electronic music, is in the generation of synthetic sound. This is made audible via the optical film projector, whereby a soundtrack is created graphically; usually by drawing or scratching directly on film, or less commonly by exposing images with the photogram technique in a dark room, or animating with an adapted camera. The varying patterns of light and dark made in the soundtrack area of film are illuminated, registered by a photocell and interpreted as voltage changes – translated into audible sound by the projector's reproducing and amplifying system. A number of amateurs were exploring synthetic sound in the 1950s, and were well advanced with audio experiments in comparison to many composers in the music world.

THE 1967 BRITISH AMATEUR TAPE RECORDING CONTEST

Entry forms complete with the rules and recording categories for the 1967 BATR Contest are already available from the offices of the sponsor magazines and the BATR Contest office at 42 Manchester Street, London W1. We shall be including the full entry form and rules in the next (June) issue of *ATR*.

1. **Speech and Drama.** This includes sketches, playlets, prose and poetry reading, fantasy and monologue. Maximum recording time 10 minutes.
2. **Documentary.** Sound stories based on fact, informative, imaginative and/or entertaining travelogues. Maximum recording time 10 minutes.
3. **Music.** Live vocal or instrumental performances Maximum recording time 10 minutes.
4. **Reportage.** Interesting sounds, interviews and on-the-spot reports on events. Maximum recording time 4 minutes.
5. **Technical Experiment.** Sound composition, electronic music, *musique concrète*, trick recording (voices, etc.) and multi-track music. Maximum recording time 4 minutes.
6. **Schools.** Recording on any subject, produced mainly by the pupils. Three classes – infants up to 7 years, juniors – 7-12 years and senior – over 12 years.

141

Letter printed in Tape Recording magazine, September 1958

THIS ISN'T MUSIC

LIKE Mr. Tams, I have been using my tape recorder to compile musique concrete, but find myself unable to share his opinion that it is a "musical tool."

The fact of the matter is that musique concrete is neither music nor art. These weird sounds may give technical satisfaction to the man who has strung them together, but can never convey emotion in the same way as conventional music.

To anyone who feels this is unfair criticism, I would ask them to listen to the work of Henry and Schæffer (available on two Ducretet-Thomson L.P.s). The work that must have gone into producing these pieces must have been considerable—various sounds are ingeniously distorted, played backwards and speeded up.

But the listener derives no pleasure from these eccentric compositions; the most he can do is to marvel at the technique.

DAVID HARDING.
Cheam.

Letter printed in ATR magazine, April 1961

Mr. B. J. WHELDON of Aughton, Nr. Ormskirk, writes:

I have been following your articles in 'ATR' with great interest — particularly those relating to Electronic Music. Your 'How to make Modern Music with a Tape Recorder' in this February magazine was fine and I would like to build the two circuits which you described as the Automatic Bell Gate and the Controlled Bell Gate. You do state in the first paragraph that the circuits are for the technical types — unfortunately I happen to be the in-between type, e.g. I can read the circuits and I can build them too, quite successfully, but I don't as yet know how to evaluate them and arrive at individual items.

Would you therefore be so kind as to tell me what the H.T. voltage would be for both the above Bell Gates and in the Controlled Gate (Fig. 3) what type of valve would be suitable — also the most suitable diode for XI.

ANSWER.—*H.T. voltages for the circuit you mention are not critical. Between 250 and 300 volts will be in order.*

The flexibility, speed and ease with which tape could be recorded on and manipulated however, tended to make optoacoustic experimentation a specialist sphere, but the results yield a distinctive form of electronic sound, and the process is still a fascinating if painstaking one to explore.

It seems that for much of the general public in Britain, the more abstract realm of music – especially that made with electronics and tape recorders – was something they struggled to understand and accept. They either dismissed it as horrible noise, or saw it purely in terms of its functional use, particularly the obvious association with science fiction. During the 1960s the saturated hobbyist magazine market was inevitably unsustainable, and one of the most interesting and useful – Amateur Tape Recording – folded in 1967, shortly after the demise of Amateur Cine World. Three years later Tape Recorder merged with Studio Sound, and this was symptomatic of the shift in magazine content towards hi-fi and professional studio gear. The bulk of features became focussed on evaluating audio equipment, while reports and enthusiasm for the activites of amateurs and tape clubs, suffered a sharp decline.

A valedictory article in Tape Recorder in April 1970 by regular columnist Dropout, summed up the prevailing downbeat mood for the new decade. With the writing on the wall he stated, "*recording clubs languish and die, and the movement can no longer hold its principal journal to its old allegiance.*" He further commented, "*The truth, as I see it, is that recording as a hobby is one of the greatest flops of all time... with reluctance, I have come to the conclusion that most amateur recordists have no interests with which tape can help them, or they have not the imagination to see what those interests might be.*"

Despite Dropout's bleak conclusion, for some hobbyists, musique concrète and electronic sound generation did fire their imagination, opening up exciting and hitherto unexplored horizons. Often lacking encouragement or a sympathetic audience, they nevertheless delved wholeheartedly into this new form of music; conducting experiments with tone generators, tape recorders, microphones, modulators and synthetic sounds. Having been neglected and unacknowledged for so long, it is now a particularly difficult task to identify and trace hobbyist tape composers and electronic enthusiasts from a bygone age; it is hoped that many more will come forward as evidence is unearthed. Here is just a small selection of some of those exploratory amateurs.

Denis B. Affleck (1906-1976)

Born: Swindon, Wiltshire
Earliest Electronic Work: Experiments with Reversed Speech (1961)
Commitment Factor: 6
Obscurity Quotient: 9
EM recording availability: Poor

In 1961 the British Amateur Tape Recording Contest (BATRC) results, showed the Technical Experiment class was won by Denis Affleck. The 55 year old telephone engineer of 248 Park Road, Peterborough, came top with his tape piece Experiments With Reversed Speech. He made further explorations into electronic manipulation of voice recordings with the track The Double Reverse, another BATRC winner in 1963, beating **Ralph Broome** into second place. That year Tape Recording magazine reviewed his efforts: "*Mr. Affleck had developed further an idea which he tried in an entry the previous year. Then he had analysed speech sounds by recording and playing backwards. This time he imitated the sound of speech played backwards, recorded his imitations and then compared that recording, played backwards, with normal speech. Double Reverse – Get it?*"

In November 63, Affleck visited the Boston Soundhunters in Lincolnshire, to discuss his tape experiments at one of their regular recording club meetings. He made one more appearance amongst the BATRC finalists with his composition Chewed Tape, in 1973, and it seems his enthusiasm for experimental recording lasted right up until his death three years later.

Denis Affleck

Ralph O. Broome (1928-1998)

Born: Sheffield
Earliest Electronic Work: Science Fiction Background (1959)
Commitment Factor: 8
Obscurity Quotient: 8
EM recording availability: Limited

Resident at 145 Sprotborough Road, Doncaster, Ralph Oscar Broome was employed as a technician in a local radio sales and repair shop. He became a member of the Doncaster and District Tape Recording Club, and was elected Technical Adviser in 1966. He is one of the very few early British electronic music amateurs to have a work released on record; his composition Nuclear Madness, was issued on a Telefunken 7" promotional disc, which featured a selection of tracks from the 9th International Tape Recording competition, held in the autumn of 1960. The piece had been a winner at the British Amateur Tape Recording Contest, and set the scene for several other well regarded entries in the Technical Experiment class.

His enigmatically titled K.U.P.P.N.N. was placed in 1962, and Eldritch, was a runner up the following year. The equipment he used on the track consisted of two home-made tape recorders, and a self-built oscillator and tremolo unit. Tape Recording magazine bluntly described Eldritch as "*a piece of electronic music of the orthodox type... but nothing in this field is orthodox. The judges felt that, while he had worked hard on its composition, its development and meaning did not emerge sufficiently clearly and that it was inadequately shaped.*"

For a competition held by the Tape Recorder magazine in 1959, Broome attended an awards presentation in London, alongside fellow prize winners **FC Judd**, **John Harper** and **Stuart Wynn Jones**. The contest for amateur tape music, saw him awarded a Simon Cadenza ribbon microphone, presented by Jean Clark, for his piece Science Fiction Background. Sadly none of Ralph Broome's equipment or tapes have survived, though a copy of the Telefunken 7" record has been unearthed at a car boot sale.

The judging panel for the 1959 Tape Recorder magazine competition for '2 minute tapes of new style music', consisted of **Desmond Briscoe, Daphne Oram, Tristram Cary**, John Borwick, Miles Henslow and Ernest Tomlinson.

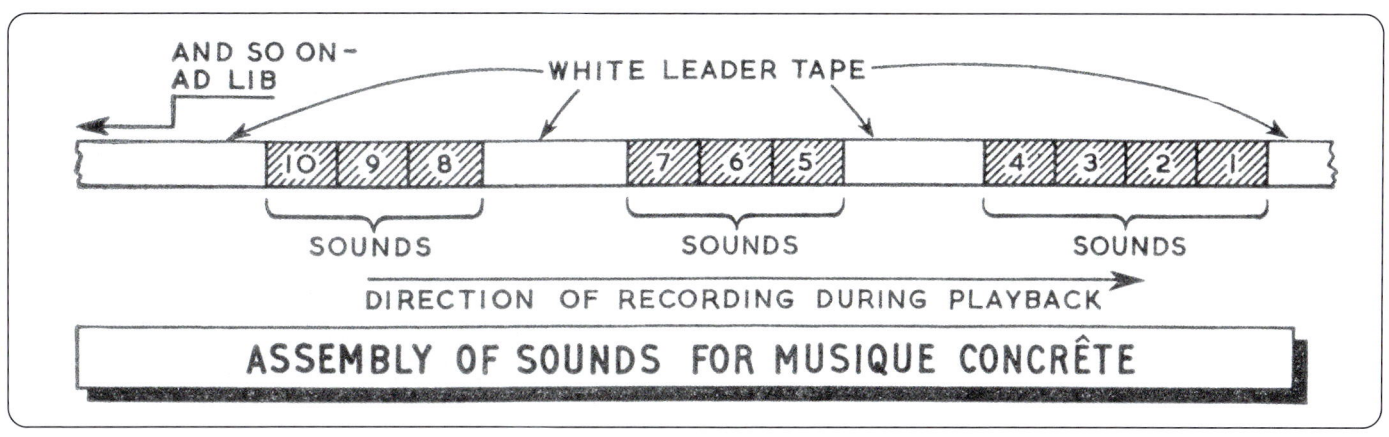

ASSEMBLY OF SOUNDS FOR MUSIQUE CONCRÊTE

Paul R. Carnell (1944)

Born: St. Albans, Hertfordshire
Earliest Electronic Work: Synthetic soundtracks (1958)
Commitment Factor: 2
Obscurity Quotient: 9
EM recording availability: Poor

Teenage film enthusiast Paul Carnell, was working with the 9.5mm cine format at home towards the end of the 1950s, and produced a number of direct animation films including Zat (1958), Snowflakes (1958), Bird Feed (1959), Oola Oops (1959), A Whale of a Whale (1959), and Men From Mars (1959). These are highly notable not only for the tender age of their creator, but for the combination of image and sound drawn directly onto the film strip. Similar to **Stuart Wynn Jones**, Carnell had seen some of the renowned animations by Scottish born Norman McLaren, and became aware of the technique of drawing or etching marks into the soundtrack area of film, to create optophonically generated synthetic sounds.

His efforts garnered some recognition in Amateur Cine World (ACW) magazine's annual Ten Best competition, but in the early 60s he switched his attention to making more conventional 16mm puppet films. His enthusiasm for 9.5mm film increased however, and he went into business distributing equipment and film prints devoted to the gauge. In 1962 he made available an abstract film, Cariolo, alongside comedies, cartoons, striptease and special interest shorts.

Trading as Nine Five Cine from 46 Hill Street, St. Albans, Herts, he offered an optical sound recording service for users of the format, initially at a cost of 9d per foot. In an interview with ACW in October 1964, he compared the advantages of 9.5mm over its more diminutive rival and stated that, "*The 8mm boffins are trying to get a quart into a pint pot!*" Carnell currently lives in London, though regrettably he no longer has the experimental films he made as a 15 year old boy.

> Besides **Paul Carnell** and **Stuart Wynn Jones**, other British amateurs who created films with synthetic directly animated sound include: Mervyn Collard: Hit (1957); Philip Grosset: Phantasmagoria in Three Violet Fits (1957); **Derek Purslow**: The Runaway Train (1959), Flight of the Bumble Bee (1959), and Oceans of Notions (1960).

35mm slide montage by Ian Helliwell

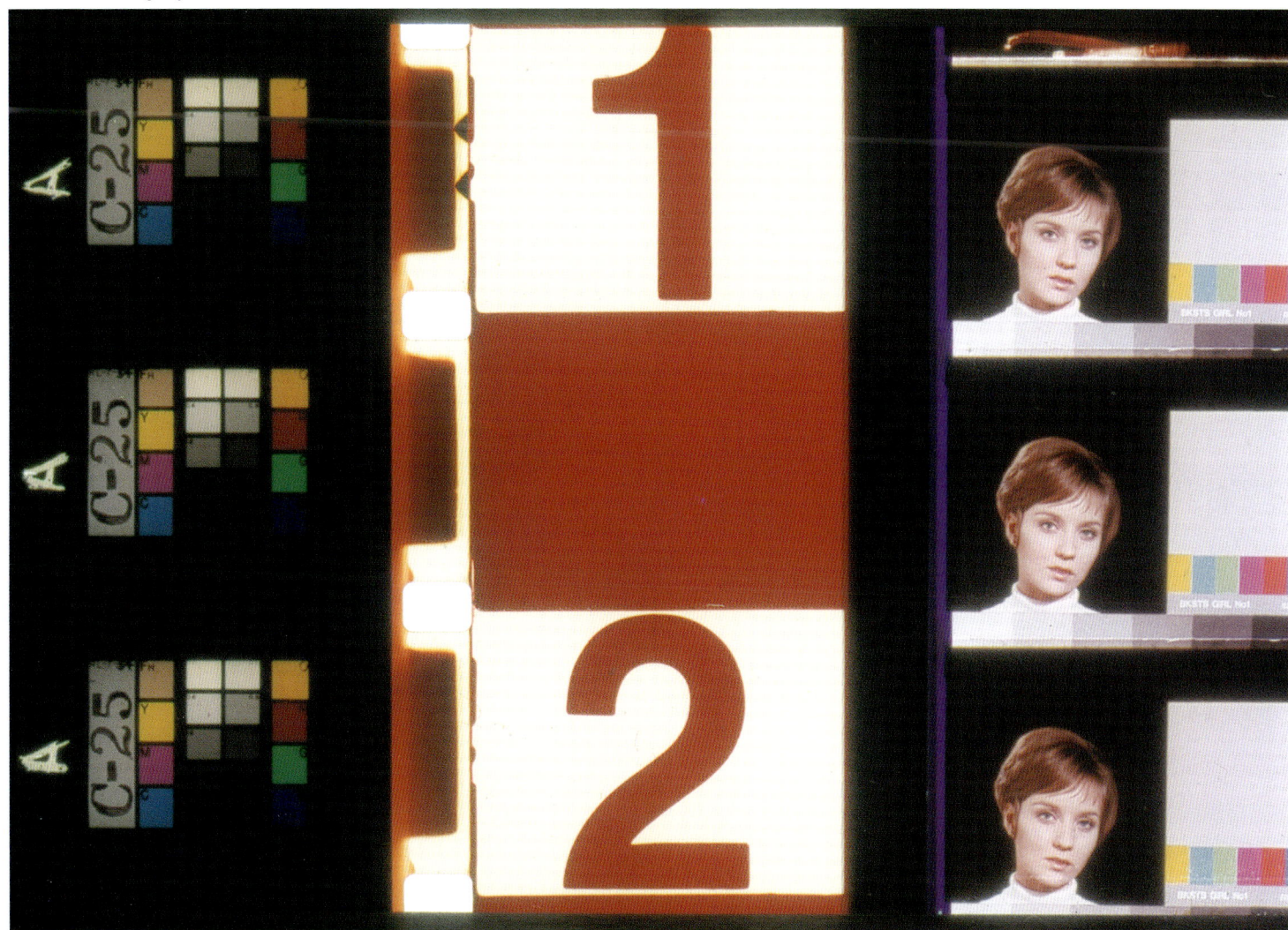

Steve Duckworth and studio, early to mid 1970s

Steve Duckworth (1948)

Born: Bardon Hill, Leicestershire
Earliest Electronic Work: Untitled tapes (1969)
Commitment Factor: 10
Obscurity Quotient: 7
EM recording availability: Limited

With a childhood interest in tape recorders, and carrying out his earliest musique concrète style experiments at the age of 10, the youthful Duckworth initially got started with the loan of a Philips tape machine from an older cousin, and was inspired by an item on television about the **BBC Radiophonic Workshop**. Harbouring a dream to work there as an adult, his abiding interest in electronic sound was further developed in 1968, with the purchase of his own Ferrograph tape recorder, which allowed for more sophisticated techniques to be explored.

He was an avid reader of any literature on electronic music that he could lay his hands on, and discovered that articles by **FC Judd** were particularly useful. Having built various circuits designed by Judd, plus his own cross-fading mixer, he purchased an off-the-shelf mixing unit from a shop in London. This proved to be less effective than hoped, but with a spot of creative soldering, he was able to rewire the circuit to feed back on itself, and generate its own electronic tones. It became his main sound producing source until he purchased an **EMS** Synthi AKS in 1973.

He composed a number of works with his synthesizer and Ferrograph machine, before picking up a second hand Akai four track recorder. Using this for layering sounds, he created the piece Ropes of Mystery, which won first prize in the BATRC Technical Experiment class in 1975. Further successful entries to the amateur tape contest followed during the second half of the 70s, including Carpathia, and Vietnam – Your Blackest Ace, in 1976, which went on to represent Britain in the CIMES international recording competition. He made Music & Movement (1975), for a teacher friend working at a school in Sheffield, and used in the classroom to stimulate dance and drama ideas amongst the children.

Duckworth has maintained his keen interest in electronic sounds, and while he has not actively sought wider recognition for his body of music, he continues to compose at his home studio in Coalville, Leicestershire. He still has his Synthi AKS, and in 2017 he recorded an interpretation of **Malcolm Pointon**'s Symbiosis.

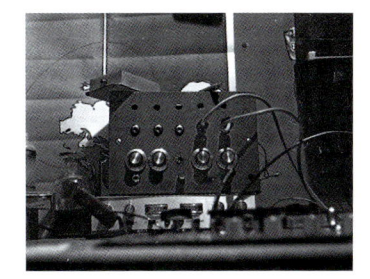

Steve Duckworth's equipment in his home studio, early 1970s

Kevin Edwards (1952)

Born: Doncaster
Earliest Electronic Work: Fragments – tape collage (1969)
Commitment Factor: 3
Obscurity Quotient: 9
EM recording availability: Poor

Schoolboy and fledgling multi-instrumentalist Kevin Edwards, benefitted from the progressive music teaching of **Roy Cooper**, at the newly merged Adwick High School in Yorkshire. He started at the comprehensive in 1963 before the merger, with music already an important part of the curriculum. On Cooper's arrival in 1965, the subject's profile was significantly boosted with imaginative initiatives, and a new school orchestra and choir. At that point the only non-traditional equipment was a standard Ferrograph tape recorder, but this was soon augmented by a stereo Brenell machine, and thereafter multivibrator circuits supplied by **Daphne Oram** and Essconics Ltd. On one of Oram's visits to Adwick she announced Edwards, who then gave an introduction to a taped musical piece he had contributed to, based on the poem Fireworks.

As well as becoming friendly with Oram, Cooper established contact with the BBC, and their cameras visited Adwick for the Music In School series. Edwards can be seen in the programme splicing tape, and Cooper is shown demonstrating a large amplified steel frame. Interested in the potential of tape manipulation and activating sounds percussively, Edwards signed up for an arts summer school in 1968 at Askham Bryan College in York. The focus of the week long course was on the construction of a similar metal frame, which could be equipped with sound amplifying and shaping devices.

At home, he had Tandberg and Philips tape recorders, and made audio collages from recording noises, speech and percussion sounds. He played flute and saxophone in an after school jazz club run by Cooper, and after leaving Adwick in 1970, he pursued the flute at the Royal Manchester College of Music. Looking for a more eclectic course, he left to attend the University of York, and in 1971 he contributed to an experimental music programme broadcast on BBC Radio Sheffield. Cooper joined the staff at York, though ironically Edwards had little further contact with him, and put his experimental music pursuits on hold, despite his student access to the University's electronic music studio. Following graduation he performed in the Grimethorpe Colliery Band, and in 1979 joined the James Shepherd Versatile Brass, staying with them until 1985. As a seasoned multi-instrumentalist he has played drums, bass, guitar, flute and electric piano, and progressed to arranging and some music teaching in Switzerland. He has been percussionist with Opera North, as well as a variety of groups and ensembles, and is now retired as assistant director of Doncaster Schools' Music Service.

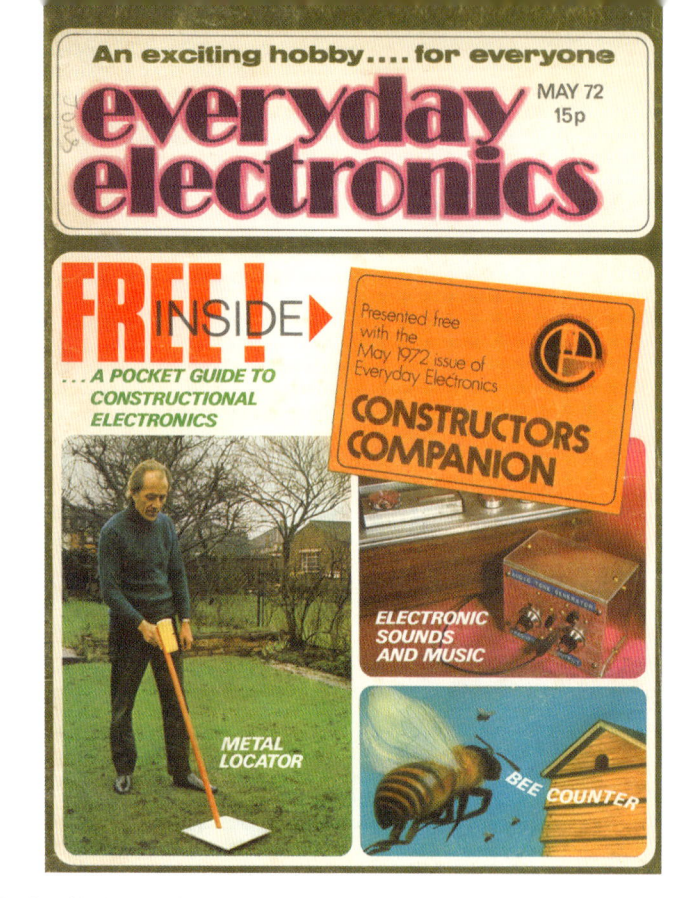

Leslie James Hills (1911-1988)

Born: Untraced
Earliest Electronic Work: ?
Commitment Factor: 5
Obscurity Quotient: 10
EM recording availability: Poor

Mr. Hills of 45 Gordon Road, Belvedere in Kent, was a keen amateur radio and electronics enthusiast, who was engaged in work with cathode ray tubes, and had patents for a number of inventions in conjunction with Jennings Musical Instruments Limited. One of his earliest, applied for in 1951, was for an electrical oscillation generator, which was perhaps designed to avoid copyright infringement in the Jennings Univox monophonic keyboard (based on the very similar but earlier French instrument the Clavioline), and erroneously claimed to have been used on the **Joe Meek** produced hit single Telstar. (Meek is said to have owned both a Clavioline and a Univox, which has added to the confusion.)

In December 1960, Hills inadvertently picked up a short wave SOS message from the Addis Ababa Amateur Radio Club. This alerted him of an attempted Ethiopian coup d'etat; the news of which he duly passed on to the authorities and the press. Since the 1950s he had been experimenting with electronic music, and was the owner of a Grundig TK9 tape recorder alongside his homemade equipment. In 1961 he is believed to have aired a musique concrète composition to the Hastings & District Tape Recording Club.

Leslie James Hills in his home studio, 1960

Trevor F. Holmes (1944)

Born: Birmingham
Earliest Electronic Work: No Title (1965) unconfirmed
Commitment Factor: 3
Obscurity Quotient: 10
EM recording availability: Poor

A 21 year old toolmaker of Redditch, Worcester, Mr. Holmes entered his electronic music composition No Title, into the 1965 British Tape Recording Contest, organised by Amateur Tape Recording magazine. Although not a winner, the panel of judges, including DJ Alan 'Fluff' Freeman and ATR editor **FC Judd** – who himself won an award in the contest for his Tempotune – decided to give a consolation prize to Mr. Holmes, of a complete set of Castle sound effects 7" records, plus a free subscription to ATR.

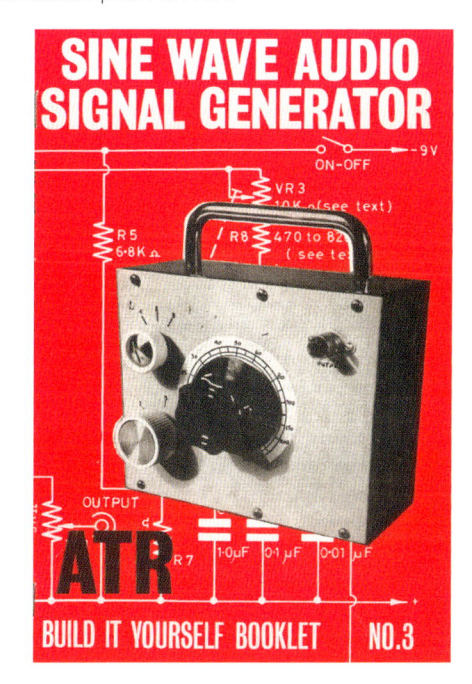

Ian Loveday (1954-2009)

Born: London
Earliest Electronic Work: Intercom studies (1968)
Commitment Factor: 6
Obscurity Quotient: 7
EM recording availability: Limited

Coming from a musical family and attending William Ellis School in north London, 13 year old Ian Loveday's amateur experiments with creatively soldering an old intercom to make electronic sounds, saw his inventiveness rewarded in 1968. His letter with circuit diagram outlining his discoveries, was published in Practical Electronics magazine on the Ingenuity Unlimited page, and detailed how he had rewired certain connections to make all kinds of electronic sounds, some of which were cyclical. In effect he had a proto-sequencer, and his approach is a model for the kind of intuitive electronics that has blossomed in more recent decades, with people taking apart toys and devices, and rewiring, modifying and creatively soldering different sound circuits. According to Ian, his adapted intercom could be used for making electronic effects for school plays, or simply "*doodled with for hours on end.*"

Leaving school without taking O-levels due to health difficulties, his self-taught engineering skills saw him work in telecommunications, and he continued his inventiveness with electronic experiments at home. He took up work as a discotheque DJ in the late 1970s, and moved into London's club scene in the 80s, progressing from an amateur to professional footing. Recognising at an early stage the new Chicago house music that was starting to appear, he began to make his own electronic dance tracks. He was in the thick of the British techno movement, and operated under various aliases including Eon, Ian B and Minimal Man, releasing two albums; Void Dweller (1992), and Sum of Parts (2003), as well as recording several John Peel radio sessions. His premature death aged 54 came suddenly after a bout of pneumonia.

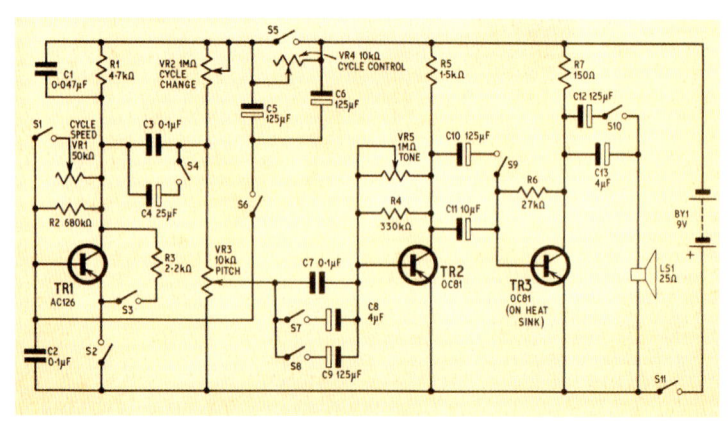

Ian Loveday's experimental circuit design

George West (1938)

Born: Oldham, Lancashire
Earliest Electronic Work: Night Circus (1963-64)
Commitment Factor: 2
Obscurity Quotient: 8
EM recording availability: Limited

No relation to **Peter West**, George West Esq. became aware of the world of tape recording around 1958, and the following year he stumbled across the hobbyist magazine The Tape Recorder, which contained a variety of articles and features on the subject of home taping. In March 1962 he had a letter included in The Tape Recorder, searching for fellow enthusiasts in his area, and after receiving 22 replies, he founded the Middleton Tape Recording Club near Manchester. 1963 was an active year; along with regular club meetings, he gave a lecture to members on echo effects in February, and in October he was featured in ATR magazine, photographed in his home recording den at 187 Oldham Road in Middleton. His spare room set-up housed three reel to reel tape recorders, turntable and mixing unit, and the published glimpse into his studio earned him one guinea.

Although aware of articles and circuit designs by **FC Judd**, he was less technically minded than some of the other club members, and was more interested in making tape documentaries, utilising the possibilities opened up by splicing and editing. For the April 1965 issue of Tape Recording, he penned an article describing the making of The Knocker-up, an audio documentary which was placed second in the British Amateur Tape Recording Contest of 1964. Prior to this he was approached regarding the creation of a musique concrète soundtrack for a dance-theatre performance, after a local hi-fi shop recommended the Middleton TRC for the job. At the end of 1963, West and club colleagues set to work on the project, and the show they scored, The Night Circus, was first performed at the Garrick Theatre in Altrincham, Cheshire in April 1964.

The following year West resigned from the Middleton TRC, and switched his allegiance to the British Ferrograph Owners Club, which was dedicated to the creative use of that make of tape recorder. Having previously run an audio service at Middleton, his initial role was to produce an audio magazine, Ferrosound, with varied contributions coming in from different members. He took over as club secretary in the late 1960s until 1975, when he could no longer commit the time; the club eventually folding in the 1980s.

Throughout his life West has maintained his ardent interest in documentaries and social history, which started in his tape club days. In 2011 his Steam: A Life on the Railway, was issued as a BBC audio book, documenting enthusiasm for railways, and the transition from steam to diesel and electric trains.

Peter West (1952)

Born: London (unconfirmed)
Earliest Electronic Work: Tape experiments (c. 1966)
Commitment Factor: 4
Obscurity Quotient: 9
EM recording availability: Poor

Attending the state funded Hampton Grammar School in Richmond Upon Thames in Middlesex, Peter West had an initial interest in contemporary music, and saved up to buy two Revox tape recorders. Experimenting with recording the sounds of acoustic instruments at school, he then subjected them to tape treatments, using speed changing, reversal and splicing. He went to a class on electronic music run by **George Brown** in Chiswick, and won a place at the Royal College of Music. During his time there he studied with **Lawrence Casserley**, and wrote an opera featuring a tape part, which was performed at the college. He visited the **BBC Radiophonic Workshop** and the **EMS** studio in this period, and following graduation joined the Cockpit Arts Centre in 1973.

Alongside **Howard Rees** he co-ran the electronic music studio at the Cockpit, which had a basic set up of VCS3 synthesizer, tape recorders and filters. His own composition work took a back seat as he became immersed in the instructional side of electronic music; teaching classes, assisting students and facilitating recording. After the closure of the Cockpit Arts Centre, he moved to a post at the Camden Music Service.

SYNTHESISER MODULES

Send S.A.E. for details of voltage-controlled modules for synthesiser construction to:

D.E.W. Ltd.

254 Ringwood Road, Ferndown, Dorset

Brian Whibley (1931-2003)

Born: Gravesend, Kent
Earliest Electronic Work: ?
Commitment Factor: 7
Obscurity Quotient: 9
EM recording availability: Poor

Living in Gravesend, Brian Horace Whibley was employed as a commercial artist in Soho, London in the 1960s, carrying out illustration and airbrush work for various clients, including Radio Times and TV Times. He was a member of a skiffle group and a keen tape enthusiast, building his own recording den at home at 85 Hillside Avenue. It was fully functional in 1963, and with the reluctant blessing of Mrs. Whibley, who endured three months of construction chaos, his recording console was built into the bay window of their living room. It housed three tape recorders, record deck, tuner, amplifier, various microphones, two self-built mixing units and a switching panel. He was paid one guinea for inclusion of a photograph of him in his lounge studio, featured in Amateur Tape Recording magazine in November 63. It was noted that his foremost interests were "*musique concrète and all main scientific advancements and historical events today.*"

Also in the Whibley lounge was an upright piano, later replaced by an electric keyboard, and in the garden were several sheds to cater for his multifarious interests. He had designated areas for woodworking, picture framing, graphics and amateur radio, and he was a fervent collector of hobbyist magazines on all manner of practical subjects. After his death, as with much experimental amateur work, virtually none of his archive or creative output was salvaged, but his passion for music and collecting has been passed on to his youngest son Andrew, who runs Retro Vinyl Records based in London.

Brian Whibley in his living room studio, 1963

Barry Witherden (1949)

Born: London
Earliest Electronic Work: Collage (1968)
Commitment Factor: 8
Obscurity Quotient: 8
EM recording availability: Limited

A music writer and composer, Barry Witherden's early exposure to the tape minimalism of Steve Reich, the musique concrète of Pierre Schaeffer, and electronic works by Karlheinz Stockhausen, all helped to consolidate his interest in experimental sound. His enthusiasm had already started as a young teenager; his first experiments with turntable manipulations began around the mid 1960s.

"When I was 14 my parents bought me a Dansette Bermuda auto-change portable record-player. I soon decided that as much fun could be had from exploiting its potential malfunctions as from just playing discs. Overloading the spindle would produce something equivalent to 'random play' on a CD player or i-Pod; adjacent discs would sometimes either lock together or slip, so that their speed would vary unpredictably. Leaving the stabiliser arm up would cause repeat plays ad infinitum, and with 10" and 12" discs, the stylus would come down at a variable point about a third of the way in. Better, you could mess around with the speed control, moving between 16, $33^{1/3}$, 45 and 78 rpm. Best of all, if you lightened the tracking weight sufficiently, you could get locked grooves which produced slightly surreal snatches and fascinating rhythmic repetitive patterns. However, apart from irritating my parents, there was little use I could put these idiosyncrasies to, until that Christmas I got a Fidelity quarter-track tape recorder with three speeds, and (most exciting and interesting) a superimpose button. I began to make tape collages using various records in my collection, plus speech and music taped off the wireless, and other sounds, including the noise of the tape recorder's own motor, collected around the home."
BW - July 2012.

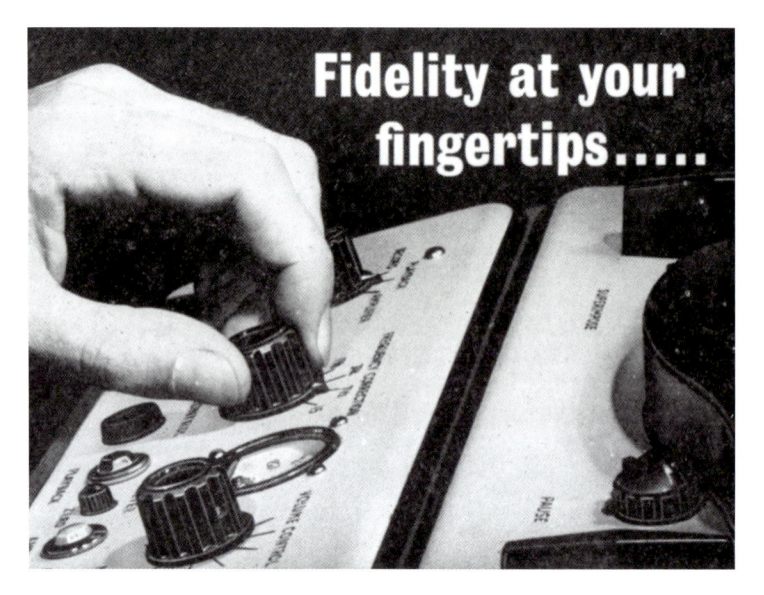

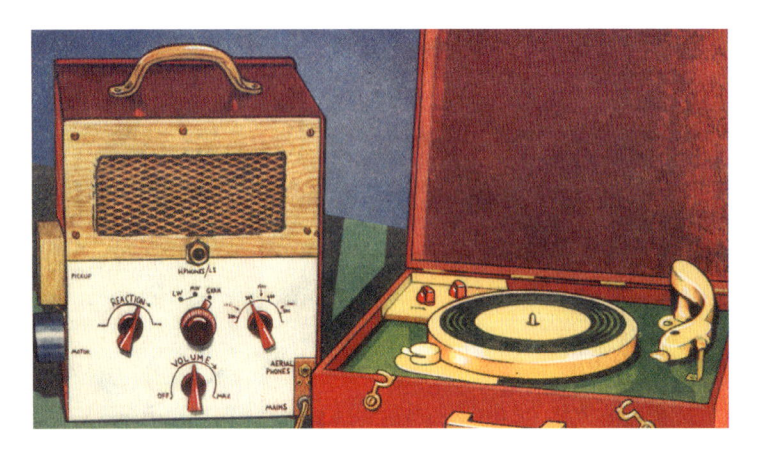

Barry continues to write, record and perform, and is one half of the Gimlet Eyed Mariners improvising electro-acoustic group, alongside Michael Fairfax, the grandson of **Ernest Berk**. He has also recorded solo under the guises of MC Warne Slippaz and Fagus the Magus.

Amateur Cine World · October 26, 1961

Stuart Wynn Jones (1919-1991)

Born: Cheltenham, Gloucestershire
Earliest Electronic Work: Opus 1 for Projector (1955)
Commitment Factor: 8
Obscurity Quotient: 7
EM recording availability: Limited

With more than a passing resemblance to Clive Sinclair, the British electronics innovator, Stuart Wynn Jones achieved a rare level of sophistication and quality in both electronic music and film, during the 1950s and 60s. By day he worked as 'ideas man' for an advertising agency; in his spare time he meticulously plotted and executed a series of abstract films, which rival the best work in the field, created at his bachelor flat at 107 Fellows Road, Hampstead, London. He had studied painting at the Derby School of Art, and music under John Pritchard, and started making home movies in 1949 with the 9.5mm format. By 1951 he had stepped up to 16mm and built his own animation table, and with access to 35mm in the mid-50s, he began investigating optical soundtracks and synthetic sound. In 1956 he made Short Spell, a completely cameraless two minute animation drawn with indian ink directly onto 35mm film, depicting a kinetic alphabet, and featuring a supremely detailed hand-drawn synthetic soundtrack.

Short Spell and his next two abstract shorts Raving Waving (1957), and Bellowing Billowing (1959), were all Ten Best award winners in the annual Amateur Cine World contest. For the latter pair, he employed a musique concrète approach for the soundtracks, recording onto magnetic tape the sounds of taps running, paper tearing and sticky tape being pulled, with splicing and mixing carried out on two Brenell tape recorders. Raving Waving was included in the prestigious experimental film competition at the Brussels World's Fair in 1958, where the selection panel included Norman McLaren, Edgard Varèse and Man Ray. The following year he began work on the cel animation The Rejected Rose, again creating a musique concrète soundtrack, this time to represent each stylised character in the film. Working on it for three years, he finally completed it in 1962 when it became another Ten Best winner. He experimented further with synthetic music by photographing images, which were translated optoacoustically into sound. This required filing the gate of his 16mm camera to widen the exposure area into the soundtrack part of the film, and the creation of a series of special cards depicting waveform images corresponding to different tones, photographed onto the film's narrow soundtrack strip.

Wynn Jones was part of the London based film and animation collective The Grasshopper Group, and edited its members' magazine, Grasshopper News. Several of the group contributed acting and production skills to his short film The Spark, in 1963, which features live action, scratched animation, and a soundtrack of narration and electronics – as well as a very brief SWJ cameo.

The Tape Recorder magazine's amateur competition for new music tapes in 1959, had seen him pick up a prize for his, Music to be Heard for its Own Sake, alongside fellow award winners **FC Judd**, **Ralph Broome** and **John Harper**. The following year he lectured at the recently opened Centre of Sound in London, concerning creative film and music making, two weeks before a lecture on sound recording by Fred Judd, the Centre's technical director. At the Photo-Cine Fair at Olympia in 1963, Wynn Jones screened a selection of his films and delivered a talk entitled, Abstract Visuals and Concrete Sounds. In March 1968 at a major concert of electronic music at the Planetarium in London, his Bellowing Billowing was screened alongside work by **Ernest Berk**, **Brian Dennis**, **Hugh Davies**, **Roberto Gerhard** and **Peter Zinovieff**.

During the latter half of the 60s, Wynn Jones made Optic Ticklers (1966); worked on Evolution of Life, a series of shorts for Halas & Batchelor; and produced animations for cartoon series Tomfoolery (1970). Employed creatively throughout the 1970s, he made titles for the 1974 Gary Glitter film Remember Me This Way, and animations for the documentary The Conservation Game (1975). He commissioned British composer Gordon Jacob to write a score for his film Duo (1975), and in 1983 penned an article for Polish magazine Animafilm, discussing moving image work with computers.

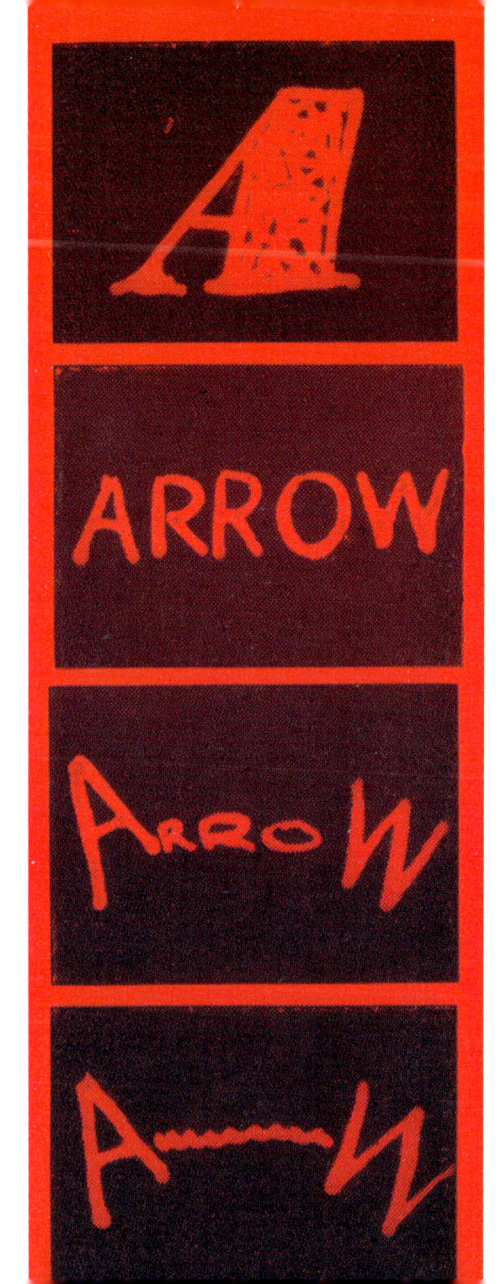

The Grasshopper Group was a disparate collective of amateur and semi-professional filmmakers and enthusiasts, established by John Daborn and Gerry Potterton in the summer of 1953. It was unusual amongst British cine societies with its emphasis on making and screening avant-garde films and animation, and having its membership drawn internationally, and not just from around its London base at 35 Endell Street, WC2. Enjoying a high profile in the amateur film-making scene, it staged the presentations of Amateur Cine World magazine's annual Ten Best competition at the National Film Theatre in London. Acclaimed animator Norman McLaren (1914-1987) – a significant inspiration for **Stuart Wynn Jones**, and an early experimenter with synthetic sound in Great Britain – became the Grasshopper Group's honorary president in 1957, and was succeeded in 1961 by Peter Sellers. The outfit carried on screenings and film production throughout the 60s, but tailed off during the following decade and dissolved formally in 1982.

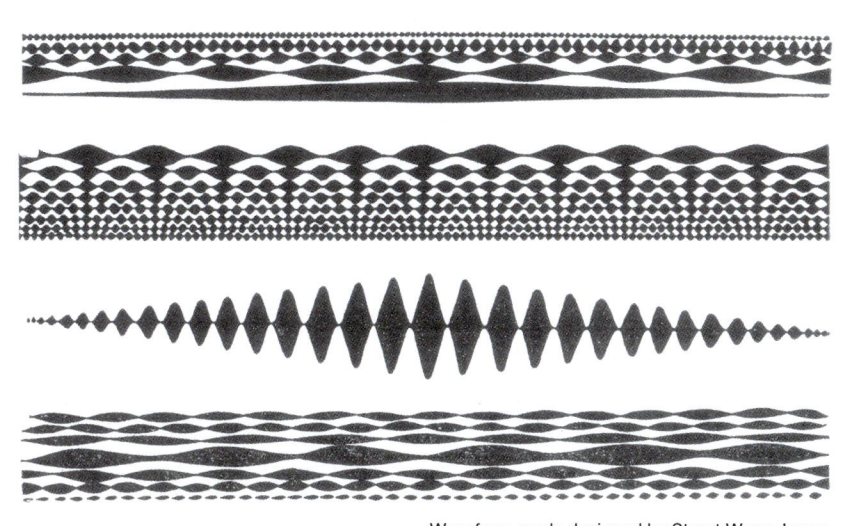

Waveform cards designed by Stuart Wynn Jones

159

Film Making Without a Camera

Cartooning from A to Z

SHORT SPELL

Stuart Wynn Jones at work, with stills from Short Spell, The Spark and The Rejected Rose

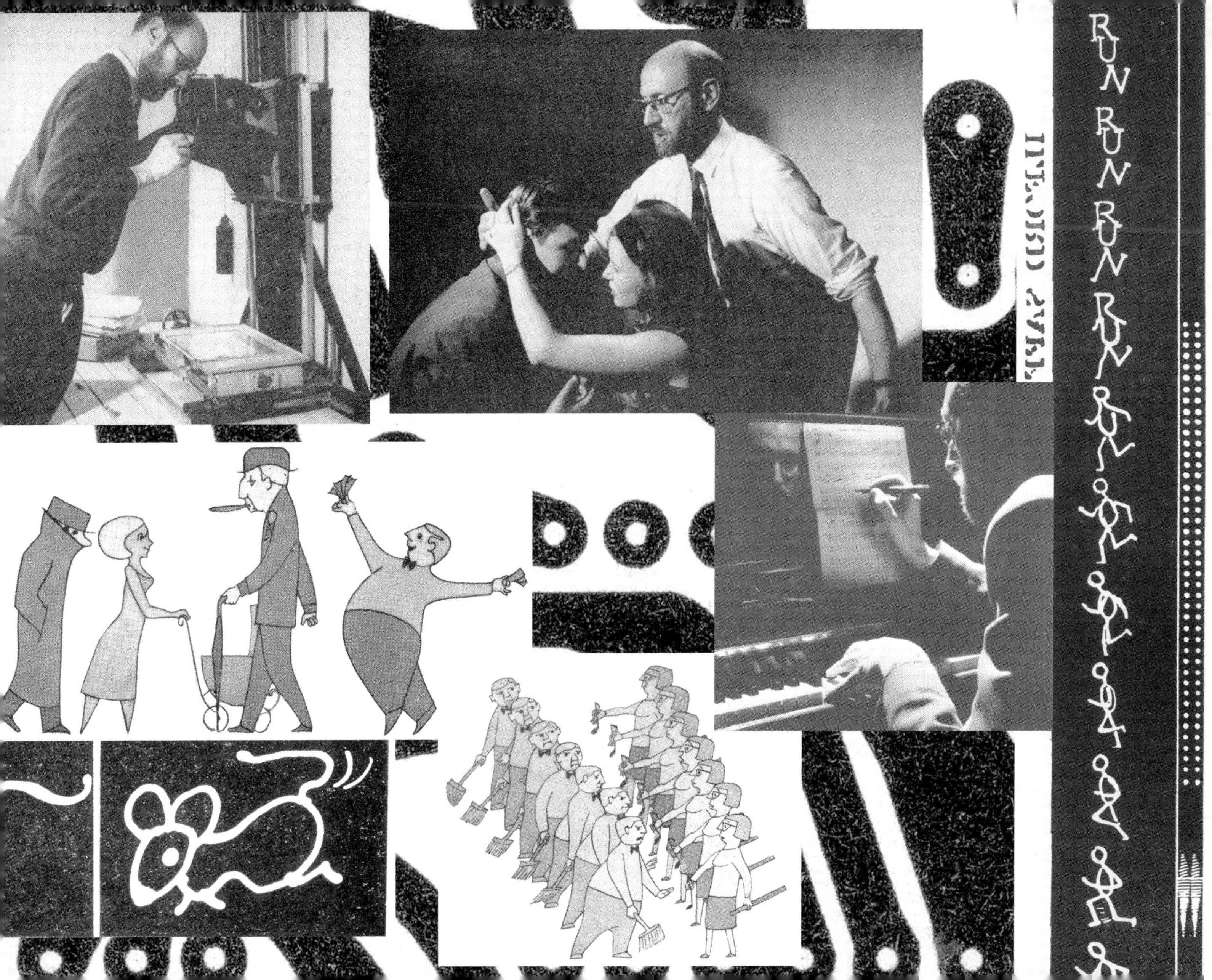
RUN RUN RUN RUN

Additional amateurs with an interest in electronic music:

R.L. Armstrong
Based on manipulated water sounds, the experimental tape piece L'eau Concrete, earned Armstrong a commendation in the 1959 British Amateur Tape Recording Contest.

Dave Dicker
Resident in Edmonton, London, Dave Dicker became a member of the North London Tape and Hi-fi Club mid-1966, and demonstrated to members his method of creating electronic music with the aid of an IBM computer. He was working on voice synthesis, and ATR magazine reported that "*words of the songs, which came over very clearly, were formed electronically.*"

Terry Draper
Mr. Draper, the chairman of Warwick and Leamington ATRS, entered his club's competition for tapes of musique concrète, and won first prize and a silver cup. His composition included the sounds of two ticking clocks, notes from a musical box, and a vase and champagne glass being struck. He lectured at his club in March 1961 on musique concrète, and demonstrated tape loops with the sound of a word repeated over and over with variable echo.

Derek C. Harker
At the Catford TRC in December 1959, secretary Mr. Harker was one of several members to make a tape for the club's competition to produce original sounds. His recording, Martians in My Piano, created at 62 Barmeston Road, Catford, SE6, was described as a "*very noisy tape indeed.*"

John S. Harper
A Brenell Mk. 5 tape machine was presented to Mr. Harper of 82 Shaftesbury Avenue, London, W1, for his award winning entry into the Tape Recorder magazine's competition for 'New Music' in 1960. His piece, A Rhythmic Mixture, received second prize behind **FC Judd**, who took top honours for his composition The Butterfly.

A winner awarded a winner!

Mr. J. S. Harper, 82 Shaftesbury Avenue, W.1 (on right), winner of the second prize (Class B) in the Tape Recorder "New Music" Competition, receives his prize — a Brenell Mk. 5 Deck. Presented by the editor of Hi-Fi News.

Brenell

Brenell performance is true-to-life performance
Details from Sole Manufacturers:
BRENELL ENGINEERING CO. LTD. 1a DOUGHTY ST. W.C.1 CHA 5809

Peter Holloway
The secretary of the West Herts tape club, Mr. Holloway tried his hand at musique concrète, and presented his experiment to fellow enthusiasts in December 1960.

Hedley R. Jones
At a meeting of the Bournemouth Tape Recording Society in October 1958, members were treated to a tape of musique concrète made by Mr. Jones, of 442 Poole Road, Branksome.

Alistair Milne and Malcolm Watt
Stalwarts of Newcastle TRC, the Geordie pair conducted experiments in 1967 with an electronic organ they had constructed. It was said to be suitable for creating electronic music on tape, and they carried out tests in conjunction with echo, speed changing and loops.

Barry Mitchell
An illustrated talk on radiophonics and tape music was presented by Mr. Mitchell, to the London Tape Recording Club in July 1966, and the following month he was enrolled as a club member. Part Two of his talk later that year, concerned the history of electronic music.

Pete Ordidge
Contributing to a club meeting at the Chesterfield Tape Recording Society in May 1959, Pete Ordidge played members his musique concrète style tape, featuring backwards piano sounds he had cut and spliced together.

Mike E. Plant
Mr. Plant of the Leeds TRC, used two Revox machines and a Butoba battery reel to reel recorder, to provide a programme of musique concrète at a club meeting in December 1963.

Derek Purslow
Born in 1930, Derek Purslow started making simple family films in 1950 with the 9.5mm gauge, but switched formats and moved into experimental work in 1959. He was an Army Bandsman stationed at Sandhurst, and vice-chairman of Reading Cine and Tape Recording Society. Inspired by **Stuart Wynn Jones**, he made four direct animation films from 1959-61. His Sound and Vision, won first prize in the Animated Cartoon section of the Cannes Film Festival; said to be the shortest film shown there up to that time.

John Ross
A member of Catford Tape Recording Club in south London, John Ross gave a demonstration of electronic music at a club meeting in the autumn of 1963, and after his lecture he encouraged members to try their hands with a variety of electronic equipment.

John Sargent
A playback and discussion of Mr. Sargent's tape Synthetic Sound, took place at a meeting of the Reading Cine and Tape Recording Society in 1964.

Peter Tassell
Musique concrète tapes were produced at the Tufnell Park TRC by Peter Tassell in 1963, and he also gave a lecture and demonstration on the subject. Colleague Keith Harris was similarly enthusiastic, and gave his own musique concrète talk later that year.

Ralph Vivian
A competition for tape pieces, organised by Brighton Tape Recording Club in July 1960, was won by the club's secretary Mr. Vivian. His recording, Journey into Space, was produced with electronic equipment in his home at 37 Ditchling Road, Brighton.

H.J. Walding
Teaching at Stimpson Avenue School, Northampton, and the owner of a Tandberg tape recorder, Mr. Walding was a runner up in the Compositions class of the 1964 British Amateur Tape Recording Contest. His piece The Dream, a three minute fantasy of voices and electronic music, was created at 48 Freehold Street, Northampton.

G.H. Wood
In February 1960, members of the Wakefield and District Tape Recording Club, were given a demonstration of musique concrète or 'sounds mysterious', by devotees Messers. Wood and Appleton. They highlighted all the techniques for cutting, splicing, reverse play and looping, and encouraged everyone to try their hand at making their own experimental tapes.

ELECTRONIC MUSIC GROUPS

3

ELECTRONIC MUSIC GROUPS - BACKGROUND

The 1960s saw a rapid evolution in musical styles and thinking, and with new smaller and cheaper transistorised components, a whole range of affordable electronic equipment became more readily available; whether commercially manufactured and bought in shops, or self-constructed at home. Changes in technology as well as society as a whole, were reflected in rock, pop, jazz and classical music, leading to new crossovers and fusions, and groups looking to explore electronic sounds both in the studio and in live performance. The increasing availability and flexibility of multi-track tape recorders, plus the incorporation of unusual sound sources and devices for modulation, all contributed to this progress.

A younger generation of experimental composers began to expand into areas previously the preserve of popular groups, and in turn, new studio recording techniques allied to a willingness to experiment, saw producers and rock and pop bands picking up on ideas and processes that had been developed in early electronic music. Initially multiple tape recorders were used to achieve superimposition and layering of tracks; bouncing sounds from one or several machines simultaneously, onto another master recorder. Gradually advances in tape recorder technology opened up multi-tracking, firstly with 4 track, and then quickly moving on to 8, 16 and many more in professional recording studios. The arrival of relatively affordable portable synthesizers at the start of the 1970s – in particular the **EMS** VCS3 and Synthi A models – also opened up new horizons for ensembles to explore, and made scored and improvised electronic music performance a far more workable option.

A further impetus for activating interest in live electronics, was in solving the problem of sterility and lack of visual focus in the playback of taped electronic music in a conventional venue setting. While the work put into tape compositions yielded exciting results, the way of transmitting them to an audience in a concert hall, required something different to the long established conventions of instrumental music. The dearth of performers during a tape piece played at a concert, inevitably stimulated some composers and musicians to work in an electro-acoustic vein to present their work, using instrumentalists playing in combination with tape. Others sought a visual counterpoint in the form of lights, projections, dancers or different elements for the audience to look at or engage with. This led to the formation of dedicated performance groups to tackle the live presentation of electronic music, often with multiple sound sources and improvisation. In the second half of the 1960s, all manner of British based rock and pop groups occasionally dallied with noises and techniques common in tape music, but very few showed more than a fleeting interest in electronics. Included here are those that made some serious forays into the experimental field.

The Beatles

Origin: Liverpool
Formed: 1960
Disbanded: 1970
Obscurity Quotient: 0
EM recording availability: Excellent

At Abbey Road studios in London, the Beatles experimentation with tape began in earnest during sessions for the Revolver LP in 1966, with the group members all having access to reel to reel recorders for making loops. Tapes can be heard on a number of tracks; in particular on Tomorrow Never Knows, which features vocals fed through a Hammond organ Leslie speaker, and noise effects from tape loops. With support from George Martin and EMI engineers, this experimental phase continued through Sgt. Pepper and Magical Mystery Tour, culminating with Revolution 9, on the White Album in 1968. Hardly a favourite amongst Beatles fans, this landmark sound collage led by John Lennon, nevertheless crossed over from the minority avant-garde tape world into the popular music arena.

The piece had been presaged however, by the much anticipated but never released Carnival of Light – a vocal and instrumental improvisation initiated by Paul McCartney, during the Penny Lane sessions in January 1967 – and made for The Million Volt Light and Sound Rave, at the Roundhouse in London. The event featured light shows and electronic music, including sounds from **Unit Delta Plus**. The Beatles recording was instigated by the design team Binder, Edwards and Vaughan, who painted a psychedelic piano for McCartney, and on delivery, David Vaughan asked him to contribute to the Million Volt event.

In the spring of 1966, McCartney rented a basement flat at 34 Montagu Square in London, owned by his band mate Ringo Starr. His idea was to set up a small demo studio for the recording and exchange of experimental sound and music, and through his connection to the Indica Gallery in London, he asked Ian Sommerville to act as in-house engineer. To get the studio up and running, Sommerville procured Revox tape recorders, speakers and editing equipment, and engineered recording sessions. Aside from McCartney, who worked on demos for Eleanor Rigby, **William Burroughs** was the other main user of the studio. In contrast to the simple set up at Montagu Square, McCartney also visited **Peter Zinovieff**'s sophisticated studio in Putney during 1966, where he spoke to members of Unit Delta Plus. It is rumoured but perhaps unlikely, that he was considering an electronic interpretation of his Beatles song Yesterday.

George Harrison's modular Moog synthesizer, patched and programmed by Mike Vickers, was utilised effectively on a number of tracks for the Beatles' Abbey Road album in August 1969, and stands out during the tremendous white noise finale on I Want You (She's So Heavy). The group's Apple label offshoot Zapple, released Harrison's Electronic Sound LP earlier that year – critically derided but highly notable for its uncompromising dissonance and freeform Moog experimentation – it hits the mark as an early example of raw synthesizer playing, without being tied to the keyboard or any conventional tonality. It clearly has an even greater oddness factor, being the avant-garde product of a member of the most famous pop group in the world. There is acrimony around the recording, and a still embittered Bernard Krause, received no royalty for his contribution to the side long track No Time Or Space.

Electronic sounds are heard briefly on Harrison's soundtrack in one scene of psychedelic oddball feature film Wonderwall (1968). His Moog had a further outing during jam sessions for his All Things Must Pass album in 1970 – electronics are featured throughout the eight minute instrumental, I Remember Jeep. It is regrettable that Zapple Records did not manage to issue any further LPs of British electronic music, and that Harrison blocked the release of Carnival of Light, when it was proposed by McCartney in 1996.

John Lennon is the Beatle most associated with experimental music through his association with Yoko Ono, and in evidence on his first three albums outside of the group; Two Virgins (1968), Life With the Lions (1969) and The Wedding Album (1969). This phase of experimentation was short lived however, and his solo work through the 1970s shows little of his previous edge and quest for new sounds during the 60s. Ringo Starr has a limited connection to the avant-garde, though he did have a starring role in Frank Zappa's offbeat film 200 Motels (1971), and was particularly taken with **John Tavener**'s The Whale; instigating and appearing on the recording for Apple Records. In the early 1970s, he contacted **EMS**, and staff member **Peter Grogono** was drafted in to Abbey Road studios, to assist Ringo with programming and patching a VCS3.

CDs:
The Beatles: Revolver (Parlophone, 1966).
The Beatles (EMI/Apple, 1968).
The Beatles: Abbey Road (EMI/Apple, 1969).
George Harrison: Electronic Sound (EMI/Apple, 1996 reissue).

> The Beatles and the Rolling Stones press driven rivalry through the 1960s, belied a close connection between the two groups. George Harrison and Mick Jagger were both early adopters of the Moog synthesizer; the instrument being affordable at the time only for rich musicians and well funded institutions. Harrison received a demonstration of a modular Moog from Bernie Krause at a Los Angeles recording studio session in November 1968, and took delivery of his own machine in February the following year. Jagger ordered a Moog in the summer of 1968; delivered from the USA by Moog man Jon Weiss. It appears with the Stones singer in the classic feature film Performance, shot that year in London, and finally released in 1970. Jagger used his Moog to supply the monotonous soundtrack for Kenneth Anger's short film, Invocation of My Demon Brother (1968), and finally sold the machine in the early 70s to a studio in Berlin, where it came into the hands of Christoph Franke of Tangerine Dream.

The Beatles drawn by Fraser Geesin

Gentle Fire

Origin: York
Formed: 1968
Disbanded: 1975
Obscurity Quotient: 6
EM Recording Availability: Excellent

In 1968 both **Hugh Davies** and **Richard Orton** were establishing electronic music studios at Goldsmiths College, and the University of York respectively. They had previously met at Cambridge and remained in contact, and in the summer of 68 formed a live electronic duo which gave a series of performances. Orton had organised experimental music sessions for students, including four events at York University; following a weekend of concerts in May 1968, and a further event at Sheffield University, once back at York the idea of a group was proposed. The core members of Gentle Fire coalesced, and the name was arrived at after consulting the I Ching. Alongside Orton, the line-up settled on Richard Bernas – a New York born composer, pianist and percussionist; Stuart Jones – composer, trumpeter and cellist; Patrick Harrex – composer and violinist; and **Graham Hearn** – composer and VCS3 player.

Hugh Davies approached Bernas and Jones regarding a series of concerts at the Arts Lab in London, and here they performed pieces by US composers Christian Wolff and John Cage, leading Davies to join Gentle Fire towards the end of 1968. The group played works by Karlheinz Stockhausen, including Spiral, and parts of Aus den sieben Tagen, and gave first British performances of Kurzwellen, and Mikrophonie II. In 1971 they participated in early renditions of Stockhausen's Sternklang, alongside the group **Intermodulation**, and later featured on the LP recording. Their own collective compositions were born out of improvisations with conventional instruments, and a wide array of sound producing devices, including amplified junk created by Davies, and a VCS3 usually operated by Hearn. As well as playing the synthesizer, Hearn was concerned with incorporating found sounds, and his contribution to one group piece – commissioned as a dance score by the Laban Dance Company, circa 1969 – involved a greatly slowed down recording of the Prelude to Das Rheingold. For a realisation of Alvin Lucier's Chambers, at around the same time, he used recordings of Frank Sinatra, placing the tape recorder's detachable speakers inside various suitcases and boxes. With all the group members able to play more than one instrument, on occasions they would swap round in order to avoid staleness and over-familiarity. Together they created a series of Group Compositions I-VI, with number VII planned to include a meal consumed on stage during the performance, with probes inside a cake connected to a VCS3.

Harrex left the group in 1970 and Michael Robinson stepped in as replacement, playing his first major Gentle Fire concert in May that year at the Purcell Room, London; after the departure of Orton, the group carried on as a quintet. Besides the strong connection with Stockhausen's music, they also performed work by Earle Brown, Christian Wolff, and Toshi Ichiyanagi, and played with John Cage, David Tudor and Gordon Mumma in 1972. That year saw Gentle Fire play at ICES-72, and make four trips to Europe for concerts and workshops. This marked the zenith of their performance activity, and after recording for the Sternklang album, the group finally wound down in 1975.

CD: Gentle Fire: Explorations (1970-1973) (Paradigm, 2020).

Gentle Fire

MONDAY FEBRUARY 1 1971 AT 7.45 p.m.

QUEEN ELIZABETH HALL

(General Manager: John Denison, C.B.E.)

programme two shillings/ten new pence

Gentle Fire in 1973

Half Landing

Origin: London
Formed: 1965
Disbanded: 1968
Obscurity Quotient: 9
EM Recording Availability: Poor

This early British electronic performance outfit went under several different names including Overcoat, and the line-up centred on **Ranulph Glanville**, Richard Bunt, Patricia Bull and John Pitchford. Glanville and Bunt were fellow students at the Architectural Association School in London in the mid-1960s, and both were enthused by a variety of influences. These ranged from Surrealism, Dada and Futurism, via Samuel Beckett and US avant-garde music. With a strong interest in using technology for performance, the group's equipment consisted of tone and pulse generators, tape recorders, mixers, ring modulator and special effects organ.

They performed at a variety of events and happenings using chance operations and improvised scores, as well as live tape splicing and remixing of recorded sounds. An early Half Landing residency at the Electric Garden venue, (a precursor of the Middle Earth club) in Covent Garden, took place circa 1966, and the group were undoubtedly one of the first in Great Britain to fully incorporate tapes and electronics into live performance.

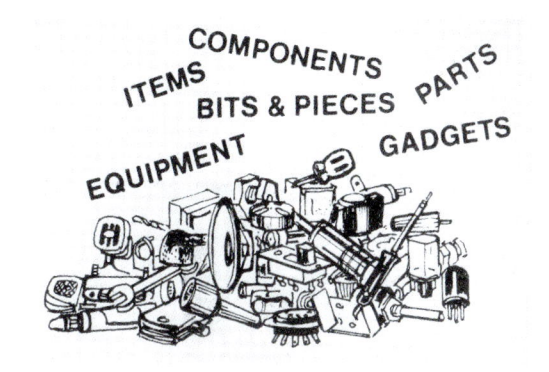

City of Leeds Education Committee

LEEDS MUSIC CENTRE

THE GENTLE FIRE

Graham Hearn	Electric Guitar
Stuart Jones	Trumpet
Richard Barnas	Piano Accordion
Patrick Harrex	
Richard Orton	Oscillators
Hugh Davies	Ring Modulators

Leeds Institute Gallery

Sunday 23rd November, 1969
at 7.30 p.m.

Hawkwind

Origin: London
Formed: 1969
Disbanded: Ongoing
Obscurity Quotient: 2
EM Recording Availability: Excellent

Hawkwind were one of the few rock groups of the 1960s and 70s to feature a band member dedicated solely to electronics; they eschewed the trained pianist with keyboard synthesizer of many other bands, and instead Dik Mik, a self-confessed non-musician, was assigned to audio generators, and appeared on their eponymously titled first album released in 1970. The original Group X were formed in the ferment of late 60s Notting Hill Gate and Ladbroke Grove counter culture, centred around busking guitarist Dave Brock, sax player Nik Turner and drummer Terry Ollis. Evolving from a loose gathering of freaks and drop outs, they organised as Hawkwind, and became a true audio-visual outfit, with acid drenched psychedelic imagery and electronic sounds very much to the fore. Their extended and regularly shifting line-up included vocalist and poet Robert Calvert, bassist Lemmy, projections from Liquid Len, curvaceous dancer Stacia, sci-fi writer Michael Moorcock and Del Dettmar on **EMS** VCS3 synthesizer.

After the extraordinary success of the single Silver Machine, which reached number 3 in the top 40 pop charts in July 1972, and their follow up Urban Guerrilla, managing 39 – despite being withdrawn after coinciding with IRA bomb attacks – the group had the finances to launch the spectacular Space Ritual road show. Featuring the full gamut of their heavy riffing, sci-fi soaked, hypnotic multi-media rock, this drew on tracks from their LPs, In Search of Space; and Doremi Fasol Latido; the quintessential early Hawkwind sound.

As key band members came and went and the energy of the early 70s counter culture dwindled, the group nevertheless persevered with the free festival scene, and still managed to preserve their ideals and make interesting albums. In fact as progressive rock completely lost its edge, and punk swept in and kick started a whole new wave of music making, Hawkwind were still producing worthwhile albums. Astounding Sounds, Amazing Music (1976), Quark Strangeness and Charm (1977), and PXR5 (1979), showed them progressing beyond their initial heavy rock template, and this carried on into the 1980s, when virtually all other groups of their generation were completely washed up. Dave Brock's interest in electronic music was much in evidence on the Church of Hawkwind LP released in 1982, featuring Harvey Bainbridge and original member Huw Lloyd-Langton. Brock worked out demos with synthesizers, and the final album was a successful mix of rock, electronics and archive voice extracts. In this period the group were actively gigging and performing at festivals, with guest appearances from Michael Moorcock and departed members Turner and Calvert. Since 1969 Brock has remained the only constant, and in 2018 he led the group into an unlikely collaboration with former Wombles pop group supremo Mike Batt. Hawkwind have recorded over 30 studio albums, and in 2021, Somnia, was released to coincide with their summer festival Hawkfest.

CDs:
Hawkwind: In Search of Space (EMI, 1972).
Hawkwind: Astounding Sounds, Amazing Music (Rock Fever, 1976).
Hawkwind: Quark, Strangeness and Charm (Rock Fever, 1977).
Hawkwind: Church of Hawkwind (Cherry Red, 1982).

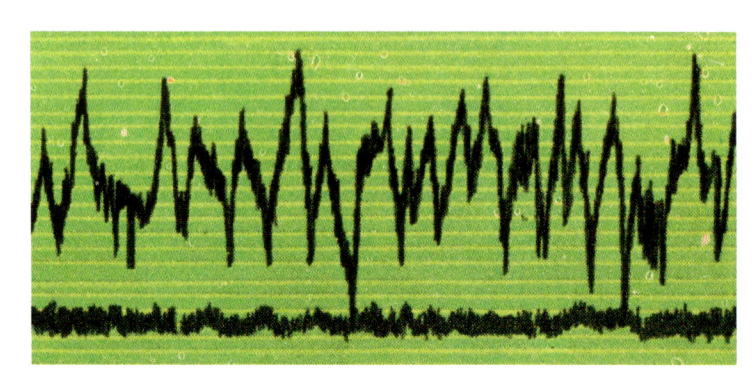

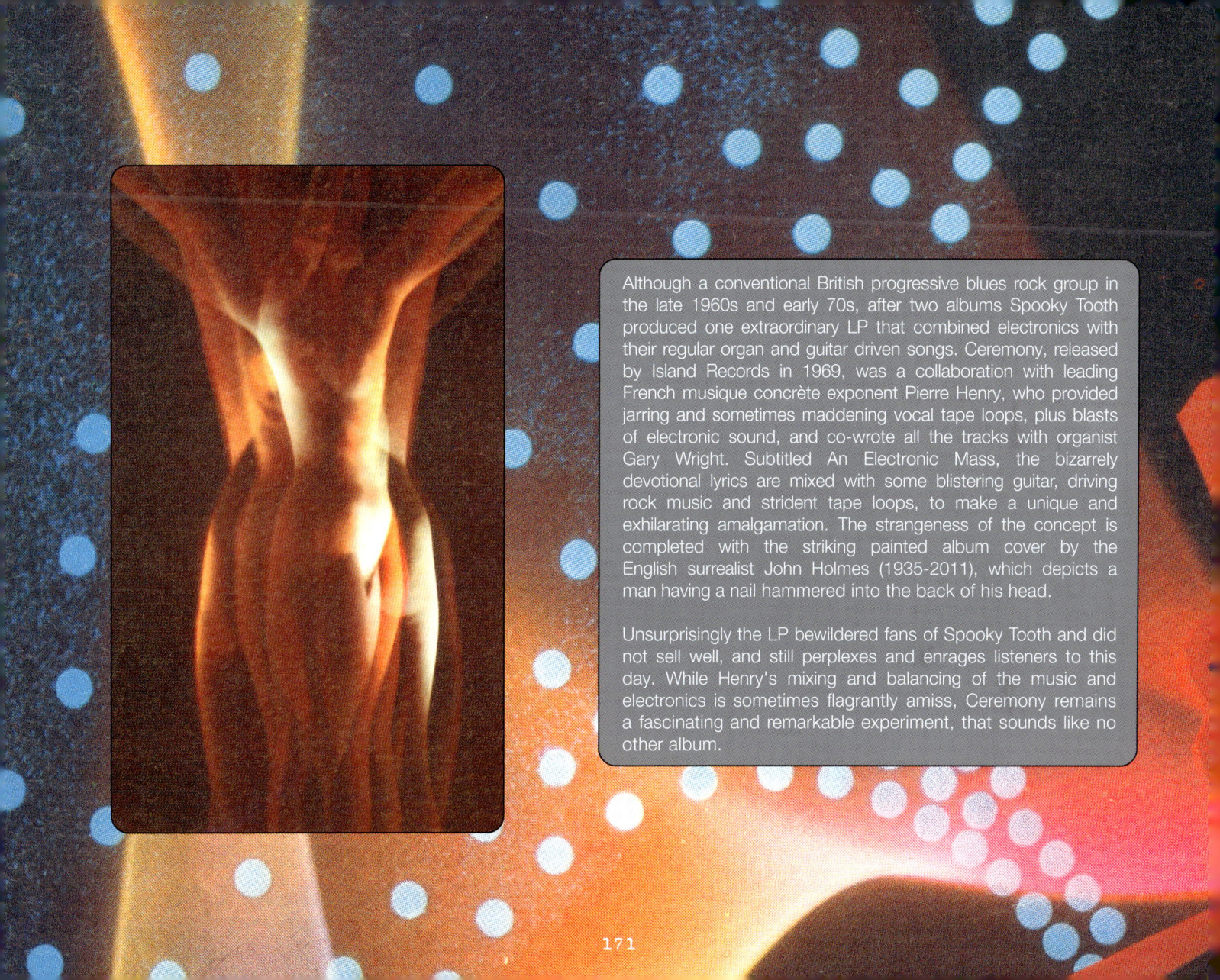

Although a conventional British progressive blues rock group in the late 1960s and early 70s, after two albums Spooky Tooth produced one extraordinary LP that combined electronics with their regular organ and guitar driven songs. Ceremony, released by Island Records in 1969, was a collaboration with leading French musique concrète exponent Pierre Henry, who provided jarring and sometimes maddening vocal tape loops, plus blasts of electronic sound, and co-wrote all the tracks with organist Gary Wright. Subtitled An Electronic Mass, the bizarrely devotional lyrics are mixed with some blistering guitar, driving rock music and strident tape loops, to make a unique and exhilarating amalgamation. The strangeness of the concept is completed with the striking painted album cover by the English surrealist John Holmes (1935-2011), which depicts a man having a nail hammered into the back of his head.

Unsurprisingly the LP bewildered fans of Spooky Tooth and did not sell well, and still perplexes and enrages listeners to this day. While Henry's mixing and balancing of the music and electronics is sometimes flagrantly amiss, Ceremony remains a fascinating and remarkable experiment, that sounds like no other album.

Intermodulation

Origin: Cambridge
Formed: 1969
Disbanded: 1976
Obscurity Quotient: 6
EM Recording Availability: Limited

Formed at Cambridge University by **Andrew Powell**, **Roger Smalley** and **Tim Souster**, Intermodulation specialised in the performance of works for instruments and live electronics. The fourth founding member was Royal Academy of Music student, Robin Thompson, with Powell being replaced by Peter Britton in the autumn of 1970. Creating a bridge between rock and classical music, they equipped themselves with **EMS** VCS3 synthesizers, and gave regular performances around the UK, appearing at the Royal Albert Hall Proms in 1970, 71 and 74. Transformation 1, by Smalley, was scored for piano, microphones, ring modulator and filter, and among the pieces Souster wrote for the group were Chinese Whispers (1970), Waste Land Music (1970), and Zorna, commissioned by the BBC for the 1974 Proms. Before his departure, Powell composed Terilament, for electric organ and amplified piano; Solo Keyboard, for electric organ, VCS3 and tape delay; and Plasmogeny, for electric organ, distorted bass guitar, plus viola and bassoon played through a VCS3.

Intermodulation's compositions were performed alongside work by more established composers, including Cornelius Cardew, Christian Wolff, Terry Riley and Karlheinz Stockhausen. The members appeared in company with **Gentle Fire** in early renditions of Stockhausen's Sternklang, scored for five groups and premiered in the open air in a park in Berlin. Both outfits featured on the double LP recording released in 1975. Smalley left Britain in 1976 and relocated to Australia, while Souster continued live performance with a new group under the name 0dB.

Light/Sound Workshop

Origin: Hornsey, London
Formed: 1962
Disbanded: 1968
Obscurity Quotient: 7
EM Recording Availability: Poor

Starting in 1962 with a single 1KW projector, the team behind the Light/Sound Workshop at Hornsey College of Art in north London, began developing complex image sequencing and light modulation in conjunction with electronics. Before long they had progressed to three projectors, allowing continuously evolving sequences accompanied by electronic music. By 1967 the unit had at their disposal a 30 speaker sound diffusion system, integrated with a 60 feet half circular projection screen, with control console for selecting, mixing and moving sounds in space. The set-up was intended for collaboration with outside electronic composers, and at the Watermill Theatre, Bagnor, Berkshire in September 1966, they were involved in a concert of electronic music staged by the group **Unit Delta Plus**. The piece Random Together 1, by **Peter Zinovieff** and **Delia Derbyshire** was played back in three sections, with the middle passage heard in darkness, and the first and last parts featuring special Light/Sound Workshop projections.

Over a period of five years during the 1960s, Hornsey College lecturer Mike Leonard (1925-2012) and his team, developed versatile lighting apparatus constructed around a metal framework, to which a variety of light sources, filters, masks, motors, relays and lenses could be attached. This was used on Top of the Pops on BBC TV in a trial for the Christmas edition in 1967, mounted on a studio gantry with back projection onto large screens behind the performers. Leonard owned a capacious house in Highgate, London, with lodgers including future members of Pink Floyd, and where he had a workshop to carry out lighting experiments.

In 1971 he participated in the Electric Theatre exhibition at the ICA in London, and was engaged in creating two of the audio-visual exhibits. He had been commissioned by Practical Electronics to build the P.E. Aurora light box, and he contributed an informative article on light effects units and their construction, for the magazine in July 71. Besides the Aurora, the Electric Theatre featured his back projected coloured light mural, with electronic music accompaniment generated from a VCS3 synthesizer.

At the Brighton Festival in 1967, the West Pier played host to a spectacular display of kinetic audio visual environments by the Light/Sound Workshop, under the title K4. The main Arena housed a 360 degree immersive projection space, with cushions on the floor, and a 14 projector system suspended from the ceiling. Electronic sound accompaniment was created by Delia Derbyshire, under the auspices of Unit Delta Plus. For the two week residency the space operated in the late evening as a discotheque, and Saturday nights were reserved for special performances. These started off with Bruce Lacey and three electronic robots, and went on to feature Pink Floyd, The Pyramid, and a kinetic arts conference, with an appearance from Les Structures Sonores and the Lasry-Baschet Group.

At the Pavilion end of the West Pier, there were further audio-visual presentations by the Light/Sound Workshop. These included Data Scatter Mosaic, a back projection sequence with multiple images and sounds, conceived as a TV set of the future. The Large Projection Environment displayed continuously changing image sequences with electronic music, put together by participants from three units of the Workshop, involving Clive Latimer, Mike Leonard, Dennis Crompton, John Bowstead, Roger Jeffs, Colin Canon and Paul Harris. Other workshop members included Tony Rickaby, Peter Cook, Martin Salisbury, Peter Kuttner and Ron Sutherland.

Coinciding with certain ideas and a couple of shared members of radical British architectural group Archigram, the Light/Sound Workshop was an experimental platform for investigations into light, colour and motion. With much left to explore in the fusion of projections and electronic music, it was prematurely dissolved after the Hornsey College protest and sit-in during May and June 1968.

P.E. Aurora lighting effects at the ICA, 1971

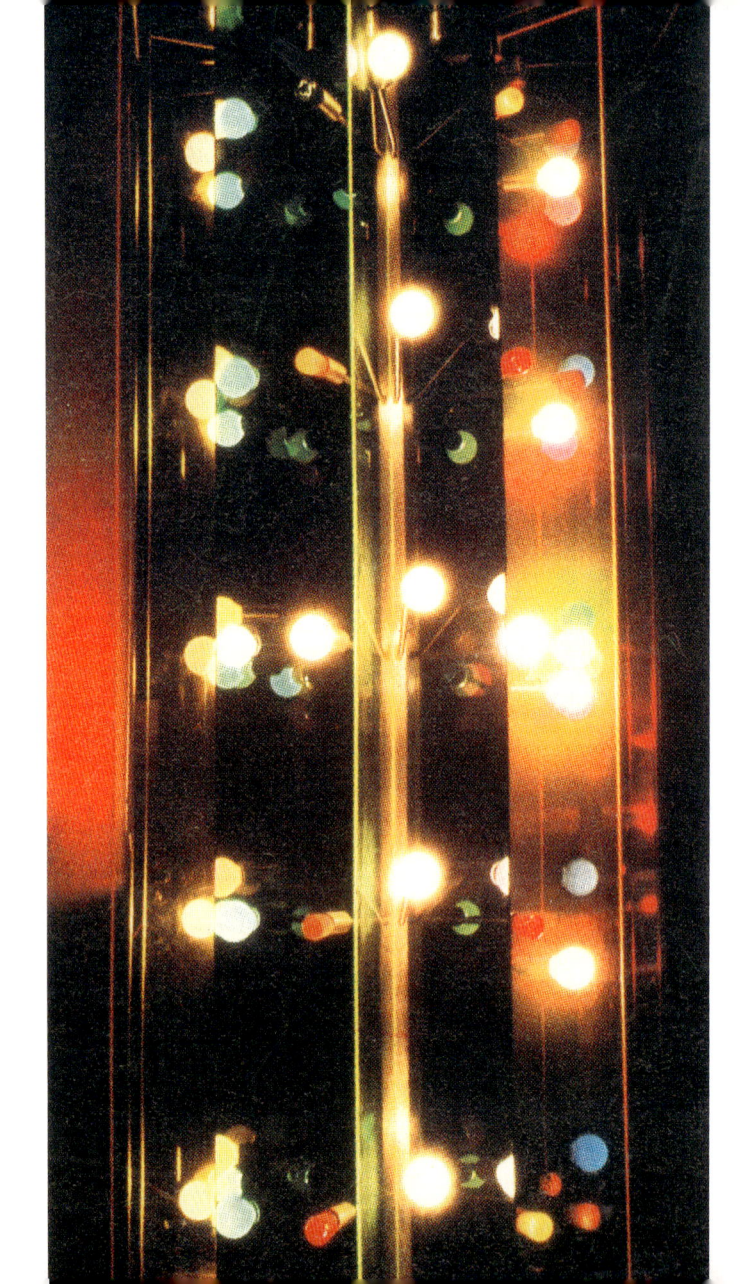

Action Space was founded in 1968 by Ken Turner, Mary Turner and Alan Nisbet. It set out to challenge the established gallery based arts scene, and redefine the role of artists in society. As part of a new wave of experimental and collective-run arts groups invigorated by the late 60s counter culture, it took interactive inflatable structures out into streets, parks, playgrounds, schools, shopping centres, derelict buildings and neglected housing estates. The members identified the need for art to reach the increasing underclass and dispossessed in London's high rise tower blocks, and for the inflatables to inspire creative play through music, drama and dance. Alan Nisbet contributed a range of skills including performance and music, and made tapes to be played at Action Space events. He sometimes used musique concrète techniques as well as electronics, to create experimental soundscapes as a backdrop for the inflatable environments. At the start of the 1980s the group restructured, with Action Space Mobile continuing to operate around the country, and Action Space London focussing on arts for people with learning disabilities.

Well established artist Bruce Lacey and his wife Jill Bruce, were working along similar lines to Action Space during the early 70s, with an interactive multi-media show, Journey Through a Black Hole to a Coloured Planet. It was housed in a giant inflatable structure, and featured costumes, lights, tape recorders, and what appeared to be a Dewtron self-built synthesizer. The work was documented in the 1973 film Outside In.

Super 8 film images by Ian Helliwell

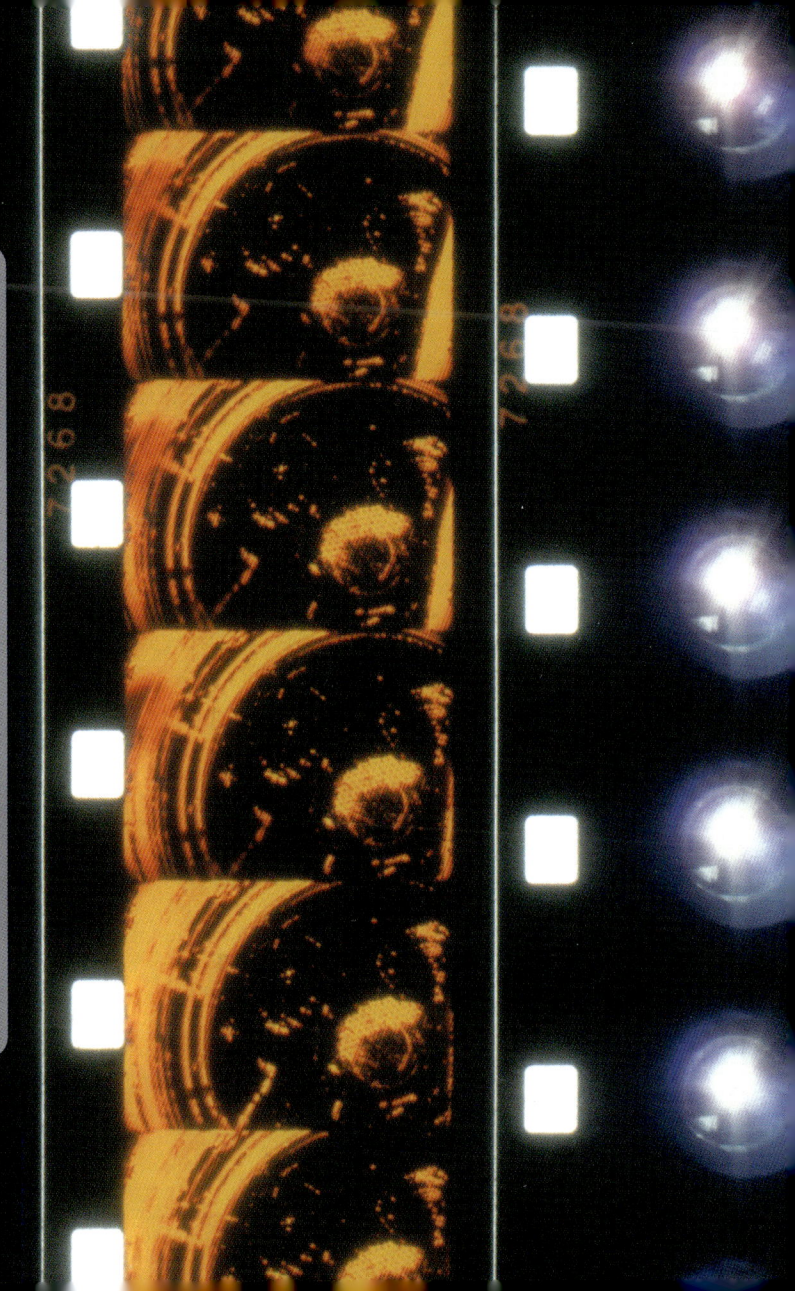

Music Plus

Origin: London
Formed: 1970
Disbanded: 197?
Obscurity Quotient: 9
EM recording availability: Poor

As part of a progressive initiative backed by the Inner London Education Authority, the Cockpit Theatre was built during 1969 in the Marylebone district of London. It opened the following year as a multi-media arts venue, hosting all manner of events, workshops and performances, often with an experimental edge. **Grahame Dudley** was appointed Director of Music, and set up an open-access electronic music studio, and established live performance groups, which could play in the theatre and give concerts around the country. Music Plus was one of three units active at the venue, along with the Cockpit Ensemble, and Sound, Light and Space – featuring members crossing over between them. The Cockpit Ensemble directed by **Malcolm Fox**, was conceived to introduce audiences to the sounds of modern music, with special projects devised for students.

It appears that Music Plus was activated first by Dudley not long after the Cockpit opened. Envisaged as a multi-media, electro-acoustic performance group, it presented live music and included lights, projections, kinetic sculpture and dance, as part of an immersive audiovisual experience. Op-artist Oliver Bevan was closely involved directing visuals, and one of his collaborations with Dudley titled Magic Squares, was presented by Music Plus at the Cockpit Theatre in December 1971. For the piece, four players sat in front of a painting featuring 12 square sections in different colours, designed to be assembled and interpreted as a musical score.

Besides Dudley, the musicians in Music Plus included Malcolm Fox, **James Ingram**, **Howard Davidson**, **Howard Rees**, and later Oliver Knussen and Irvine Arditti. They performed their own electro-acoustic compositions alongside contemporary British works, and gave UK premieres of pieces by Cage, Kagel and Stockhausen.

Naked Software

Origin: London
Formed: 1970-71
Disbanded: 1973
Obscurity Quotient: 8
EM Recording Availability: Poor

Naked Software involved **Howard Rees** (reeds), **John Lifton** (voice, electronics), **Hugh Davies** (electronics), **Anna Lockwood** (various sound sources) and Harvey Matusow (Jew's harp and devices). They experimented with all sorts of non-standard instruments, and performances were often triggered by some form of graphic information, which could be interpreted as a score. This could be anything from pressed seaweed, detailed maps or football programmes, to form the basis of group improvisations and multi-media spatial sound. The group appeared at ICES-72 in London, and for their Arnolfini concert in Bristol in the early 70s, they used Lockwood's glass instruments as the core of the performance. Other shows involved 12 Philips cassette tape recorders operated by a single switch, devised by Lifton and Matusow. The machines were set up in a circle for an immersive 360 degree spatial sound system, with tapes running in and out of phase. Naked Software dissolved when Matusow and Lockwood left Britain for the USA in 1973, and all the members went their separate ways.

Naked Software in the early 1970s

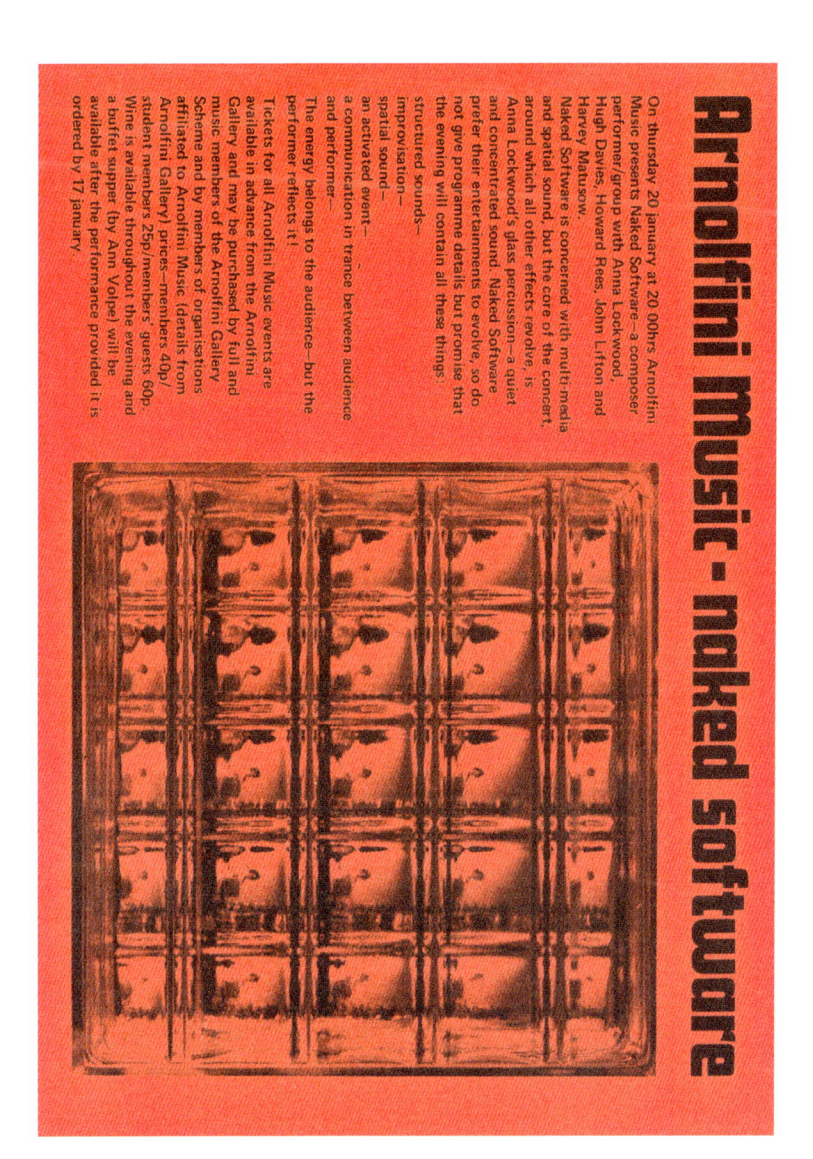

Arnolfini Music – naked software

On thursday 20 january at 20.00hrs Arnolfini Music presents Naked Software - a composer performer/group with Anna Lockwood, Hugh Davies, Howard Rees, John Lifton and Harvey Matusow.

Naked Software is concerned with multi-media and spatial sound, but the core of the concert, around which all other effects revolve, is Anna Lockwood's glass percussion – a quiet and concentrated sound. Naked Software prefer their entertainments to evolve, so do not give programme details but promise that the evening will contain all these things:

structured sounds—
improvisation—
spatial sound—
an activated event—
a communication in trance between audience and performer—

The energy belongs to the audience - but the performer reflects it !

Tickets for all Arnolfini Music events are available in advance from the Arnolfini Gallery and may be purchased by full and music members of the Arnolfini Gallery Scheme and by members of organisations affiliated to Arnolfini Music (details from Arnolfini Gallery) prices—members 40p/student members 25p/members guests 60p. Wine is available throughout the evening and a buffet supper (by Ann Volpe) will be available after the performance provided it is ordered by 17 january.

Quiet Pavement Ensemble

Origin: London
Formed: 1968
Disbanded: 197?
Obscurity Quotient: 10
EM Recording Availability: Poor

Established by Adrian Nutbeem (born 1946 in Ilford, London) and John Bucklow (born 1947 in Oldham, Lancashire), the [Gentlemen of the] Quiet Pavement Ensemble, was a platform for their activites with live performance and sound transformation. Their first show was for the Bluecoat Arts Forum at the Royal Institute Galleries, and they went on to create an installation for the 1968 Festival of Sound in London. At the Eye and Ear Concert at Mountford Hall, Liverpool University, in January 1969, the programme included tape pieces by **Donald Henshilwood**, Pierre Henry and Luciano Berio, plus Object-Text-Light-Interval, by the QPE.

Nutbeem and Bucklow were fellow students at Camberwell College of Arts, and both were pursuing experiments with sound and electronic technology. They collaborated on the Computer Arts Society exhibition Event One, at the Royal College of Art in March 1969, which involved work by **John Lifton**, and many other leading practitioners of electronic and computer based art. Their piece was based on picking up vocal and environmental sounds in the exhibition, with those signals activating a bank of lights, which in turn was sensed by photocells. The light modulated photocells triggered tone generators to feed electronic sounds back into the network.

Bucklow had begun by making art from transient materials, dependent on outside changes of light or temperature. Over a five year period he examined the generation and interaction of electronic sound and light, and proceeded to explore cymatics and liquid crystals, continuing his activities based in New Zealand. Nutbeem qualified as a design engineer, and through his career has investigated audio, photography, video, electromechanical engineering and amphibious vehicles. He was chairman of Amfibian Research and Development based in Suffolk, until the company went under in 2011.

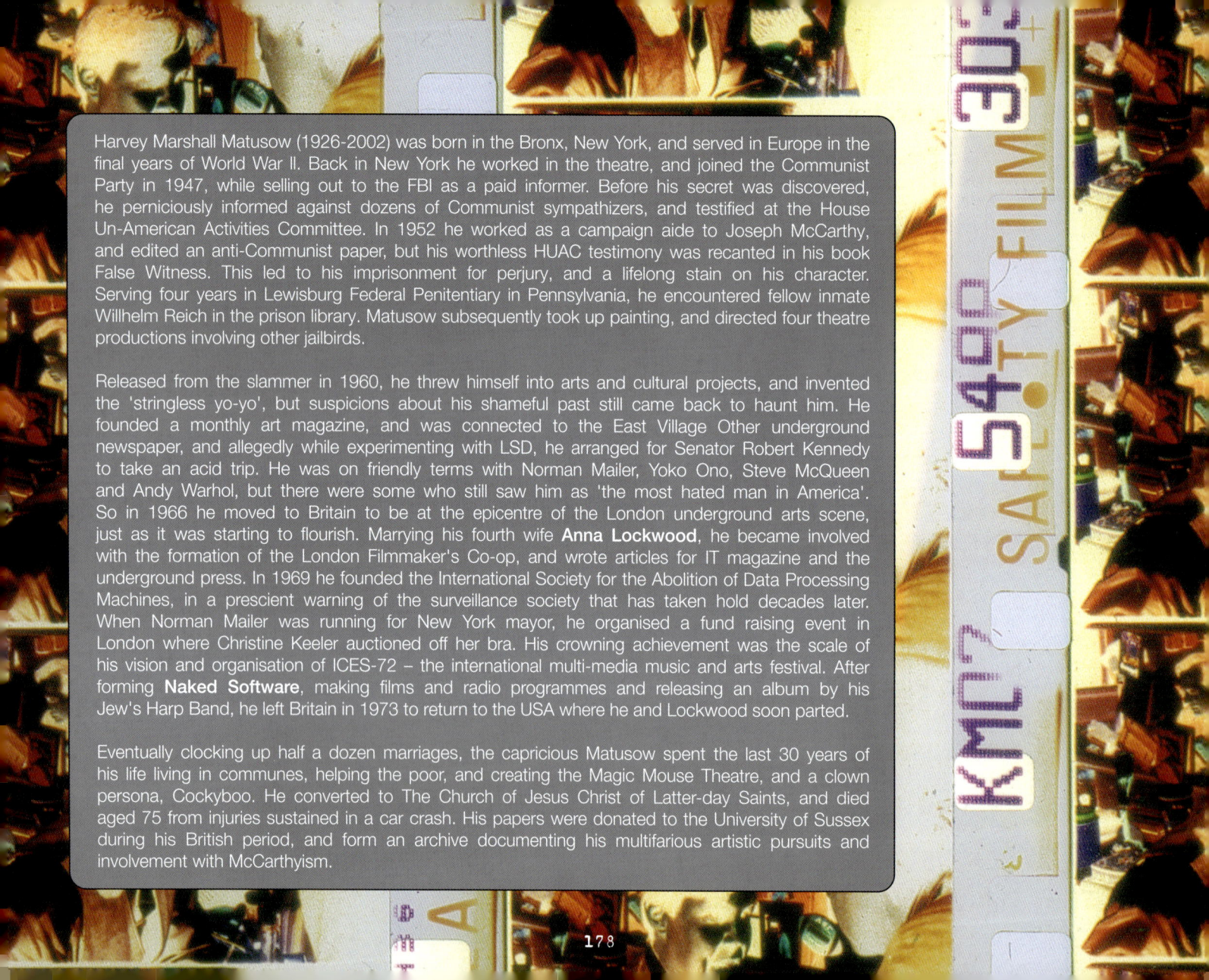

Harvey Marshall Matusow (1926-2002) was born in the Bronx, New York, and served in Europe in the final years of World War II. Back in New York he worked in the theatre, and joined the Communist Party in 1947, while selling out to the FBI as a paid informer. Before his secret was discovered, he perniciously informed against dozens of Communist sympathizers, and testified at the House Un-American Activities Committee. In 1952 he worked as a campaign aide to Joseph McCarthy, and edited an anti-Communist paper, but his worthless HUAC testimony was recanted in his book False Witness. This led to his imprisonment for perjury, and a lifelong stain on his character. Serving four years in Lewisburg Federal Penitentiary in Pennsylvania, he encountered fellow inmate Willhelm Reich in the prison library. Matusow subsequently took up painting, and directed four theatre productions involving other jailbirds.

Released from the slammer in 1960, he threw himself into arts and cultural projects, and invented the 'stringless yo-yo', but suspicions about his shameful past still came back to haunt him. He founded a monthly art magazine, and was connected to the East Village Other underground newspaper, and allegedly while experimenting with LSD, he arranged for Senator Robert Kennedy to take an acid trip. He was on friendly terms with Norman Mailer, Yoko Ono, Steve McQueen and Andy Warhol, but there were some who still saw him as 'the most hated man in America'. So in 1966 he moved to Britain to be at the epicentre of the London underground arts scene, just as it was starting to flourish. Marrying his fourth wife **Anna Lockwood**, he became involved with the formation of the London Filmmaker's Co-op, and wrote articles for IT magazine and the underground press. In 1969 he founded the International Society for the Abolition of Data Processing Machines, in a prescient warning of the surveillance society that has taken hold decades later. When Norman Mailer was running for New York mayor, he organised a fund raising event in London where Christine Keeler auctioned off her bra. His crowning achievement was the scale of his vision and organisation of ICES-72 – the international multi-media music and arts festival. After forming **Naked Software**, making films and radio programmes and releasing an album by his Jew's Harp Band, he left Britain in 1973 to return to the USA where he and Lockwood soon parted.

Eventually clocking up half a dozen marriages, the capricious Matusow spent the last 30 years of his life living in communes, helping the poor, and creating the Magic Mouse Theatre, and a clown persona, Cockyboo. He converted to The Church of Jesus Christ of Latter-day Saints, and died aged 75 from injuries sustained in a car crash. His papers were donated to the University of Sussex during his British period, and form an archive documenting his multifarious artistic pursuits and involvement with McCarthyism.

Unit Delta Plus

Origin: London
Formed: 1965
Disbanded: 1967
Obscurity Quotient: 6
EM Recording Availability: Limited

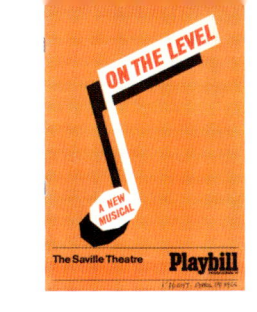

As a venture for supplying electronic music commercially as well as in lectures and presentations, the collaboration between **Delia Derbyshire**, **Brian Hodgson** and **Peter Zinovieff** was cemented in the mid-1960s, with Unit Delta Plus based at Zinovieff's advanced home studio in Deodar Road, Putney, London. Various commissions soon started to come their way; The John Arden play The Business of Good Government, has the group's stamp with Derbyshire having created the score. It was first performed in West Wickham, Kent in late 1965. On The Level (1966), a musical by Ron Grainer, also has the Unit Delta Plus credit, with Derbyshire working on it between August 1965 and February 66. Around this time she also created electronic sound for Esso, Philips, and ICI Fibres, who sponsored a fashion show by students of the Royal College of Art.

Although there was a tendency for the three members to work individually on projects, the full group staged a concert at the Watermill Theatre near Newbury, in September 1966. In attendance were Radiophonic colleagues **Desmond Briscoe** and David Cain, and poet John Betjeman, with the event involving slides and kinetic projections by the Hornsey **Light/Sound Workshop**. On the bill were the pieces Amor Dei, Tarantella, Moogies Bloogies, Fragment, Potpourri and Random Together 1; the latter a three part composition created jointly by Derbyshire and Zinovieff, with the first and last sections designed for special projections by the Light/Sound Workshop. The programme notes for the evening explained that Unit Delta Plus specialised in electronic switching and sequencing, and the harnessing of controlled randomness.

UDP participated in the Million Volt Light and Sound Rave, at the Roundhouse in London, over two nights in Jan/Feb 1967; the event being a showcase for projections and electronic music, including Carnival of Light by **The Beatles**. Also that year a production of Macbeth, staged by the RSC at Stratford-upon-Avon, featured a score by Guy Woolfenden and electronic music by Unit Delta Plus. The group made its final appearance at the Royal Academy of Music in November 67, though details for the event are sketchy. With Zinovieff's studio undergoing upheavals to install new equipment, recording access for the trio was restricted, and as their diverging interests pulled in opposing directions, a split by the year's end was perhaps inevitable.

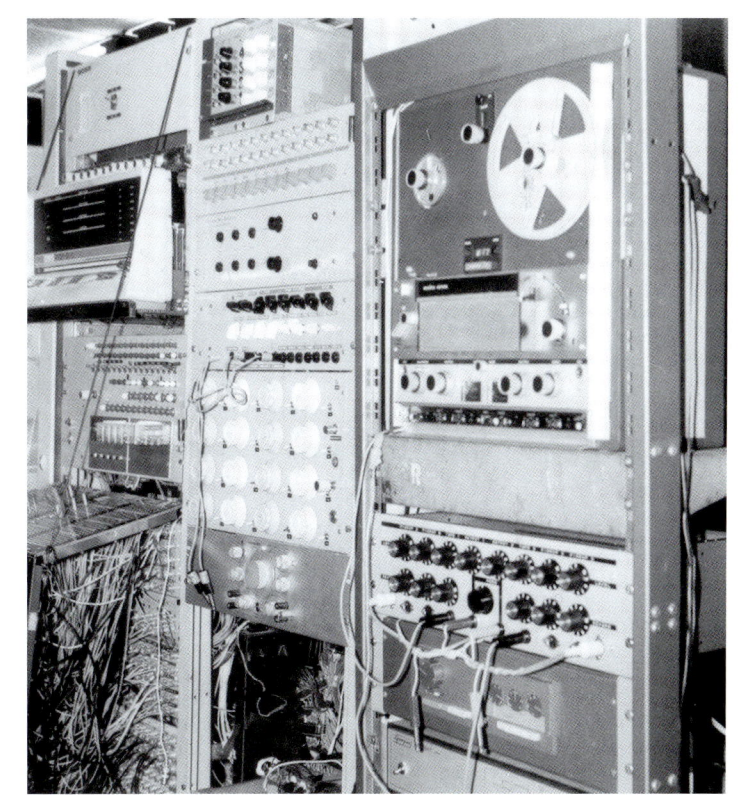

A section of Peter Zinovieff's Deodar Road studio

White Noise

Origin: London
Formed: 1968
Disbanded: Ongoing
Obscurity Quotient: 4
EM Recording Availability: Excellent

From the ashes of **Unit Delta Plus**, a new collaboration crystallized between experienced **BBC Radiophonic Workshop** composers **Delia Derbyshire** and **Brian Hodgson**, and young American born musician **David Vorhaus**. Following an inspirational college lecture in London by Unit Delta Plus members in 1967, Vorhaus approached Derbyshire and Hodgson, and an alliance was formed later that year. White Noise came into being in 1968 with the recording of a 2 track demo, and the intention of attracting a singles deal. While Derbyshire and Hodgson were under contract to the BBC, Vorhaus approached Island Records boss Chris Blackwell, who was looking instead towards the progressive LP market. He advanced the group £3000 to record an album; a huge sum of money in the late 1960s for an unknown quantity.

Although Derbyshire and Vorhaus were the driving forces behind the album's conception, the three electronic tunesmiths worked in their recently established Kaleidophon studio in Camden, equipped with multiple tape recorders and home-made devices. They also carried out recording surreptitiously in the evening at the Radiophonic Workshop, and for the making of one particular track Vorhaus explained in an interview, "*My Game of Loving, had just about everybody I met in it over that month or two. A French girl did one version, then a German girl, then a Swedish girl. Each version a different country. They're all for real. In fact there was even an electronic orgy in it and a real orgy, and you'd be hard pressed even now to tell which was the real one.*" The recording took a year, and when Island issued an ultimatum for the finished product, the final track was completed in a few days. An Electric Storm was issued to little fanfare in 1969; White Noise played no gigs, but the album sold slowly and steadily and remained in print throughout the 1970s, achieving the number one spot in Holland.

While the group was put on ice following the first LP, Vorhaus did some sessions in the early 1970s with ex-Soft Machine musician/composer Kevin Ayers, and through this connection, struck up a friendship with Virgin supremo Richard Branson. With the personnel stripped down to just Vorhaus, White Noise 2 was released on Virgin Records in 1975, featuring the four movement Concerto for Synthesizer. On the LP cover he explained. "*In this concerto, the synthesizer, a solo instrument, now also creates its own ensemble since I built a 16 track tape recorder for company. The Kaleidophon Synthesizer includes a couple of VCS3s, but is basically a console of electronic modules I've designed since 'White Noise 1' to bring to life all the sounds I imagined.*"

Further releases have been sporadic, with the albums White Noise 3-5 appearing between 1980 and 2000. More recently there has been regular live performance activity, with Vorhaus playing alongside Mike Painter under the White Noise banner.

CDs: White Noise: An Electric Storm (Island, 2007 reissue).
    White Noise 2 (Virgin, 1975).

35mm slide montage by Ian Helliwell

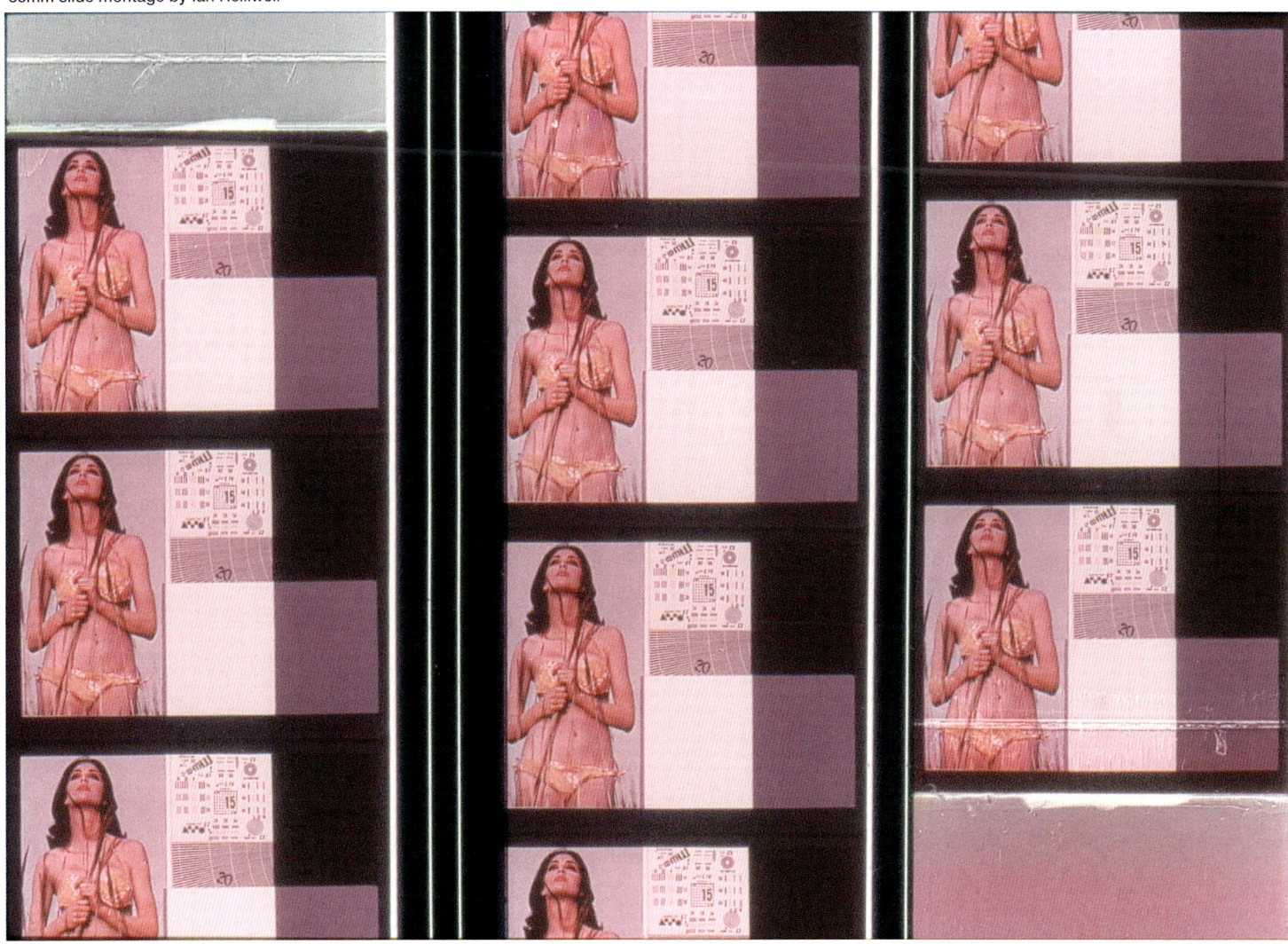

④ EMS – ELECTRONIC MUSIC STUDIOS

EMS - BACKGROUND

In its dual role as a pioneering computer-controlled studio and leading synthesizer manufacturer, EMS played a significant part in early British electronic music, and was known across the world for its innovative products. From the early 1960s **Peter Zinovieff** had been building up his own collection of electronic music equipment, and continuing at his home at 49 Deodar Road in Putney, SW London, he initially bought ex-government and war surplus test equipment from electronics shops in Lisle Street, London, and set up his gear in a garden outhouse overlooking the Thames. With its increasing complexity and evolution into the first computer-driven private studio in Britain by 1967, expenditure on new apparatus and upkeep was proving costly. The personal backing and wealth of Zinovieff's wife could only stretch so far, and to generate extra revenue, the idea of a company to manufacture and sell electronic music equipment to fund the studio, was an ambitious but realistic way forward.

The seeds for the creation of EMS had been sown through the working relationship with Mark Dowson, and then engineer David Cockerell, who had the ability to translate Zinovieff's ideas for electronic gadgetry, into designs for fully functional circuits. In time they realised that the next logical step was to harness the capabilities of computer process control, hitherto used in manufacturing industries, and by 1967 Zinovieff had bought a DEC PDP-8/S; the first computer to be installed in a private house in Britain. After the sale of his wife's tiara to fund his extravagant purchases, it was decided that a new company should be formed, and EMS - the Electronic Music Studios (London) Ltd. – came into being most likely during the latter part of 1968, though only formally constituted as a limited company in 1969. Zinovieff had earlier become aware that he was not alone in Britain, in trying to get together a sophisticated and versatile facility to make electronic music; over many years **Tristram Cary** had built up one of the best equipped analogue studios in the country. After the demise of **Unit Delta Plus** in November 1967, it was a propitious time to launch EMS with a partnership between Zinovieff, Cary, and Cockerell. **Alan Sutcliffe** and Humphrey Evans also had a connection, with Sutcliffe becoming a co-director in 1973.

Back at the start, a commission for an electronic sound generator for **Don Banks**, was fulfilled with the prototype Don Banks Music Box, the first of three such units. An initial model of the EMS Electronic Studio Mark 1 was offered for sale in early 1969 for £260, though this never actually went into production. After further research and development, later that year the team came up with the VCS3; Cockerell creating the circuitry, and Cary building the distinctive cabinet. This was a classic design, and similar in portability to the Synket synthesizer, developed in Rome by Paul Ketoff in 1963. It saw EMS launch itself into manufacturing a revolutionary new range of semi-affordable machines;

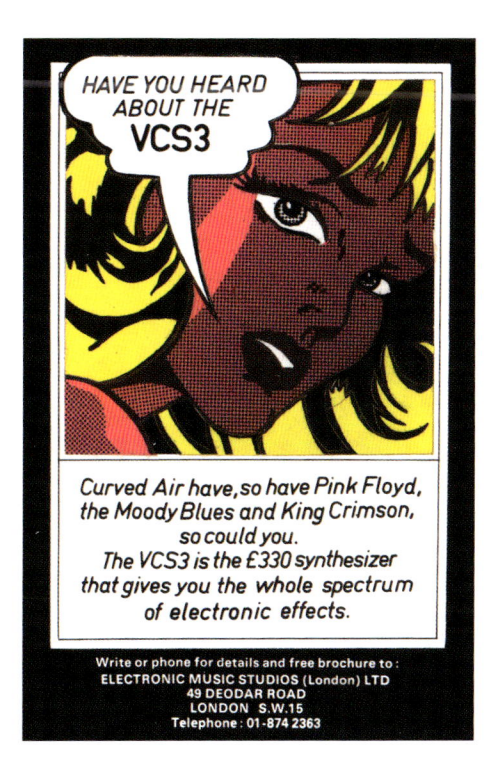

the first European company to enter the nascent but rapidly expanding synthesizer market. The VCS3, and suitcase Synthi A which was launched in 1971, both featured joystick and pin matrix patch system, proving to be highly suitable for pop and experimental music, and ideal for education, being bought by many colleges and universities across Britain. (The Synthi E was later designed to cater more specifically for this educational market, and introduced in 1975.)

There was an admirable utopian streak in Zinovieff's approach, which chimed perfectly with the counter-cultural times of London in the late 1960s and early 70s. While showing scant regard for commercial electronic music or rock and pop, he was initially sceptical of the need to supply a keyboard with the VCS3. He had not anticipated British rock groups such as **Hawkwind**, Pink Floyd, King Crimson, Curved Air, Roxy Music and Zorch, picking up on the instruments' potential. In February 1969 the company masterminded, and supplied sound equipment for a major concert of British electronic music at the Queen Elizabeth Hall in London. The terrific line-up included pieces by Cary and Zinovieff, as well as composers who had worked at EMS; Don Banks, Alan Sutcliffe, **Justin Connolly** and **Lawrence Casserley**. The printed programme for the event carried several pages devoted to the company, and the various products and services it could offer. Among these were the design, manufacture and installation of equipment, and facilities for hire for the composition and recording of electronic music. Among the products offered for sale were the EMS Dynamic Filter for £90, a twin ring modulator for £60, and a complete computerized electronic music system from £20,000; a colossal sum of money in 1969. While Zinovieff's Deodar Road home remained the nerve centre of studio operations, the company opened up a nearby shop at 277 Putney Bridge Road, from which to sell the EMS Synthi range.

Besides David Cockerell, EMS designers, programmers and engineers included **Peter Grogono**, Jim Lawson, Peter Eastty, Richard Monkhouse, Tim Orr, and Synthi A designer Brian Rodgers. When Grogono joined EMS in early 1969, Zinovieff's new PDP-8/L, christened Leo, had recently been acquired. Leo was an order of magnitude faster than the existing DEC computer named Sofka, which was already connected to various electronic music devices. These included a huge bank of oscillators, with outputs passing through envelope shapers, filters, and a mixer to produce the final signal. It was decided that Leo should do the computing and pass results to Sofka for delivery, and Grogono's first job at EMS was to write code for Leo, to cooperate with its slower counterpart. This became the music software MUSYS/1, which Grogono developed further, and by 1978 it had evolved into the programming language MOUSE.

EMS was certainly not short on ideas and innovation, and various prototypes for new machines were built but never marketed. One that did go into production was the EMS Spectre/Spectron colour video synthesizer, developed by Richard Monkhouse in 1974. Although it is reckoned only 15 were built, this was a complex analogue-digital hybrid that offered fantastic possibilities in video synthesis. It allowed audio signals to generate and manipulate images, and featured the trademark EMS pin matrix patch system. The Spectron can be seen in the Chris Marker film Sans Soleil (Sunless), made in 1983.

As well as the competitively priced portable machines at the lower budget end of the synthesizer market, from 1971 EMS also supplied the massive Synthi 100 to academic institutions and broadcasting stations. In Britain these included the **BBC Radiophonic Workshop**, and universities at Cardiff, East Anglia, and Glasgow. Internationally it was first ordered by Radio Belgrade in what is now the capital of Serbia, and subsequently purchased by the Institute for Psychoacoustics and Electronic Music (IPEM) in Ghent, Holland; Carleton University, in Ottawa, Canada; the University of Melbourne, Australia; and at Indiana University South Bend Electronic Studio, USA. More than 25 Synthi 100's were built and installed, and a few still survive today, including the machines in Belgrade and Melbourne. The instrument employed VCS3 technology expanded into one gargantuan unit; with 12 VCOs, 2 keyboards and a 256 step monophonic digital sequencer, it also featured two 64 x 64 patch matrices and a built in oscilloscope. This analogue leviathan has never been topped for sheer size.

Cary and Zinovieff were conscious of the lack of an accessible national electronic music studio for composers to use, and to press for such an amenity, both were closely involved with the formation of the short lived British Society for Electronic Music (BSEM). The small but sophisticated EMS studio became a de facto centre, hosting visits and recording by Hans Werner Henze, **Harrison Birtwistle**, **David Lumsdaine** and **David Rowland**, as well as Cary's RCM students. At the start of the 70s **FC Judd** visited EMS, and his

EMS Spectre

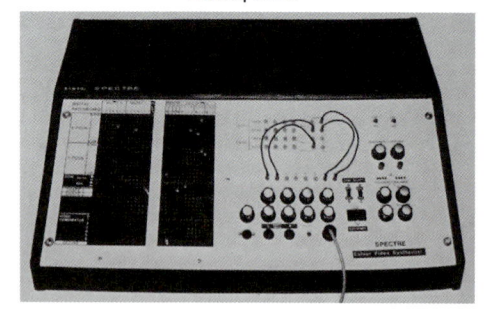

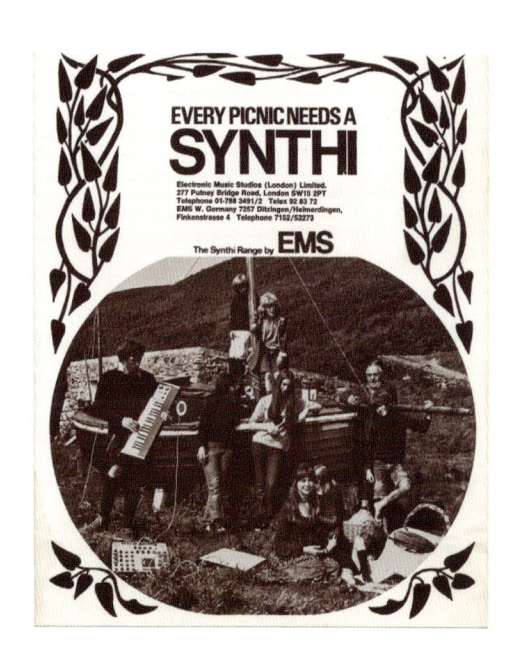

EMS studio in 1973. L-R: Jim Lawson, John Holbrook, Peter Zinovieff and Tristram Cary

1972 book Electronics In Music, carried adverts for the company and a Synthi 100 pictured on the cover. In the text he explained that the previous year, Zinovieff had offered his studio and all its equipment to the nation, valued at that time at around £40,000. The offer was free of charge providing a suitable venue and upkeep were offered in return. It was not taken up, and some years later when EMS was in need of rescue, a potential lifeline was held out by the National Theatre in London. This proved to be an unfortunate state of affairs; the National appeared to have agreed to house the equipment, and effectively create the world class, accessible studio that had been envisaged and campaigned for by the BSEM. However, for reasons now difficult to discover, the National withdrew from the deal, and some of the valuable EMS gear they had been storing in the Theatre's basement, ended up falling into disrepair and was eventually destroyed.

As Zinovieff's first marriage dissolved, and financial difficulties with the company became apparent, EMS moved from Putney to his new home in Great Milton, Oxfordshire during 1976. There were discussions about space at Oxford University being allocated in conjunction with **Robert Sherlaw Johnson**, though the idea never got off the ground. David Cockerell left EMS in 1974, and Tristram Cary followed suit the same year. Zinovieff had spent much time up in Scotland working on the Mask of Orpheus libretto for Harrison Birtwistle, and consequently his attention had shifted, and he became much less involved in directing the company. While manufacture of Synthis carried on throughout the 70s, several products, including the Synthi Hi-Fli, failed to take off, and stiff competition from Japan and the USA contributed to the demise of EMS. It finally folded in 1979, and the assets were bought by Datanomics. They were a company that made hospital beds and medical gear, based in Wareham, a small town in Dorset, where EMS manufacturing was already being carried out. Datanomics managed to produce vocoders, the two popular Synthi models, as well as developing the Datasynth, but they bailed out of the commercial synthesizer market, and EMS was sold again in 1984. Well established composer and VCS3 user **Edward Williams** took over, and The Soundbeam and upgrades to the vocoder were made during his ownership. Eventually Robin Wood, who had been an employee of the company since 1970, acquired the full rights in 1995. From his base near Truro, Cornwall, he keeps the EMS flag flying, and produces a small number of Synthi As and VCS3s, though not without a sizeable waiting list.

P.E. SOUND SYNTHESISER

Get away to a flying start with this exciting Space Age project. Precision cut metal parts to form modular units as described in the March issue are available NOW.
A. Power supply subframe with tab drillings only **£1·35** (P. & P. 25p).
B. Circuit board support plates fully drilled, 94p.
Panels drilled with locating holes only: C. 20mm, 18p; D. 38mm, 21p; E. 60·5mm, 28p; F. 64mm, 31p; G. Module locking rods complete, £1·20 ea. SAVE MONEY by obtaining a complete kit of hardware which comprises 1 off each A, C, D, F, 5 off E, and 7 off B, G **£17·42**, Post Free.

EATON AUDIO
P.O. Box No. 3
ST. NEOTS
HUNTINGDON
PE19 3JB

TERMS: MAIL ORDER ONLY. C.W.O. Cheques or crossed P.O. payable to Eaton Audio. Minimum order £2. Where P. & P. charges are not shown please add 10p in the £1 to orders under £5. Orders over £5 will be sent free of P. & P. All prices subject to V.A.T. increases from 1st April.

The EMS studio at Great Milton in the late 1970s

Next Month...
we enter our Second Decade

with the PE MINISONIC

breaking the "Sound Barrier"

...it's down in size!
...it's down in cost!

Next month we mark ten years of lusty existence with the "Minisonic", a miniature battery operated synthesiser for the experimenter, which can provide endless varieties of sound.

Not a toy but a creative instrument with two log v.c.os, two envelope shapers and v.c.a.s with variable attack and decay. A voltage controlled low-pass filter, ring modulator, white noise generator and two 250mW amplifiers with monitor speakers complete the circuit line-up.

A novel stylus operated integral keyboard provides control of the v.c.os. Alternatively, this can be achieved by adding a 'normal' keyboard or applying external control voltages.

For less than £50 you can programme your own kaleidoscope of exciting synthi-sounds.

A Synthesiser for less than £50!

also in this issue:
- CAR ANTI-THEFT SYSTEM
- NOVEL TRANSISTOR TESTER
- BATTERY ELIMINATOR FOR CASSETTE RECORDERS

PRACTICAL ELECTRONICS
NOVEMBER ISSUE ON SALE MID-OCTOBER, 1974

A VERSATILE INSTRUMENT FOR THE COMPOSER, MUSICIAN OR KEEN EXPERIMENTER IN THE CREATION OF SOUNDS IMITATIVE OR UNIQUE

By G.D. SHAW

Sound Synthesiser

Practical Electronics February 1973

Following on from the breakthrough in British synthesizer design and manufacture by **EMS**, the company D.E.W. LTD. founded by Brian Baily, took up the supply of synth kits. These were in fact modules with leads to be connected and power supplies added, sold under the name Dewtron, from 254 Ringwood Road, Ferndown, Dorset. Trading as Dewtron Engineering (Wokingham), Baily had started placing small ads in Practical Electronics magazine in 1965, and by 1971 he was listing for sale a variety of mail order synthesizer modules which he had designed. The Dewtron Project X was a build yourself synth, which could incorporate all the devices for a fully equipped unit, and was followed up by the Apollo and Gypsy synthesizers. These were offered as self-assembly or ready-made, and rock group Led Zeppelin are rumoured to have bought an Apollo. Adopting a similar patching arrangement to EMS which avoided leads, Dewtron boasted of a "*man-sized robust patchboard*," with a pin matrix to connect modules, all for a fraction of the price of a commercial machine. Retailing at £330 in 1969, the EMS Synthi VCS3 was well over 10 times the average weekly wage in Britain, leaving many keen electronic music devotees and hobbyists, with no way to afford a machine of their own.

With affordability in mind, Practical Electronics magazine commissioned designer GD Shaw, to come up with a low cost synth project for home constructors to build. This resulted in the 'P.E. Sound Synthesiser' first appearing in February 1973; an ambitious home engineering challenge which ran through 13 issues, concluding in February the following year. Building from scratch represented a monumental task for any but the most circuit-savvy synth solderer, and as a result, in November 1974, Practical Electronics published Shaw's next design for the battery powered, stylus activated Minisonic synthesizer. Although a more modest and simpler affair to build, it still offered a wide array of electronic sounds, and was backed up with articles by **Malcolm Pointon**. In June 1975 his description and graphic score of his composition Symbiosis, was published to inspire use of the Minisonic.

BUILD A
PROJECT 'X' SYNTHESISER

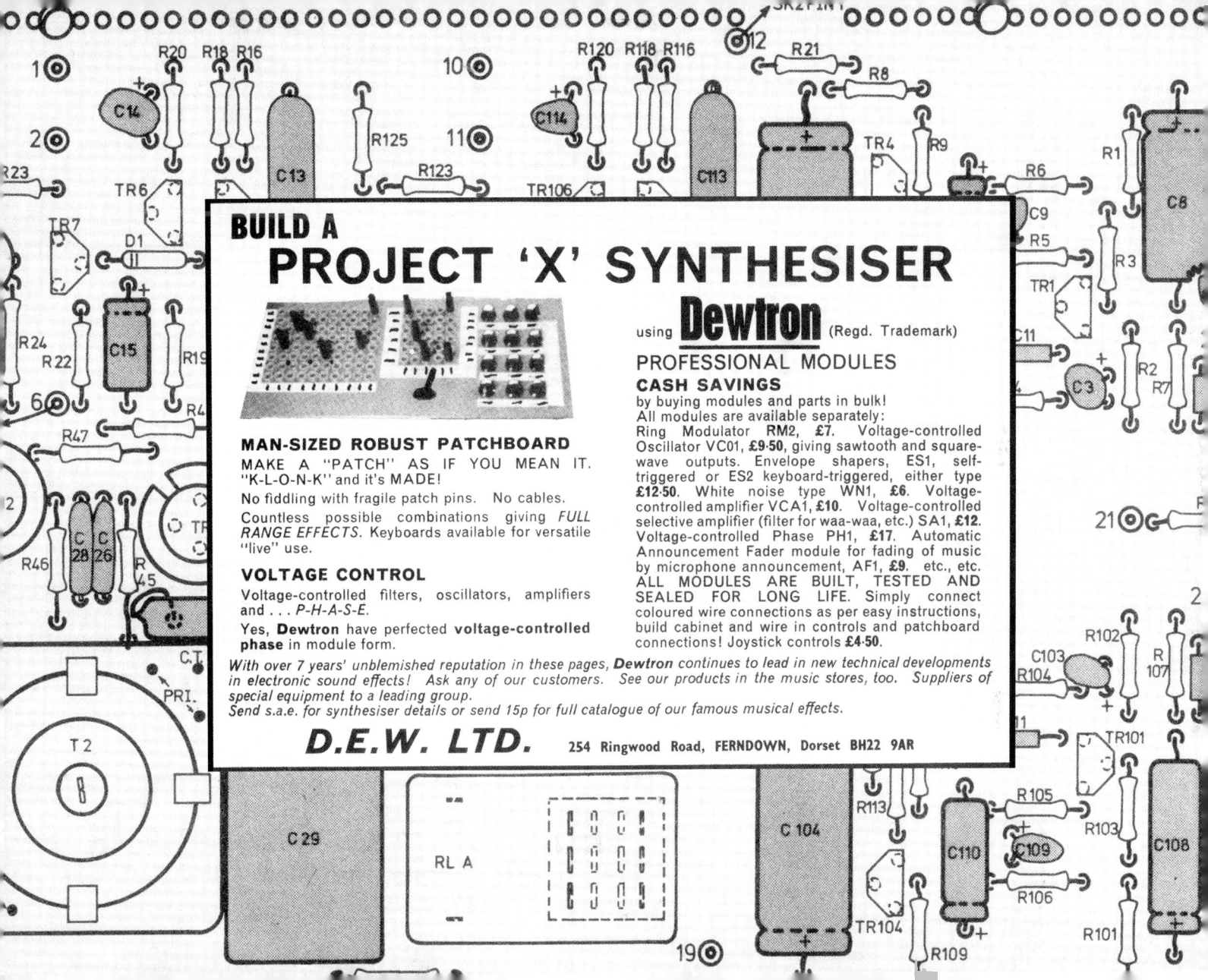

using **Dewtron** (Regd. Trademark)

PROFESSIONAL MODULES

CASH SAVINGS
by buying modules and parts in bulk!
All modules are available separately:
Ring Modulator RM2, **£7**. Voltage-controlled Oscillator VC01, **£9·50**, giving sawtooth and squarewave outputs. Envelope shapers, ES1, self-triggered or ES2 keyboard-triggered, either type **£12·50**. White noise type WN1, **£6**. Voltage-controlled amplifier VCA1, **£10**. Voltage-controlled selective amplifier (filter for waa-waa, etc.) SA1, **£12**. Voltage-controlled Phase PH1, **£17**. Automatic Announcement Fader module for fading of music by microphone announcement, AF1, **£9**. etc., etc. ALL MODULES ARE BUILT, TESTED AND SEALED FOR LONG LIFE. Simply connect coloured wire connections as per easy instructions, build cabinet and wire in controls and patchboard connections. Joystick controls **£4·50**.

MAN-SIZED ROBUST PATCHBOARD
MAKE A "PATCH" AS IF YOU MEAN IT. "K-L-O-N-K" and it's MADE!
No fiddling with fragile patch pins. No cables. Countless possible combinations giving *FULL RANGE EFFECTS*. Keyboards available for versatile "live" use.

VOLTAGE CONTROL
Voltage-controlled filters, oscillators, amplifiers and ... P-H-A-S-E.

Yes, **Dewtron** have perfected **voltage-controlled phase** in module form.

With over 7 years' unblemished reputation in these pages, **Dewtron** *continues to lead in new technical developments in electronic sound effects! Ask any of our customers. See our products in the music stores, too. Suppliers of special equipment to a leading group.*

Send s.a.e. for synthesiser details or send 15p for full catalogue of our famous musical effects.

D.E.W. LTD.   254 Ringwood Road, FERNDOWN, Dorset BH22 9AR

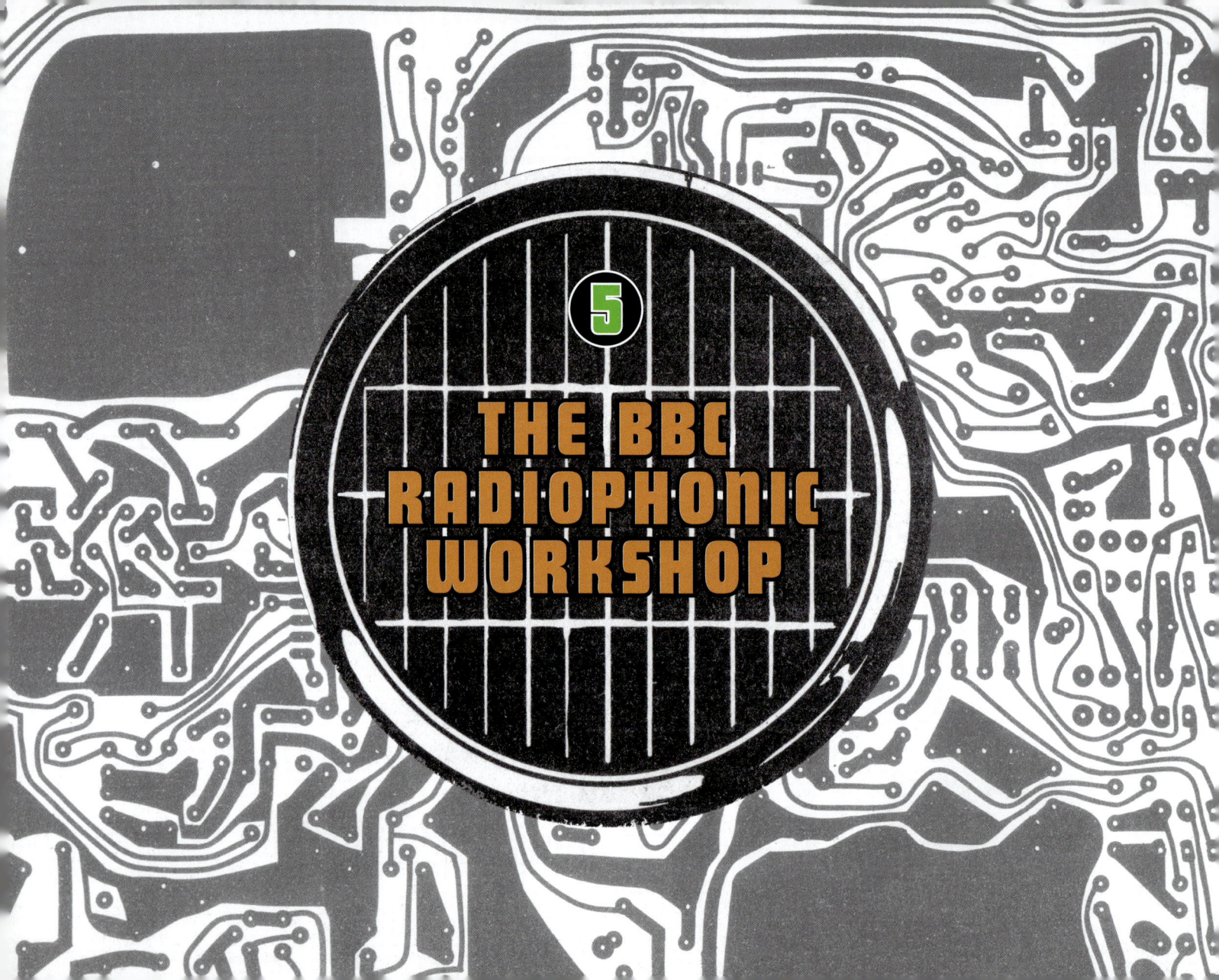

THE BBC RADIOPHONIC WORKSHOP

5

BBC RADIOPHONIC WORKSHOP - BACKGROUND

The celebrated BBC sound unit was established under the auspices of the Drama Department, and was officially opened on the 1st April 1958. In the run up to its formation, the Electrophonic Effects Committee (EEC), made up of producers, studio managers and BBC officials, was convened in December 1956, to examine how the Corporation should proceed in the production and application of electronic music. With figures in the Music Department displaying an unconcealed dread of the lunatic fringe taking over the airwaves, and undermining the musical output of the nation, the stakes were high, and traditionalists were set firmly in opposition to enthusiasts in the Drama Department.

Producers such as Donald McWhinnie, proposed that experimental work should be conducted for its own sake, without it necessarily being used for broadcast. After a visit to Paris and consultation with Pierre Schaefer and his colleagues, he recommended the equipment for a basic electronic studio. The BBC Music Department was essentially hostile to musique concrète, and tried to head off radical developments with the purchase of a 'multi-colour tone organ', an ill-suited substitute for the essential tools of tape recorders, tone generators, modulators and filters. By March 1957 the EEC evolved into the Radiophonic Effects Committee, and producer Douglas Cleverdon organised monthly listening sessions, for the playback of electronic music recordings for interested staff. The venue of the Radiophonic Workshop was eventually decided upon, and the former Maida Vale skating rink, converted in the 1930s into BBC studios for music recording, was the chosen site.

Daphne Oram had been pressing for such a unit through most of the 1950s, and along with fellow studio manager **Desmond Briscoe**, she had worked on programmes which cemented the need for the Workshop's formation. Outside composers such as **Humphrey Searle**, **Tristram Cary** and **Roberto Gerhard**, had also carried out experimental work for BBC productions prior to its opening, but once it came into existence its scope was limited as a service department, largely making sounds for radio and television. This dashed the hopes of experimentalists both beyond and within the Corporation, who felt that Britain should have an accessible national electronic studio, to rival that of broadcasters RTF in Paris, and WDR in Cologne. Nonetheless, once up and running, the Workshop produced a wide variety of electronic music and special sound effects, which found a home in all kinds of programmes. Much of its work involved quite simplistic signature tunes, ditties and call signs, yet this was balanced out by experimental and provocative pieces, particularly for radio. This cutting edge lasted through the 1960s and into the 70s – composers including **Daevid Allen**, **George Newson**, **Roger Smalley** and **Marc Wilkinson**, as well as concrete poets **Bob Cobbing**, Barry Bermange, Brion Gysin and Lily Greenham – all gained the opportunity to work there. In its first year of existence, the small staff included founders

Daphne Oram and Desmond Briscoe, with Dick Mills and Jimmy Burnett, plus technician Richard 'Dickie' Bird. After 15 years with the BBC, Oram resigned in January 1959, and Briscoe took over as studio head officially in March 1960. Following Bird's death three years later, David Young was appointed resident engineer, and he contributed significantly to the equipment and technical set-up of the Workshop. He was a World War II veteran, and used his war time ingenuity to build his own electronic organs, and fashion useful devices out of second-hand junk, for the Radiophonic composers to utilize creatively.

For many British people their first and lasting experience of electronic music was through popular TV programmes, particularly Doctor Who, where the science fiction setting allowed a good deal of experimentation to reach the hearts and minds of viewers innocently watching at home. As the 1970s wore on and the original 60s staff, and the musique concrète techniques they used were replaced, the sensibility inevitably changed, and new generations of composers were employed. They came predominantly from a traditional instrumental background, where keyboards or guitars were the mainstay of their musical composition.

EMS synthesizers which had first been introduced in 1970 – with the VCS3 and the Synthi 100 offering vast and almost limitless potential for the experimenter – were eventually seen as past their sell by dates, and were replaced by modern and much slicker equipment. As this kit became cheaper and more accessible to independent musicians in private studios, the Workshop lost its unique place as a provider of experimental soundscapes. It ended up using the same generic gear as others in the field, leaving its increasingly lightweight output with only a tenuous link to its musique concrète origins. Library music labels providing off-the-shelf signature tunes, were covering a similar function, while producers and songwriters working in the pop world scoring chart hits, could make a far better job of electronic pop than the Radiophonic composers. In the second half of the 1970s, a new wave of British synthesizer experimentalists, took up the gauntlet that the Workshop had previously held.

Along with the urge to replace and update equipment, and get rid of old but still useful gear, a phenomenon common across electronic music throughout its history, there came a drive for profits above experimentation at the BBC. This was especially true during the John Birt era, when as Director-General, he introduced 'Producer Choice'; a form of outsourcing embracing market forces, which left the Workshop to limp on until its closure in 1998. Nevertheless, there is a terrific legacy of music from the first half of its existence, represented in a number of worthwhile CD compilations. Unfortunately the Doctor Who theme tune becomes rather ubiquitous on these releases, though the ones listed here all contain some excellent tracks.

BBC Radiophonic Workshop

Origin: London
Established: 1958
Disbanded: 1998
Obscurity Quotient: 1
EM Recording Availability: Excellent

The Radiophonic composers who joined the unit prior to 1971, serving for more than three months, are presented as a list for reference, and only those with their own studios or making experimental electronic music outside the BBC, have been credited with a full entry in the main A-Z section.

Name	Joined
Anthony Askew	1964
Norman Bain	1960
John Baker	1963 See p.16
Desmond Briscoe	1958 See p.24
Jimmy Burnett	1958
David Cain	1967
Roger Charlton	1966
Malcolm Clarke	1969 See p.33
Charles Clark-Maxwell	1961
Delia Derbyshire	1962 See p.46
Margaret Etall	1963
Janet Gibson	1965
Maddalena Fagandini	1960
John Harrison	1960
Brian Hodgson	1962 See p.68
Paddy Kingsland	1970
Geoff Leonard	1960
Bridget Marrow	1965
Dick Mills	1958
Dennis Morgan	1959
Daphne Oram	1958 See p.97
Keith Salmon	1965
Geoffrey Smith	1959
Clive Webster	1966
Jenyth Worsley	1961
Richard Yeoman-Clark	1970
Phil Young	1959

CDs:
BBC Radiophonic Music (BBC Music, 2008)
The Radiophonic Workshop (BBC Music, 2008)
30 Years at the Radiophonic Workshop (BBC Enterprises, 1993)
BBC Radiophonic Workshop A Retrospective (BBC Music, 2008)
Doctor Who at the BBC Radiophonic Workshop Volume 1 (BBC Music, 2000)
Doctor Who at the BBC Radiophonic Workshop Volume 2 (BBC Music, 2000)
Doctor Who – The Krotons (Silva Screen, 2013)

Delia Derbyshire talking to George Newson at the Radiophonic Workshop in 1966

6
TAPE LEADERS
EARLY BRITISH
ELECTRONIC
MUSIC CD

CD TRACK NOTES

Steve Duckworth: M52 (1974)

Recorded in his home studio on 22nd September 1974, Duckworth's track consists of several overlapping sound elements. A tape loop made from the noise of an aerosol spray was treated with his **EMS** Synthi AKS synthesizer, as well as an Electro Harmonix 'Electric Mistress' flanger. He also included the sound of an apple being bitten, a flushing toilet and various electronic tones from the Synthi.

Tristram Cary: Trios (1971)
Abridged performance

The **EMS** Synthi and dice composition Trios, was given its premiere at the Cheltenham Music Festival in 1971, and the first London performance at the Queen Elizabeth Hall came in April the following year, at a concert also featuring pieces by **Harrison Birtwistle** and Karlheinz Stockhausen. It was originally presented by Tristram and his two sons using VCS3 and keyboard, two turntables and vinyl records, plus two specially made containers each holding three dice. To encourage performances, the two LP records and a booklet with the score, were issued by EMS in a limited edition gatefold set. The synthesizer player follows the 16 page score, while the turntable operators select tracks from the records according to throws of the dice, which continue being made throughout the piece. This allows for predetermined synthesized sounds, played in tandem with randomly chosen LP tracks, thus making every performance different.

As the key elements for realising Trios are specialised and now exceedingly rare, Tristram did make allowances in the instructions to accept a variety of equipment and personnel configurations depending on availability. The players in this recording – Ian Helliwell and Simon James – use the original dice throwers which Tristram left to Ian, to continue their use in future performances. The synthesizer part can be played with a VCS3 or Synthi A, and can be taped and played back in concert if required. With the vinyl records transferred directly to CD, Helliwell and James, along with Vicky Fenlon playing a DK1 keyboard, made a recording of the Synthi in August 2012, which was then copied onto quarter inch reel to reel tape. This realisation was performed at the Hackney Picturehouse, on 17th March 2013, during the Pioneers of Electronic Music festival.

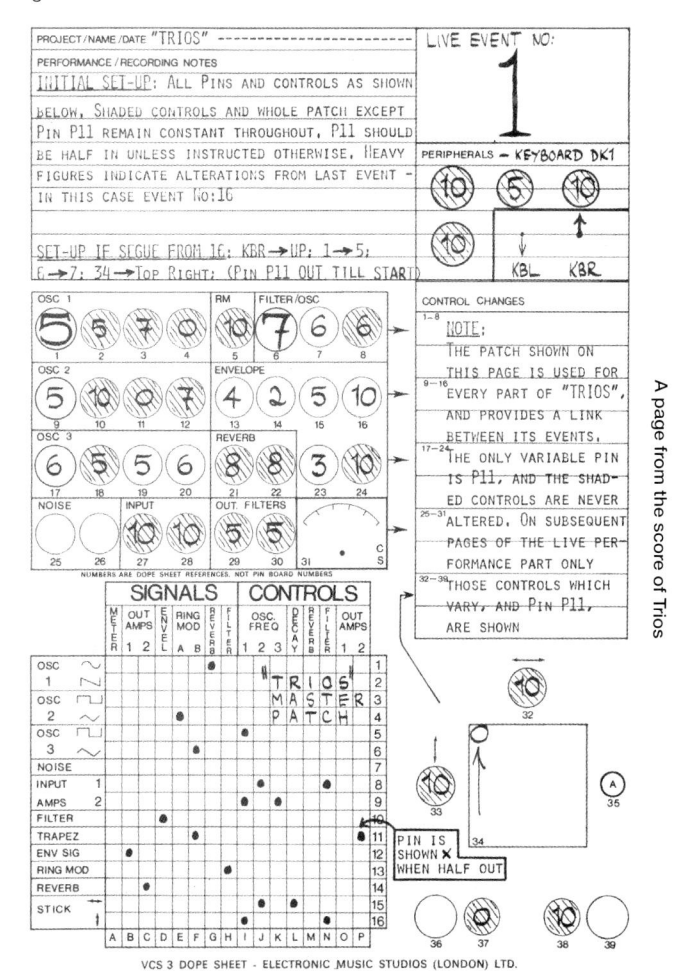

A page from the score of Trios

Ralph Brooome: Nuclear Madness (1960)
Original 7" edit.

Nuclear Madness was a winner in the Technical Experiment class of the 1960 British Amateur Tape Recording Contest. It went on to enter a continental championship, and was issued in abridged form on a German Telefunken 7" promotional disc. This featured a selection of tracks from the 9th International Tape Recording competition, which was organised at Radio V.A.R.A. studios in Hilversum, Holland, evaluating more than 50 amateur tape recordings in five categories. The sleeve notes for the record describe the excerpt of Nuclear Madness thus: "*This technical montage by the Englishman R. O. Broome, shines a macabre light on our current way of life. Altered oscillation effects, echoing and timbral distortion are used to conjure up a vision of the most barbarous invention of the present day. The acoustic impression is all the more alarming as a vague yet terrifying allusion in the free space of fantasy, forms atop the already familiar bizarre picture of flash and mushroom clouds.*"

Broome penned an article for Tape Recording magazine in the autumn of 1960, describing the genesis and recording of Nuclear Madness. He was interested in the control of noise, and decided the ultimate manifestation of a controlled release of energy and sound, is exemplified in an atomic explosion. To make his track he combined the noise of hammering metal, with tones from his self-built oscillator, along with a ticking clock and voice countdown. Although the 7" contains a truncated version of the piece, it is significant in that it is very likely the only official record release of British amateur electronic music to come out in this period.

Ernest Berk: Chigger Sound 1 (1968)
No Fish or Oh Mr. Bard (1962)

Chigger Sound is the first of five 'electronic pop' tracks Ernest Berk made for the Morgan Record Company. Although the bulk of his compositions were experimental, and most often intended for use in his dance work, he made several other tracks in a pop vein, and worked with **Basil Kirchin** on a few more commercial pieces. Some of them were recorded for labels Conroy, CBS and EMI, though none were made widely available. Chigger Sound is notable for using the same basic track minus the vocals, of Wake Up Cherylina, a 1967 single B side by English beat combo The Smoke.

No Fish or Oh Mr. Bard was created as a soundtrack for an experimental film by British artist John Latham (1921-2006), and this short titled Talk Mr. Bard, is available on the anthology DVD, John Latham Films 1960-1971. However, the film does not feature Berk's soundtrack, and there is no reference to it in the accompanying notes in the DVD booklet. It appears that it was originally shown with Berk's sound, as this is mentioned in his studio log, and sometime later in the 1960's Latham decided to replace it with a different voice collage soundtrack. He did something similar with his next film Speak, which is said to have soundtracks commissioned from Pink Floyd, Joe Harriott, and allegedly from Ernest Berk.

Peter Grogono: Datafield (1971)

Working with the digital tape drives for the PDP-8 computers at **EMS**, Grogono managed to find a cheap source of used industrial magnetic tape, and one day decided to try out an experiment. Out of curiosity he ran the computer tape on a regular half inch analogue Ampex reel to reel tape deck, achieving some very promising results. Mindful not to overload the audio amplifier with digitally recorded tape, he found that the outcome was much more interesting than anticipated, producing a range of timbres that caught his ear. He set about recording the most exciting sections, using speed changing to achieve greater variety, and adding reverb and then cutting, splicing and balancing to produce the final mix of Datafield.

Donald Henshilwood: Sonata 7 (1968)

In his home studio at 130 Frankby Road, West Kirby in Cheshire, Henshilwood created a whole series of numbered electronic music sonatas. Unfortunately it is probable that most of these pieces have not survived after his death, except for Sonata 7. By a happy accident, a recording was found amongst the personal tape collection of **George Newson**, which he had received from Henshilwood in 1968. Although only a mono mixdown, thanks to Newson, this terrific discovery has at least preserved two compositions plus two keyboard transcriptions, and at present remains the only accessible taped evidence of Henshilwood's electronic music.

FC Judd's home studio circa 1965

FC Judd: Voltage Control 3 (1963)

One of three short works created by Fred Judd using tape loops and his prototype synthesizer, this track is estimated to be from 1963, the year that he built his unique voltage controlled synth. The experimental instrument featured a 48 note keyboard that switched multivibrator circuits, with filtering and envelope shaping built in. Two of the keys were used for switching a mixing circuit to activate external sources, and there was an input to modulate signals from other devices. Voltage Control 1 and 2 appeared on the Electronics Without Tears anthology, released in 2011.

George Newson: Oute (1969)

Based on a 1968 chamber piece for six instruments written by Newson, titled The Six of Us, this was subsequently renamed Genus. Finally an electronic realisation became Oute, or alternatively One Under the Eight. It was composed and recorded while he was based at the University of Utrecht during 1969, and though inspired by his instrumental work, all the sound material was generated in the studio using electronic equipment.

Peter Zinovieff: Tarantella (1966)

Conceived as a stylised electronic folk dance, Tarantella was played at the **Unit Delta Plus** concert at the Watermill Theatre, Bagnor, Berkshire on the 10th September 1966. It was described in the programme as an imitative piece, in that electronic timbres were reminiscent of flute, reed and percussion sounds, and based on a scale that might have been used by a peasant group of musicians in central Europe. For the most part the time interval between notes was rigidly set, but the choice of notes in the scale, and their volume within a set range, was subject to random probablility. On occasions Zinovieff was apt to make revisions to some of his earlier pieces, and Tarantella has been incorporated into his 2014 violin concerto OUR TOO.

Ken Gray: Electrosculpture (1976)

This composite track made from two recordings of Ken Gray in action, features audio from an ITV Southern regional report on his Phantasmagoria Today exhibition, during the Brighton Festival in 1976. The reporter introduces the Electrosculptures displayed in the Brighton Museum Art Gallery, interviews Gray about his work, and conducts a vox pop with visitors to the exhibition. A further interview took place two years later at the gallery of James Rushton, in Eastern Road, Brighton, where sonic sculptor Gray talked about his audio-visual pieces, and demonstrated some of the sounds that visitors could activate with special probes. For an article in the Brighton and Hove Gazette he explained, "*I want people to enjoy a tactile experience... it is pretty complicated, but I want people to come out of the exhibition beaming and more optimistic about the future.*"

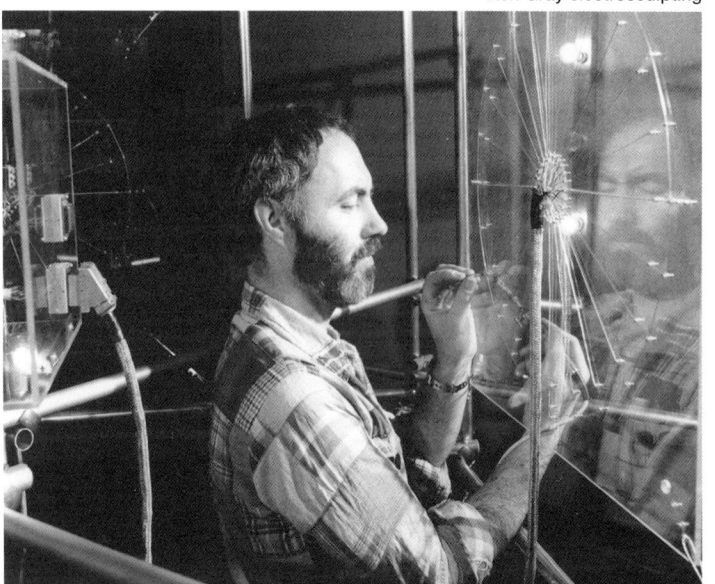

Ken Gray electrosculpting

George West: Night Circus (1964)

Abridged version.

In 1963 George West was contacted by Ronnie Yerril, a member of the My Fair Lady musical cast, which had played in London and moved north to give provincial performances at the Manchester Opera House. As a choreographer, Yerril put together a separate group with other cast members, to stage a show in aid of Oxfam to be called Night Circus, and envisaged a soundtrack of musique concrète and electronics. During his search for a suitable sound source or collaborator, a local Manchester hi-fi shop recommended the Middleton Tape Recording Club, and he made contact with George West, the club chairman. At the end of 1963, the Middleton tape activists discussed the scenario and sonic requirements, and set to work on the project. Operating to a tight schedule over six weeks, West was responsible for producing and editing special sound effects, with finished sequences delivered each week for the dancers to rehearse to. The 25 minute show was first performed in April 1964 at the Garrick Theatre in Altrincham, Cheshire, to an estimated 900 strong audience.

The characters in the story consisted of a Dancer, Tightrope Walker, Ringmaster, two Clowns, and a pair of Siamese Twins; these being two female dancers in one costume. Yerril wanted the characters to have their own individual taped motifs, and West and his team came up with themes associated with each one. The sounds of violin, tuba and metronome were recorded on tape, and treated or made into loops, and appeared according to the actions on stage.

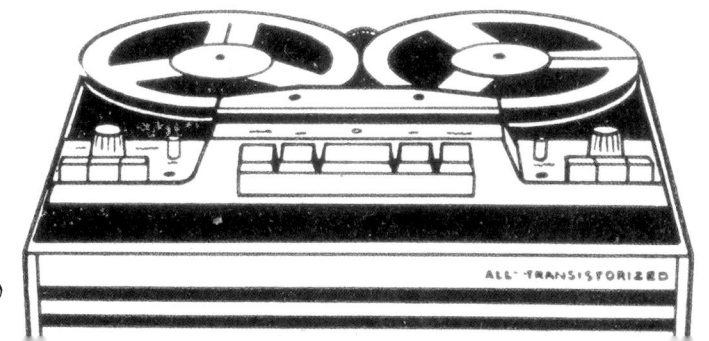

David Piper: Mare Crisium (1970)

Abridged version.

In response to the second moon landing in November 1969 by Apollo 12, Piper set about programming and patching the Moog synthesizer, housed at Manchester University in the small studio he had co-founded. Without a written score and using only the Moog as a source, he generated sounds in real time and reacted intuitively to the machine, in what he described as "*a kind of interfered with improvisation.*" These electronic sequences were recorded directly to tape, and the process of editing and shaping the material was undertaken to make the complete composition. The full 20 minute piece stands alongside other early extended modular synthesizer works, such as George Harrison's Electronic Sound, Michael Czajkowski's People the Sky, and Andrew Rudin's Tragoedia, all of which gained an official album release. Mare Crisium has never been issued, and has remained unheard in Piper's archive since its original concert airings in Manchester during 1971.

Stuart Wynn Jones: Short Spell (1956)

Short Spell is a cameraless two minute animation painstakingly drawn with indian ink directly onto 35mm celluloid, depicting a kinetic alphabet with each letter cleverly metamorphosing into the next. Even more remarkable is the synthetic soundtrack also applied physically to the film strip, revealing a mastery of the direct animation technique. In its creation, Wynn Jones first calculated divisions of a frame based on frequency ratios, and was then able to generate different pitches and timbres through varying the size, shape and spacing of hand drawn dots and lines. Short Spell was a very popular film, and an 'Oscar' winner in the annual Ten Best competition organised by Amateur Cine World. It received numerous screenings, and appeared on TV on the BBC Tonight programme in January 1958.

The animation was released commercially by Adventure Film Productions, who made available 8mm and 16mm prints for home viewing, of various short films that had featured in the Ten Best. Comedian, game show presenter and early video enthusiast Bob Monkhouse, owned a copy of Short Spell, and rang Wynn Jones to enquire about the direct animation method. Monkhouse came up with an idea inspired by the SWJ film, and in 1964 this was translated by Keith Learner of Biographic Films, into an award winning TV commercial for Kit-Kat biscuits.

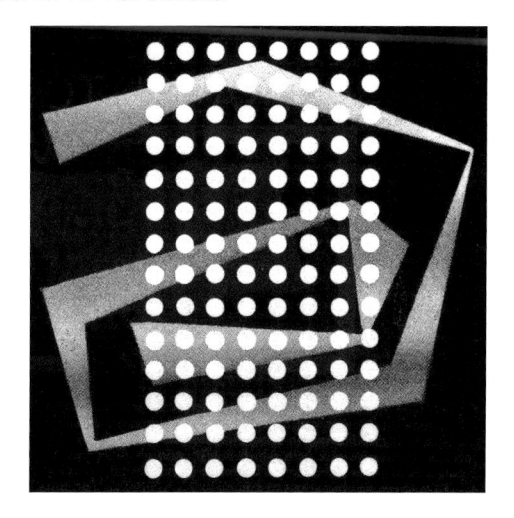

Laurie Scott Baker: Music for Maths (1971)

An early convert to **EMS** equipment, Baker bought his own VCS3 in 1969 and a Synthi A a few years later. In the early 70s he was considering the assembly of a series of electronic tracks for use as library music. Although never released as an album, among the selection was this piece, used in a TV documentary on mathematics in the long running BBC Horizon series.

To purchase the CD please visit velocitypress.uk
For their permission and generous support for the compilation, special thanks to:
Laurie Scott Baker, John Cary, Steve Duckworth, Ann Gray, Peter Grogono, Freda Judd, George Newson, Deirdre Piper, Matthias Tiefenbacher, George West and Peter Zinovieff.

7

INFORMATION, CREDITS AND INDEX

TAPE LEADERS - A PERSONAL ACCOUNT BY DEIRDRE PIPER

Ian Helliwell's Tape Leaders documents an important, but little told part of music history in Britain. No one could deny that the 1960s and 70s were an unsettling, yet exhilarating time, and for a young developing composer, the musical landscape then was both exciting in its technical novelties and aesthetic challenges, and mind-changing in its new structural theories and philosophical implications. The 'New Music' was heard in abundance via the BBC, and all that was fresh and revolutionary in contemporary composition could be experienced, simply by tuning in to the Third Programme. As an undergraduate in music, and later as a post-graduate during the mid-late 60s, I benefited enormously from this resource, making (rather bad) home tape recordings off the radio. It was in this context that I developed a keen awareness of electronic music, and an intention to pursue it at graduate level. I was most fortunate in being able to persuade Professor Hans Redlich, at the University of Manchester, to supervise and support my work, which also included studies in electronic circuitry at the John Dalton College of Technology. Under his aegis we were able to establish a small, but admirably functional analogue studio in 1967, for the production of electronic and tape music.

Thus I was an actor on the electronic music stage in Britain during the 1960s, and Helliwell's book brings to the surface a host of memories of that exciting time – personal memories of people and events which have lain buried for many years. Its publication has also led me to resurrect old and decaying documents of that period, which I have carried around in my personal archives for several decades. One of these recalls my attendance at the Queen Elizabeth Hall, for what was billed as 'The First London Concert of Electronic Music by British Composers'. It was held on 15th January 1968, featuring works by **Delia Derbyshire**, **Ernest Berk**, **Tristram Cary**, **Daphne Oram**, **Jacob Meyerowitz**, **George Newson**, and a real-time computer-composed piece by **Peter Zinovieff**. During this latter performance, I recall being absolutely transfixed by the array of blinking lights of the equipment as the piece gradually unfolded. Critical response to the concert was guarded; Martin Cooper, writing in the Daily Telegraph the following day observed, "... *the electronic composer's position today is comparable to that of a painter with a virtually limitless palette and no graphic, linear convention. It is on the discovery or creation of such a convention that the future of electronic music depends.*"

Hugh Davies, the director of the Electronic Music Workshop at Goldsmith's College, London, came to visit the studio in Manchester during 1969. As the compiler of the International Electronic Music Catalog, he had listed the newly developing Manchester studio, but without any information as to its correct location or musical output. It was a welcome opportunity to meet one of the leading lights in the electronic movement in Britain. The Manchester studio had recently imported a large Moog synthesizer, but it amused me that

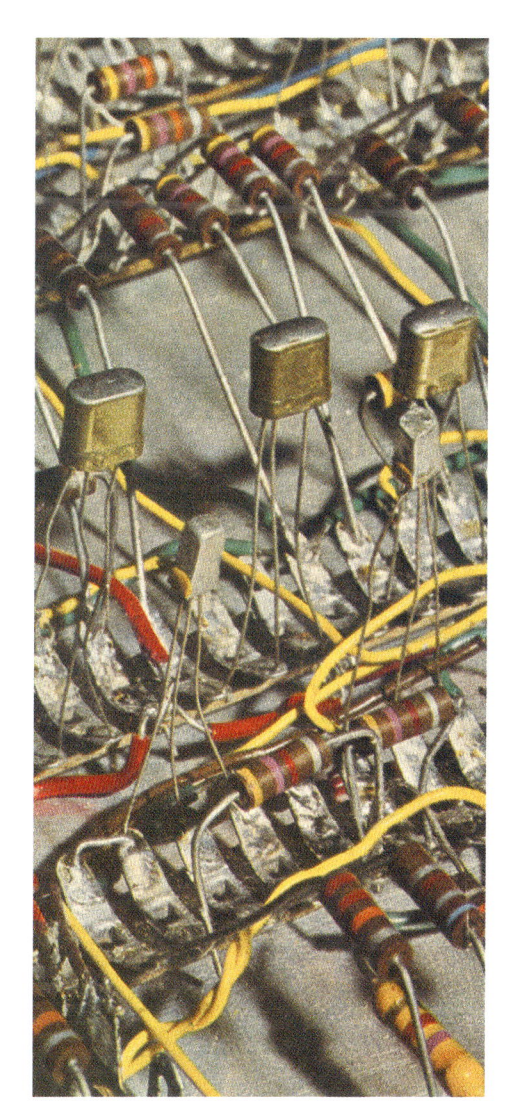

Hugh's interest in our equipment centred rather on the two commercial band-pass filters we were using! One of the last pieces I composed in Manchester was Mare Crisium. This piece received two or three public performances before languishing unheard for several decades in my personal tape archives. Recently it was transferred to digital format, and I had the strange experience of hearing it fresh again. It is a 20 minute work, and my first reaction was that it took too long. True, the piece develops slowly, but the killing of time is partly what it's about. I like the textural contrast between the two audio channels during the first part, and their mutual interplay during the second. While earlier pieces of mine still exist on archival tapes, this composition is the first I would publicly acknowledge.

While my memories of those years in Britain remain elusive as to details, the sense I had then of being part of something radical and of historic potential is still strong. We were a small community sharing visions of a new music for a new age, and the remarkable thing was that wherever we presented concerts, the public attended seemingly in droves. I am so glad to have had the privilege of playing a part in that movement.

Deirdre Piper, May 2014

MAN
ON
THE
MOON

PHILIPS

Ian Helliwell (1966)

Born: Newcastle upon Tyne
Earliest Electronic Work: Rose Tinted Spectacles (1991)
Commitment Factor: 10
Obscurity Quotient: 6
EM recording availability: Limited

Starting life in the north east of England, Helliwell spent his early years growing up in Newton Hall, Durham. His electrician father secured a job at Portland Prison in 1972, and the family moved to Weymouth, Dorset. Attending Weymouth Grammar School in the immediate aftermath of punk rock, the 12 year old Helliwell was captivated by punk 7" singles played to him by his older brother, and it was then that he first heard tracks by late 70s British electronic groups. Despite not pursuing music or art as O-Level subjects, his passion for music led to the purchase of a second hand drum kit, and the formation of his first group at school aged 14. Leaving education at 16 in 1983 armed with six O-Levels, a move to Brighton followed two years later, with long spells of unemployment, punctuated by occasional dead end, poorly paid jobs.

Out of bedsitter land in 1988 he formed a new group, the Giant Clams, with guitarist Adrian Shephard, and first worked with a four track cassette recorder, making initial experiments with a tape echo unit and reel to reel tape loops. With a move to a rented flat at 59 Ship Street, Brighton in 1991, and the demise of the Clams, Helliwell threw himself into solo four track recording, playing guitar, bass, drums, Jen synthesizer and radio. Despite a paucity of gear he made his first serious forays into electronic music with a radio and simple multivibrator circuits, and worked on his earliest collages of sound. With no training in music or electronics, but a fascination for building and adapting his own equipment, he realised that the best way forward was via his own 'intuitive electronic' and 'creative soldering' approaches. He developed techniques for rewiring 9 volt sound generating kits, and from the early 1990s continuing to the present day, he has constructed a unique range of machines, including a series of Hellitron tone generators and Hellisizer synths, all housed in carefully styled, Dymo labelled cabinets.

At the close of the 1980s he became increasingly interested in visual arts, particularly light projections and filmmaking, and with no previous knowledge or experience, he set about painting abstract slides, and drawing and scratching directly onto super 8. By 1992 he was working on abstract collage films, and shooting a no-budget sci-fi movie, using his self-built circuits to create the soundtracks. Experimental film and animation combined with electronic music, has formed the core of his filmmaking output ever since.

His independent research into electronic music history started gradually through the 1990s, and in 1998 he put together several electronic pioneers events for the Brighton Fringe festival, including a Stylophone Procession, in the town centre streets. In 2003 he wrote a letter to **Tristram Cary**, and the following year he organised a small exhibition, screenings, and a performance of Tristram's work staged at Brighton University. In 2007 Helliwell created super 8 animation sequences for What the Future Sounded Like, a documentary on **EMS**, and a year later he branched out into radio with the ongoing Tone Generation series, covering various aspects of early electronic music. At the end of 2009 he began work on Practical Electronica, an unfunded documentary concerning **FC Judd** and early British tape recording. In that time he made a number of experimental short films including Expo 67 – An Audiovisual Collage (2010).

It is fair to say that Helliwell's independent, self-taught and self-funded approach, has failed to make any commercial headway. After more than 30 years of dedicated work, interest in his instruments, slides, collages, electronic music and over 150 short films has been limited. British establishment indifference has not diminished his enthusiasm and creativity however, and in Germany several of his abstract shorts were included in the 2010 Celluloid exhibition; a major retrospective of direct animation at Frankfurt's Schirn Kunsthalle Museum. In 2019 he released Project Symbiosis, a compilation based on **Malcolm Pointon**'s 1975 graphic score. His creative work with music, films, electronics, collage, and machine building progresses; while his research into early electronic music, abstract film and world's fairs, remains an ongoing study.

CDs:
Sonic Postcards (Sonic Arts Network, 2001) – includes Helliwell's, New York NY.
Delaware Road (Buried Treasure, 2015) – includes Helliwell's, Water Gardens.
Project Symbiosis (Helliwell Industries, 2019) - 10 composers interpret Symbiosis.

Home studio with equipment built by Ian Helliwell

SOURCES AND INFORMATION

Interesting examples and references for early British electronic music.

Books
Analog Days (2002) – Trevor Pinch & Frank Trocco.
BBC Radiophonic Workshop – The First 25 Years (1983) – Desmond Briscoe & Roy Curtis-Bramwell.
Electronic Music For Schools (1981) – Richard Orton.
International Electronic Music Catalog (1968) – Hugh Davies.
The Sound of Tomorrow (2012) – Mark Brend.
Special Sound (2010) – Louis Niebur.

Films/TV
Alchemists of Sound (Dir: Roger Pomphrey, 2003) BBC TV documentary on the Radiophonic Workshop.
An Untitled Film (Dir: David Gladwell, 1964, music: Ernest Berk) Eerie slow motion short film included on the Requiem for a Village DVD.
Berlin Horse (Dir: Malcolm Le Grice, 1970, music: Brian Eno) Looped and optically printed found footage film.
Between the Tides (Dir: Ralph Keene, 1958, music: Edward Williams) Documentary on the Off the Beaten Track DVD.
The Delian Mode (Dir: Kara Blake, 2010) Documentary on Delia Derbyshire.
Guinness For You (Dir: Anthony Short, 1972, music: Tristram Cary) Short promo film for bottles of Guinness Extra Stout, released on the Roll Out the Barrel DVD set.
Myth Makers – Tristram Cary (Reeltime Pictures, 2005) DVD features an engaging interview with Tristram Cary from a Doctor Who perspective.
The New Sound of Music (Dir: John Mansfield, 1979) Educational documentary eloquently presented by Michael Rodd.
The Offence (Dir: Sidney Lumet, 1973, music: Harrison Birtwistle & Peter Zinovieff) Classic feature film starring Sean Connery as a disturbed detective.
Practical Electronica (Dir: Ian Helliwell, 2011) Documentary on FC Judd and early electronic music.
The Sea Devils (Dir: Michael Briant, 1972, music: Malcolm Clarke) Doctor Who at its best, featuring The Master and Clarke's Synthi 100 score.
Shaped For Living (Dir: Peter deNormanville, 1967, music: Tristram Cary) Striking documentary on design made for Expo 67.
Space Patrol (Dir: Frank Goulding, 1963, music: FC Judd) Landmark TV puppet series released as a DVD box set.

Short Spell (Dir: Stuart Wynn Jones, 1956) Ace two minute direct animation with synthetic sound.
The Stone Tape (Dir: Peter Sasdy, 1972, music: Desmond Briscoe) Haunting TV drama released on DVD.
Trios Performance (Dir: Ian Helliwell, 2013, music: Tristram Cary) Video documenting a complete presentation of Trios.
What the Future Sounded Like (Dir: Matthew Bate, 2007) Informative documentary on EMS.
Workshop: Same Trade As Mozart (Dir: David Buckton, 1969) Vintage documentary featuring some of the key British electronic composers.

Radio/Podcast
A Sound British Adventure – Radio 4 documentary written by Mark Brend. (2012).
Blue Veils and Golden Sands – dramatisation of the Delia Derbyshire story starring Sophie Thompson. (2002).
Electric Tunesmiths – focus on the BBC Radiophonic Workshop, including interviews with a number of the staff composers. (1971).
Sculptress of Sound: The Lost Works of Delia Derbyshire. (2010).
The Tone Generation – an extensive audio series that deals with early electronic music, including episode 1 on British composers, and episode 25 on the 1968 QEH concert. (2008-present).

Tape Leaders glossary
Berkchandise – Music and material of Ernest Berk.
Juddrabilia – Equipment and ephemera relating to FC Judd.
Intuitive Electronics – Creative soldering as practiced by teenager Ian Loveday in 1968.
Meek-Geek – An individual with an obsessive interest in the life and work of Joe Meek.
Oram-Forum – A discussion centred on the music and career of Daphne Oram.

Credits
Grateful thanks for support, conversation and materials to:
Brigid & Laurie Scott Baker, Janet Beat, Oliver Bevan, Lawrence Casserley, Rose Clouts, Steve Duckworth, Grahame Dudley, Julia and Mick Dunn, Ron Geesin, Anthony Gilbert, Elizabeth Glasser, Ann Gray, Patrick Harrex, Per Hartmann, Graham Hearn, Freda Judd, George Newson, Deirdre Piper, Barbara Pointon, Deborah Rees, James Siddons, George West, Andrew Whibley, and Judy Williams.

For their help and information, thanks go to the following:
Mark Ayres, Pattie Benjamin, Mark Brend, George Mowat-Brown, Dick Bunt, David Butler,

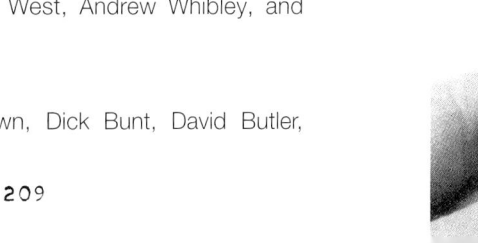

Paul Carnell, Julian Cowley, Howard Davidson, Stephen Deutsch, Terence Dwyer, Kevin Edwards, Archer Endrich, Fraser Geesin, Paul Gilby, Tom Hall, Isobel Hiom, Aartje Hulstein, James Ingram, Simon James, Nicola LeFanu, John Lifton, Annea Lockwood, Terry Martini, Karolyn Milam, James Mooney, Mark Orphan, Jim Pennington, Andrew Powell, Caroline Salzedo, Doug Shaw, Dave Thompson, Stephen Trowell, David Vorhaus, Peter West, Teresa Winter, Alex Wilson, Trevor Wishart, Barry Witherden, Robin Wood at EMS and Richard Yeoman-Clark.
In memoriam: Daevid Allen, Ranulph Glanville, Peter Grogono, David Lloyd-Howells, Richard Orton, Alan Sutcliffe and Peter Zinovieff.

For their additional research and generous information sharing, special thanks to Daniel Wilson and James Gardner.

If any readers have first-hand knowledge, were friends or relatives of electronic composers, or have new information to add about any of those mentioned, please contact the author. Tape Leaders is part of a process of gathering facts and widening the history, and updates will be made as research continues. Every effort has been made to trace image copyright holders; please contact the author regarding any concerns.

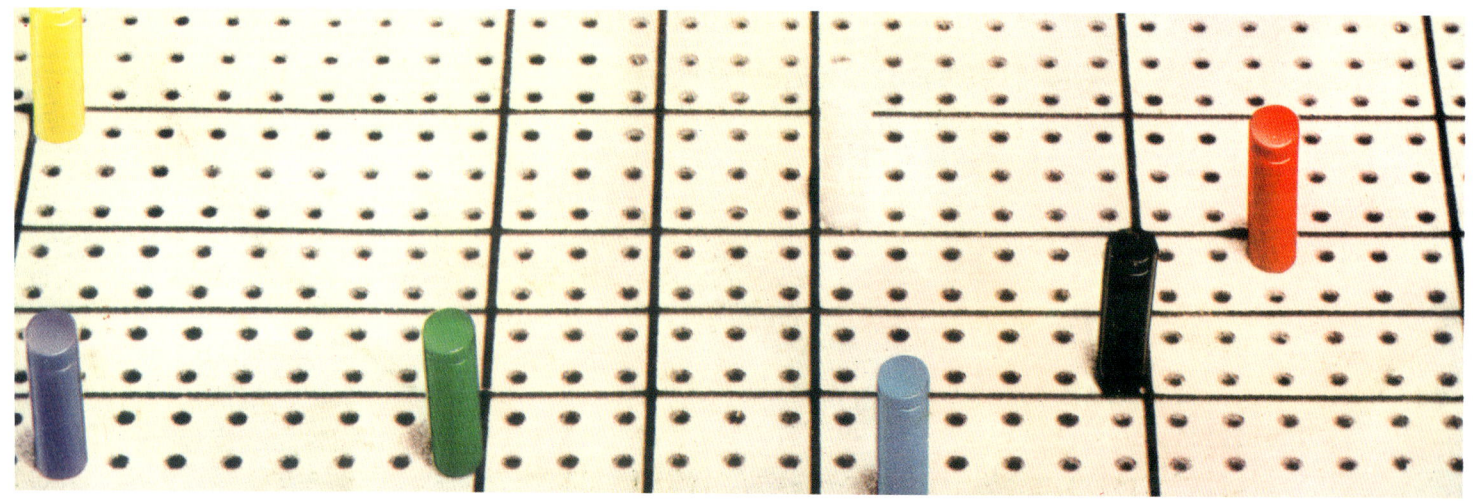

INDEX

A
Action Space 175
Affleck, Denis B. **144**
Alchemists of Sound 24, 33
Allen, Daevid **14**, 193
Alston, Richard 86, 87
AMM 59
Anderson, Barry **15**, 23
Anderson, Lindsay 34, 57, 128
Anderson, Ruth 87
Arden, John 179
Ardley, Neil 130
Armstrong, RL 162
Ayers, Kevin 14, 20, 180

B
Babbitt, Milton 18, 25, 34, 42, 131, 218
Badings, Henk 19, 111
Bailey, Derek 44
Baily, Brian 190
Bainbridge, Harvey 170
Baker, John **16**, 195
Baker, Laurie Scott **17**, 201
Balch, Anthony 27
Ballard, JG 84
Ballet Rambert 25, 54, 69, 112, 126
Banks, Don **18**, 28, 31, 89, 92, 96, 109, 112, 118, 120, 131, 183
Bartok, Bela 15
Beat, Janet **19**, 99
Beatles, The 14, 65, 92, **166-67**, 179
Beckett, Samuel 24, 39, 120
Bedford, David **20**, 45, 59, 89, 96
Bennett, Richard Rodney 96, 119
Bennink, Han 44
Bentley, Andrew 102
Berberian, Cathy 45, 95

Berg, Alban 113
Berio, Luciano 45, 47, 67, 73, 95, 128, 177
Berk, Ailsa 21
Berk, Ernest 18, **21**, 28, 31, 44, 45, 47, 78, 89, 156, 158, 198, 203, 208, 209
Berk, Lotte 21
Berkeley, Lennox 20, 89, 123
Bermange, Barry 47, 193
Bernas, Richard 168
Bernelle, Agnes 47, 80
Betjeman, John 179
Better Books 37
Bevan, Oliver 45, 49, 176
Birtwistle, Harrison 15, 18, **23**, 25, 26, 31, 44, 59, 64, 70, 96, 112, 120, 135, 186, 197, 208
Blackwell, Chris 180
Blades, James 108, 113
Blake, Michael **24**
Boland, Bridget 57
Borwick, John 100, 125, 145
Boulanger, Nadia 94, 114
Bowen, Meirion 125
Boulez, Pierre 49
Bowie, David 53
Bradbury, Ray 28
Bragg, Billy 20
Branson, Richard 180
Briscoe, Desmond **24**, 56, 69, 97, 145, 179, 193, 194, 195, 209
British Society for Electronic Music 7, 18, 39, 130, 131, 186, 188
Britton, Peter 119
Brock, Dave 170
Brook, Peter 217
Brooke-Rose, Christine 118
Broome, Ralph 72, **145**, 158, 198

Brown, Douglas 139
Brown, George **25**, 28, 31, 42, 70, 154
Brown, Earle 45, 70, 168
Bryars, Gavin 44, 53, 109, 112, 130
Bucklow, John 177
Bull, Patricia 169
Buller, John **25**, **26**
Bunt, Richard 169
Burnett, Jimmy 194, 195
Burroughs, William S. 14, 24, **27**, 166

C
Cage, John 34, 53, 59, 168, 176
Cain, David 179, 195
Cale, John 53
Calvert, Robert 170
Cardale, John 217
Cardew, Cornelius 17, 52, 59, 108, 172
Carnell, Paul R. **146**
Cary, Tristram 6, 7, 17, 18, 21, 24, 25, **28-30**, 31, 33, 42, 44, 49, 50, 54, 64, 67, 71, 72, 78, 89, 93-6, 112-13, 120, 125, 131, 135, 145, 183, 193, 197, 203, 206, 208, 209
Casserley, Lawrence 18, 25, 28, **31-32**, 37, 42, 44, 49, 54, 89, 120, 154, 185
Chase, Leonard 217
Chopin, Henri 37
Ciamaga, Gustav 103
Clarke, Malcolm **33**, 50, 195, 208
Cleverdon, Douglas 95, 113, 128, 193
Clouts, Cyril **34**, 93, 125
Cobbing, Bob 32, **37**, 86, 193
Cockerell, David 17, 28, 89, 134, 183
Cockpit Ensemble 32, 42, 49, 53, 54, 109, 176

Cohan, Robert 69, 85
Collard, Mervyn 146
Collins, Glyn 85
Colourscape 32
Composers' Guild of Great Britain 28, 94, 128
Computer Arts Society 83, 89, 120, 121
Condron, Nicholas 217
Connolly, Justin 18, 26, **39**, 64, 131
Cooper, Roy 6, **40**, 45, 46, 99, 150
Costello, Elvis 20
Cowie, Edward **42**
Coxhill, Lol 20
Cunningham, Merce 34
Curved Air 64, 184
Cybernetic Serendipity 82-83, 120, 135
Czajkowski, Michael 201

D

Daborn, John 159
Dallapiccola, Luigi 18
Dankworth, John 18
Davidovsky, Mario 131
Davidson, Howard 25, 28, 31, **42**, 53, 54, 70, 109, 176
Davies, Hugh 5, 17, 18, 23, 25, 26, 31, **43-44**, 45, 59, 60, 66, 84, 86-7, 92, 99, 102-03, 112, 116, 118, 125, 131, 158, 168, 176, 203, 208
Dennis, Brian 6, 17, 20, 21, 26, **45**, 46, 50, 67, 118, 126, 158
de Palma, Brian 90
Derbyshire, Delia 24, 25, 28, 31, **46-47**, 57, 67, 68, 93, 95, 120, 126, 134, 173, 179-80, 195, 203, 208-09
Desorgher, Simon 32
Dettmar, Del 170

Deutsch, Stephen 32
Devo 53
De Wolfe 78
Dicker, Dave 162
Dik Mik 170
Downes, Bob 17, 217
Dowson, Mark 183
Draper, Terry 162
Dress, Michael **47**
Dryden, John 72
Doctor Who 18, 24, 30, 33, 46, 56, 57, 68, 69, 71, 80, 113, 194, 195, 208
Duckworth, Steve **148-49**, 197
Dudley, Grahame 28, 32, 42, 45, **49**, 54, 176
Dufrene, Francois 37
Downes, Bob 217
Dunbar, Geoff 17
Dwoskin, Stephen 55
Dwyer, Terence **50**, 104

E

Eastley, Max 44, 53
Edgar Broughton Band 20
Edwards, Kevin **150**
Electroacoustic Cabaret 32
Electrophon 46, 47, 69
Ellis, Merrill 116
Ellitt, Jack **51-52**
EMS 17-19, 23-24, 31, 33, 50, 52, 64-66, 69, 86, 89, 102, 112, 114, 120, 129, 130, 134-35, 149, 154, 165, 172, 179, **183-88**, 190, 194, 197-98, 201, 206, 209
Eno, Brian **52-53**, 78, 109, 208
Evans, Humphrey 183
Expo 58 28, 95, 97, 158
Expo 67 28, 206, 208

Expo 70 56

F

Feldman, Morton 25, 70
Flanders, Michael 28
Fox, Malcolm 28, 42, 49, **54**, 109, 176
Franklin-White, Eddie 32
Freeman, Alan 151
Frink, Elisabeth 80
Fripp, Robert 52

G

Geesin, Ron 47, **55-56**, 87
Gellhorn, Martin 102, 217
Gentle Fire 37, 44, 52, 57, 66, 89, 102, 114, 118, **168**, 172
Gerhard, Roberto 7, 18, 47, **57**, 79, 131, 158, 193
Gilbert, Anthony **59**, 89
Gill, Dominic 21
Gilmour, David 108
Ginsberg, Allen 14
Gladwell, David 21, 78
Glanville, Ranulph **59**, 169
Glasser, Stanley **60**, 85
Godfrey, Bob 56
Goehr, Alexander 23, 25, 42, 54, 59, 96
Gong 14
Graham, Martha 34
Grainer, Ron 46, 71, 179
Grant, Steven 24
Grasshopper Group 158, 159
Gray, Barry 217
Gray, Ken **61-63**, 200
Greenham, Lily 193
Greenwood, Tony 119
Grierson, John 158

Grogono, Peter 23, 39, **64-65**, 86, 112, 167, 185-86, 198
Grosset, Philip 146
Gysin, Brion 14, 27, 193

H

Haggard, Piers 128
Halas & Batchelor 18, 28, 59, 158
Half Landing 59, **169**
Hall, Peter 79, 179
Hall, Richard 25, 111
Hammer Films 18, 28, 112
Harker, Derek 162
Harper, Don 68
Harper, John S. 72, 144, 158, 162
Harrex, Patrick 168
Harrison, George 166, 167, 201
Hartmann, Per 32
Harvey, Jonathan 95, 96, 218
Hawkwind 170, 184
Haynes, Stanley 218
Hearn, Graham **66**, 168
Heath, Ted 78
Helliwell, Ian 197, 206-07, 208, 209
Hendrix, Jimi 27
Henry, Pierre 67, 171, 177
Henshilwood, Donald 18, 31, 44, **67**, 120, 198
Henslow, Miles 145
Henze, Hans Werner 135, 186
Herd, Keith 78
Hillage, Steve 20
Hills, Leslie James **151**
Hobson, Michael 218
Hoddinott, Alun 123
Hodgson, Brian 16, **68-69**, 126, 134, 179-80, 195

Hodell, Ake 37
Holger, Hilde 85
Holmes, John 171
Holmes, Trevor F. **151**
Holloway, Peter 163
Hopper, Hugh 14
Howells, Herbert 31, 111, 112
Humble, Keith 109, 130
Hydra 32

I

ICES-72 32, 83, 86, 89, 109, 168
Ichiyanagi, Toshi 168
Ingram, James **70**, 176
Intermodulation 89, 108, 118-19, 168, **172**
IRCAM 15, 23, 96, 108

J

Jacob, Gordon 54, 111, 158
Jenkins, Mark 180
Jones, Geoffrey 71, 99
Jones, Stuart 168
Josephs, Wilfred **71**
Joseph Weinberger 80, 125
Judd, FC 5, 24, 46, 67, **72-77**, 78, 91, 95, 99, 104, 139, 140, 145, 149, 151, 153, 158, 186, 199, 206, 208, 209

K

Kagel, Mauricio 176
Keating, John 125
Keen, Jeff 37
Keene, Peter **78**
Kerouac, Jack 27
Ketoff, Paul 183
King Crimson 52, 184

Kirchin, Basil 21, **78-79**, 198
Knussen, Oliver 176
Koenig, Gottfried Michael 86
Komorous, Rudolf 67
KPM 46, 55, 68, 127
Krause, Bernard 166

L

Lacey, Bruce 173, 175
Laine, Cleo 18
Lasry-Baschet Group 173
Latham, John 21, 198
Learner, Keith 201
Le Caine, Hugh 103
Le Fanu, Nicola 89
Le Grice, Malcolm 52, 84, 121, 208
Lemmy 170
Lennon, John 27, 123, 166
Leonard, Mike 173
Leppard, Raymond **79**
Leslie, Desmond 18, 21, 47, **80-82**
Les Structures Sonores 173
Levy, Don 71
Lewis, John 69
Leyton, John 91
LFMC 37, 178
Lifton, John **83-84**, 86, 89, 176
Light/Sound Workshop 47, **173**, 179
Lilburn, Douglas 86
Liquid Len 170
Lloyd, Ronald **85**
Lloyd-Howells, David **85-86**
Lloyd-Langton, Huw 170
Lockwood, Anna 28, 37, 64, **86-87**, 89, 176
Logan, Peter 68
Loveday, Ian **152**, 209

Lucier, Alvin 168
Luening, Otto 90
Lumsdaine, David **89-90**, 123, 186
Lutoslawski, Witold 42, 67
Lye, Len 51, 52

M

MacBeth, George 14, 59
Mackay, Andy 52
Macnaghten Concerts 25, 26, 39, 57, 118
Maderna, Bruno 73, 95, 128
Manfred Mann's Earthband 17
Marker, Chris 186
Martin, George 166
Mathieson, Muir 129
Matthews, Max 135
Matusow, Harvey 18, 37, 83, 86, 89, 176, 177, **178**
Maxwell Davies, Peter 23, 49, 59, 96, 131
McCartney, Paul 27, 102, 166
McDowell, John Herbert **90**
McLaren, Norman 51, 52, 146, 158, 159
McWhinnie, Donald 24, 193
Meek, Joe **91**, 151, 209
Messiaen, Olivier 59, 114
Metcalf, John **92**
Metcalfe, Hugh 37
Metzger, Gustav 37
Meyerowitz, Jacob 28, 34, **93**, 96, 203
Mills, Dick 46, 57, 68, 194-95
Milne, Alistair 163
Mitchell, Barry 163
Monkhouse, Richard 129, 185, 186
Monkman, Francis 64
Moog, Robert 24, 95, 116
Moog synthesizer 103, 116, 166, 203
Moorcock, Michael 170

Muir, Jamie 44, 112
Mumma, Gordon 168
Musgrave, Thea 28, **94**, 99
Music Improvisation Company 44
Music Plus 42, 49, 54, 70, 89, 109, **176**

N

Naked Software 83, 86, 109, **176**, 177, 178
Neve, Rupert 80
Newley, Anthony 47
Newson, George 28, 47, 67, 93, **95-96**, 103, 193, 198, 199, 203
Nicholson, George 218
Nikolais, Alwin 21
Nisbet, Alan 175
Nono, Luigi 20, 95
Nucleus 130
Nutbeem, Adrian 38, 177
Nyman, Michael 26, 53, 109

O

Oldfield, Mike 20
Oliveros, Pauline 34, 87, 103
Ollis, Terry 170
Ono, Yoko 27, 166, 178
Oram, Daphne 6, 19, 24, 28, 43, 44, 71, 72, 73, 78, 93, 94, 95, **97-100**, 104, 120, 129, 134, 145, 150, 193-95, 203, 209
Ordidge, Pete 163
Orton, Richard 26, 44, 66, 67, 85, 92, **102**, 118, 131, 132, 168, 208
Oxley, Tony 112

P

Parker, Evan 44, 130
Partch, Harry 85

Paynter, John 50, 92
Pedrell, Felipe 57
Peel, John 55, 152
Pert, Morris **102**
Pertwee, Jon 30, 33
Phillips, Tom 52
Pickett, Richard 102, 218
Pierrot Players 23, 131, 218
Pike, Jennifer 37
Pink Floyd 55, 59, 108, 173, 184, 198
Piper, David **103**, 201, 203-05
Pitchford, John 169
Plant, Mike 163
Pointon, Malcolm 6, **104-07**, 139, 149, 190
Pousseur, Henri 128
Powell, Andrew 102, **108**, 118, 119, 172
Powell, Mel 39
Practical Electronics 117, 139, 140, 152, 173, 174, 189, 190
Purslow, Derek 146, 163

Q

Quiet Pavement Ensemble 67, **177**
Quiet Sun 53

R

Racine Fricker, Peter 39, 45, 86, 111, 112, 118
Radiophonic Workshop 4, 7, 14, 16, 17, 24, 25, 28, 30, 33, 34, 37, 46, 47, 50, 56, 57, 68, 69, 95, 97, 99, 113, 116, 118, 123, 128, 149, 154, 186, **193-95**, 208, 209
Randall, JK 131
Rands, Bernard 92, 130, 218
Ratledge, Mike 14
Rawsthorne, Alan 28

Redlich, Hans 103, 203
Rees, Howard 26, 86, **109**, 154, 176
Reich, Steve 156
Reich, Wilhelm 93, 178
Rhys, John Marlow **111**
Richardson, Tony 218
Ridout, Alan **111**
Riley, Terry 14, 108, 172
Robinson, Michael 168
Ross, John 163
Rowland, David 44, 70, 86, 89, **112**, 186
Roxburgh, Edwin 25
Roxy Music 52, 184
Rudin, Andrew 201

S

Salzedo, Leonard **112**
Same Trade As Mozart, The 16, 24, 39, 45, 135, 209
Sargent, John 163
Schaefer, Pierre 156, 193
Schafer, R. Murray 103
Scherchen, Hermann 18, 113
Schlesinger, John 55
Schmidt, Peter 53, **113**
Schneemann, Carolee 83
Schoenberg, Arnold 57
Schuller, Gunther 59
Scott, Raymond 78
Scott, Ridley 16
Scratch Orchestra 17, 52
Searle, Humphrey 25, 54, 79, 112, **114**, 193
Seiber, Matyas 59, 60
Self, George 45, 50, 126
Shansky, Marjorie 70
Shaw, GD 32, 139, 190

Sherlaw Johnson, Robert 92, **115**, 188
Siddons, James **116**
Simmons, John 218
Simpson, Dudley 69
Sinclair, Clive 135, 158

Smalley, Roger 42, 45, 70, 108, **118**, 119, 172, 193
Smith Brindle, Reginald 130
Smyth, Gilli 14
Soft Machine 14, 20
Sommerville, Ian 27, 166
Sonnabend, Yolanda 47
Souster, Tim 108, 118, **119**, 172
Southern Library 16, 57
Spooky Tooth 171
SPNM 59, 86, 89, 94, 125, 128, 131
Stacia 170
Standard Music Library 46
Starr, Ringo 65, 123, 166, 167
Stevens, John 17
Stockhausen, Karlheinz 15, 19, 25, 26, 31, 42, 43, 45, 52, 67, 70, 104, 108, 118, 119, 156, 168, 172, 176, 197
Stravinsky, Igor 15, 28
Studio G 72
Summers, Elaine 90
Surman, John 59
Sutcliffe, Alan 99, **120-22**, 135, 183, 185
Swain, Robert **123**
Swann, Donald 28
Synthesiser Music Services 32
Synthi A 19, 50, 149, 165, 188, 197, 201
Synthi 100 24, 33, 50, 68, 103, 130, 186

T

Takemitsu, Toru 73, 116

Talking Heads 53
Tassell, Peter 163
Tavener, John 89, **123**, 167
Taylor, Jonathan 25
Taylor, Paul 90
Theremin, Leon 78
Thompson, Robin 108, 112, 118, 172
Tilbury, John 21, 44
Tippett, Michael 42, 111
Tomlinson, Ernest 28, 145
Tornados, The 91
Trowell, Stephen **125**
Tube Sculpture 32
Tudor, David 168
Turner, Ken 175
Turner, Nik 170

U

Unit Delta Plus 46, 68, 69, 126, 134, 166, 173, **179**, 180, 183, 199
Ussachevsky, Vladimir 116, 131

V

Vanderbeek, Stan 64
Varèse, Edgard 95, 116, 128
Vaughan, David 166
VCS3 17, 24, 28, 31, 52, 65, 66, 89, 116, 154, 165, 168, 170, 172, 173, 180, 183, 186, 188, 190, 197, 201
Vetter, Edgar **125**
Vivian, Ralph 163
Vorhaus, David 25, 68, **126-27**, 180

W

Walding, HJ 163
Walton, William 113
Warham, Peter 45, 102

Waters, Roger 55
Watt, Malcolm 163
Webern, Anton 89, 113
Weeks, Stephen 55
Weidenaar, Reynold 103
West, George **153**, 200
West, Peter 153, **154**
Whibley, Brian **154**, 155
White, John 45, 118
White Noise 46, 68, 127, **180**
Whitman, George 25
Wigman, Mary 21, 47
Wilkins, Margaret Lucy **128**
Wilkinson, Marc **128-29**, 193
Williams, Edward 99, **129**, 188, 208
Williams, Richard 28
Winter, Keith 50, 89, **130**
Wire 119
Wishart, Trevor 66, 102, **132**
Witherden, Barry **156**
Wolff, Christian 168, 172
Wonder, Stevie 84
Wood, GH 163
Wood, Robin 129, 188
Woolfenden, Guy 179
Wrench, Graham 97, 99
Wright, Geoffrey **133**
Wyatt, Robert 14, 17
Wynn Jones, Stuart 21, 45, 51, 72, 145, 146, **158-61**, 201, 209

X
Xenakis, Iannis 59, 132

Y
Yamashta, Stomu 102, 108
Yardbirds, The 59
Yeoman-Clarke, Richard 123, 195

Yerril, Ronnie 200

Z
Zappa, Frank 167
Zinovieff, Peter 6, 18, 19, 21, 23, 28, 31, 39, 44, 45, 59, 64, 69, 89, 93, 96, 99, 120, 126, 131, 132, **134-35**, 137, 158, 166, 173, 179, 183, 186, 199, 203, 208
Zoline, Pamela 84

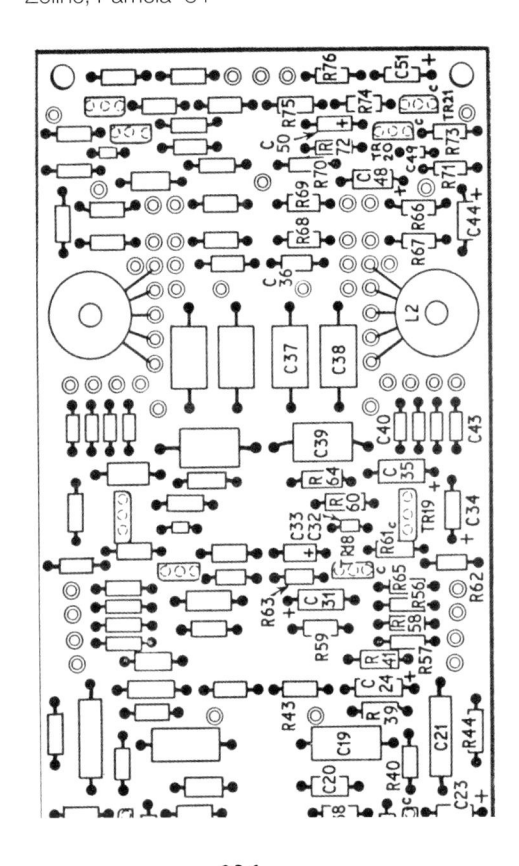

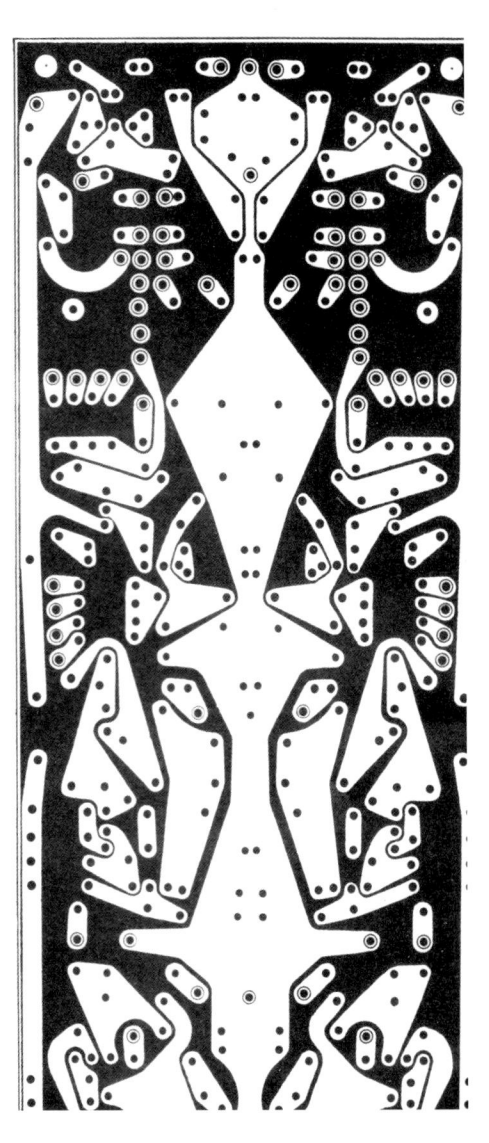

APPENDIX

The following is a list of additional composers not featured in the first edition of Tape Leaders, and acknowledged to have created experimental works for electronics or tape in the period covered by this book. Included after the name, is the title of the individual's first tape piece or another recognised early work.

Peter Brook (1925) - Titus Andronicus (1955)
Opening at the Shakespeare Memorial Theatre in August 1955, this was an uncommon revival of Shakespeare's much maligned play Titus Andronicus, starring Lawrence Olivier and Vivien Leigh. Notably, Brook directed and created a musique concrète score; the Evening Standard described the way he, "*clashed experimentally with pots and warming pans, played with pencils on Venetian glass phials, turned wire baskets into harps*". For his production of The Tempest, Brook again provided a musique concrète soundtrack; the play opened at Stratford-upon-Avon in August 1957.

John Cardale (1949) - Dionysus (1970)
Cardale studied at Durham and the Royal College of Music prior to his postgraduate study in composition at York University, where he created Dionysus. This was a tape work derived from superimposed sound patterns generated with electronic oscillators, and included on the Electronic Music from York compilation album in 1973.

Leonard Chase (19??) - Othello (1955)
Alongside Tony Richardson, Chase composed a musique concrète score for a two part BBC production of Othello, which screened in December 1955. Much is made of the recording being the earliest surviving example of dramatised Shakespeare on British television. Overlooked but equally significant, is that it features perhaps the earliest surviving use of musique concrète in a British TV play.

Nicholas Condron (19??) - Electronic studies (late 1960s)
Attending public school and moving on to a job as a tape operator at CBS Studios, London, the occult absorbed Condron attended the Beckenham Arts Lab, and penned an article for The Stage in 1968, concerning electronic music in the theatre. He purchased a Moog synthesizer and contributed to the Chappell Recorded Music album Electronic Music - The Machines, released in 1973. After a name change to Rikki Sylvan, in 1976 he formed punk/glam outfit Rikki and the Last Days of Earth, which released several singles and an LP on the DJM label before its demise in 1978. Shortly after, he worked with Gary Numan to mix the Replicas and Pleasure Principle albums. Certain key facts about his life remain unclear, but it is thought he died in the 1990s.

Bob Downes (1937) - New Sounds for Percussion, Flute and Synthesizer (1970)
Flautist and leader of the Open Music Trio, Downes has played with a number of noteworthy British jazz luminaries including Mike Westbrook, Keith Tippett and Barry Guy; while in the pop world he has worked with Julie Driscoll, John Barry, Manfred Mann and Alex Harvey. The New Sounds... LP was released in 1970 on the JW Theme Music library label, including the track The Dream. His Open Music Trio album, Diversions, also featured this piece with **Laurie Scott Baker** on VCS3 synthesizer.

Martin Gellhorn (1945) - Essay (1962)
Attending the Guildhall School of Music, and while a student there, Gellhorn appeared on the BBC radio quiz programme It Strikes A Chord, in August 1968. Prior to this, he received the opportunity while still a teenager, for hands-on experience at **Daphne Oram**'s studio in 1962, working alongside **Hugh Davies** to co-create the piece Essay. Studying at York University, he composed several works for tape there in the early 1970s; his Compression ICES'72, was created especially for the festival of the title. In this period he also worked at Goldsmiths, Cardiff and the University of East Anglia.

Barry Gray (1908-1984) - Hoover Keymatic promotional film soundtrack (1960)
Gray started assembling his own home recording studio at 242 Dollis Hill Lane, north London, around 1950, and over the years kitted it out with a very early 4-track tape recorder; Baldwin electric harpsichord; Clavioline; Hammond organ; test oscillator and ring modulator; Miller Spinetta; and an Ondes Martenot. His work for television created for Gerry Anderson was mainly in a catchy and commercial style, though a more experimental approach can be heard in his background electronic music; an example is credited in the main titles for the Dr. Who and the Daleks feature film from 1965.

Jonathan Harvey (1939-2012) - Cantata III (1968)
After studying at Cambridge, Harvey joined the faculty of Southampton University in 1964, and a Harkness Fellowship enabled further study at Princeton University during 1969-70. Working on the live electronic manipulation of sound, Cantata III, was completed before he left for the USA, and written for the Pierrot Players. Impressed by Milton Babbitt and advances in American computer music, he created the tape piece Time Points in 1970. Back in Britain, Harvey worked in the electronic music studio at Cardiff University, and in 1980 he was commissioned by IRCAM in Paris, and composed Mortuos Plango Vivos Voco, based on bell and vocal sounds. He was Professor of Music at Sussex University from 1977-93, and died in Lewes aged 73.

Stanley Haynes (1950) - Variants 1 (1970)
Studying at York University at the same time as John Cardale and George Nicholson - Haynes, Nicholson and **Richard Orton** founded the University's Electronic Music Society. Graduating in 1971, Haynes spent a year in Paris on a scholarship to study composition and electroacoustic music at the GRM. He then embarked on four years of research with computer music at Southampton University, and from 1976-78 he was a Research Fellow at City University in London. In 1977 he was again in France to work at IRCAM on his best known piece, Prisms, for piano and computer synthesized tape.

Michael Hobson (1922-1958) - Vampaera (1956)
Based on the tale of Dracula, Vampaera was mentioned in entertainment weekly The Stage, of 21st June 1956: "*When the newly formed Western Theatre Ballet presented its first production on June 18th at the Royal, Bristol, a work was danced for the first time in this country to musique concrète... the ballet Vampaera was devised by Peter Darrell.*" Permission to use music by Debussy, to which the dance had been choreographed was denied, and so Hobson, musical director of the Ballet Workshop, formed in 1951, stepped in to compose a musique concrète score. Before his premature death at the age of 36 he composed a further musique concrète piece in conjunction with Ronald Fouracre, for another Peter Darrell ballet titled Impasse.

George Nicholson (1949) - Equation (1970)
An intensive study in tape editing, Equation was Nicholson's only purely electronic work and incorporated a number of untreated source materials, mostly from commercial recordings cut together according to a ground plan of durations. He conducted further experiments in the electronic studio at York University until graduating in 1971, and four years later he began a PhD supervised by Bernard Rands and then David Blake. He made one further excursion into the studio in 2010, for a piece for trombone and live electronics.

Richard Pickett (1949) - Light Black (1970)
Studying at York University from 1968-71, Pickett's tape work Light Black, was originally produced as accompaniment for a shadow puppetry performance staged at the University.

Tony Richardson (1928-1991) - It Should Happen to a Dog (1955)
For this BBC production, the then up and coming young film director Richardson, created the musique concrète soundtrack. The play was filmed under his direction in August 1955, and starred Alfie Bass and David Kossoff. He worked with Leonard Chase on Othello, for TV, and later directed Shakespeare's Pericles, for the theatre, which premiered at Stratford in July 1958, with an electro-acoustic score by **Roberto Gerhard**. The following year he directed the film version of Look Back in Anger, launching his acclaimed career in features.

John Simmons (1932-2009) - Escapement (1957)
Establishing the company Soundrama - offering electronic music and original special effects - Simmons worked under this label on the Nigel Kneale penned film, The Abominable Snowman (1957). He created electronic sounds for Escapement - a British black and white sci-fi film released in 1958, and retitled in the USA as The Electronic Monster. In his role as head of production at Soundrama, Simmons stated in 1957 that electronic music's potential was, "*extraordinary and exciting*". In September the following year he received the opportunity to discuss it further on the BBC Light Programme, Movie-Go-Round.

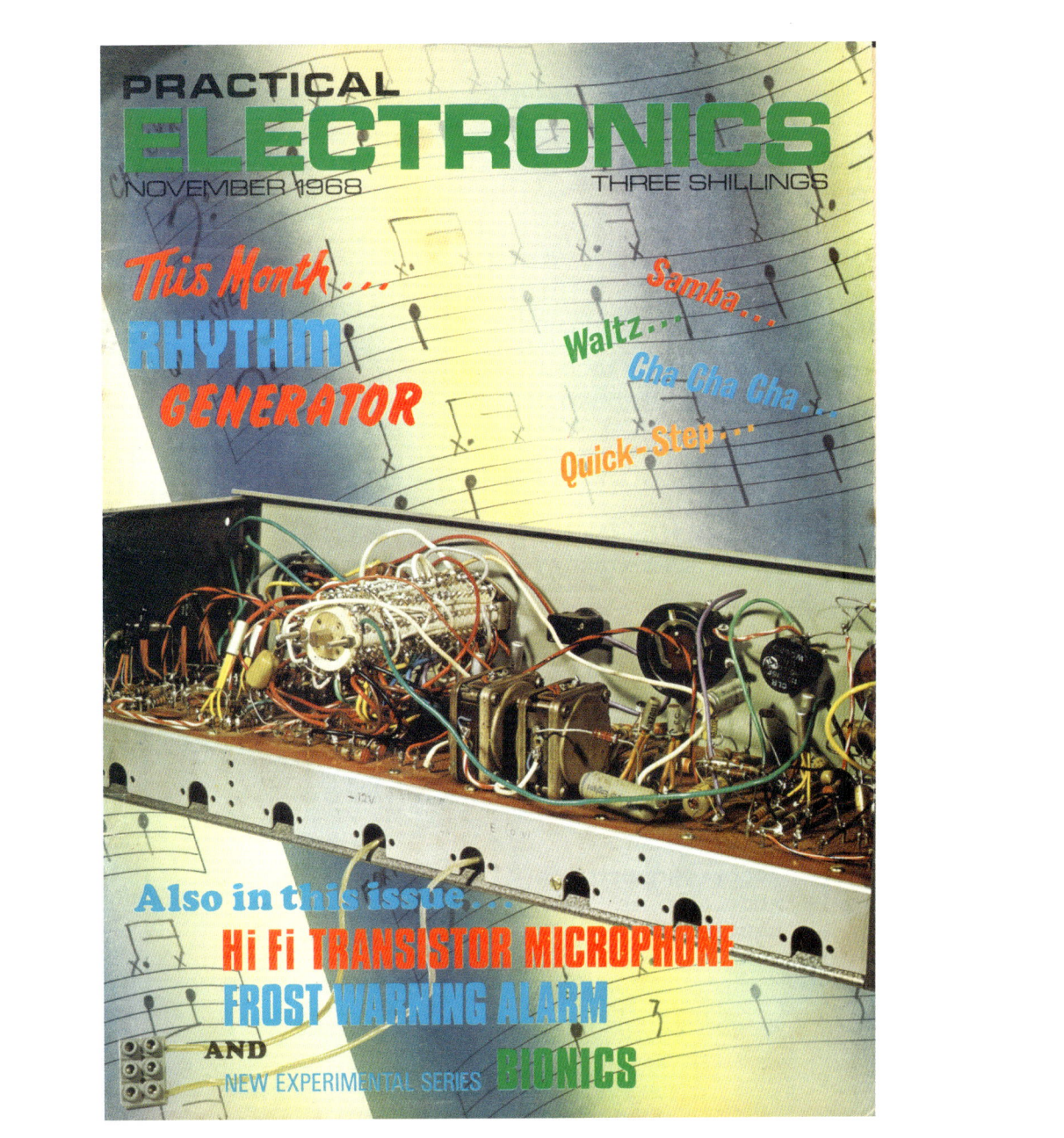

PRACTICAL ELECTRONICS

NOVEMBER 1968 THREE SHILLINGS

This Month...
RHYTHM GENERATOR

Samba...
Waltz...
Cha-Cha-Cha...
Quick-Step...

Also in this issue...
Hi Fi TRANSISTOR MICROPHONE
FROST WARNING ALARM
AND
NEW EXPERIMENTAL SERIES **BIONICS**